THE CURRENCY OF CONFIDENCE

A volume in the series
Cornell Studies in Money
edited by Eric Helleiner and Jonathan Kirshner

A list of titles in this series is available at
www.cornellpress.cornell.edu.

THE CURRENCY OF CONFIDENCE

How Economic Beliefs Shape the IMF's Relationship with Its Borrowers

Stephen C. Nelson

CORNELL UNIVERSITY PRESS   ITHACA AND LONDON

Cornell University Press gratefully acknowledges receipt of a grant from the Kaplan Institute for the Humanities, Northwestern University, which aided in the publication of this book.

First published 2017 by Cornell University Press
Printed in the United States of America

Library of Congress Cataloging-in-Publication Data

Names: Nelson, Stephen C., 1980– author.
Title: The currency of confidence : how economic beliefs shape the IMF's
    relationship with its borrowers / Stephen C. Nelson.
Description: Ithaca : Cornell University Press, 2017. | Includes bibliographical
    references and index.
Identifiers: LCCN 2016035600 (print) | LCCN 2016036594 (ebook) | ISBN
    9781501705120 (cloth : alk. paper) | ISBN 9781501708299 (epub/mobi) |
    ISBN 9781501708305 (pdf)
Subjects: LCSH: International Monetary Fund. | Loans, Foreign. | Financial crises. |
    Neoliberalism.
Classification: LCC HG3881.5.I58 N45 2017 (print) | LCC HG3881.5.I58 (ebook) |
    DDC 332.1/52—dc23
LC record available at https://lccn.loc.gov/2016035600

Contents

Tables and Figures

Acknowledgments

It has become a habit to read the acknowledgments of every book I pick up. A not-insubstantial share open with something along these lines: "this book took far longer to finish than I care to admit."

This book took far longer to finish than I care to admit.

Many people earned my gratitude for helping me to actually complete it. Since it started its life in the Department of Government at Cornell University, I thank Peter Katzenstein, Jonathan Kirshner, Nic van de Walle, and Chris Way for their guidance when I started down this path. Tom Pepinsky served as an additional reader and supplied, as expected, tough and trenchant comments that aided in the process of writing this book. Peter, in particular, must be singled out for more than living up to his legendary reputation as a mentor. He has been there with sound advice and deep insight every step of the way. The seeds of the book lie in a paper written for Peter's graduate seminar in international relations. That paper marked my first look into the world of the International Monetary Fund (IMF). And Peter has been there every step of the way since.

I have been very lucky to work on this book while a member of the Political Science Department at Northwestern University. I owe my colleagues Karen Alter and Hendrik Spruyt sizable debts for the detailed and incisive comments they provided on a first draft of the book. Bruce Carruthers gave me extremely helpful feedback on what became chapter 6 and has been a consistent source of inspiration, on this and many other projects. Henry Bienen's interest in my work on the IMF and its borrowers was a strong signal that I should keep at it. Jordan Gans-Morse generously shared his expertise on the concept of neoliberal economic beliefs that is at the core of my argument in this book. I have benefited from the kindness and wisdom of many of my political science colleagues in Scott Hall and in the broader Northwestern community; it would be impossible to thank each individual at Northwestern who in some way helped me during this process, but rest assured, I know that I owe you one.

I discussed some of the core ideas in this book with the very smart students in my graduate seminars at Northwestern. The seminar participants probably do not remember the incisive comments that they offered, but I do. Several Northwestern undergraduates helped me collect data for the analyses in chapters 3 and 7. I thank Sarah Green, Nandi Mehta, and Dor Srebernik for their perspicacious work.

Many scholars spent a valuable currency—their time—reading my work and offering their feedback on it. Sections of this book have been presented to seminars and workshops hosted at Brown University, Cornell University, Georgetown University, Northwestern, the University of Chicago, Johns Hopkins, the University of Wisconsin, and the University of Minnesota. Too many people offered helpful critiques and suggestions before, during, and after these seminars to thank each individually; I will, however, single out Bentley Allan, Mark Blyth, Mark Copelovitch, Chris Forster-Smith, Ron Krebs, Kate McNamara, Abe Newman, Jong-Hee Park, Len Seabrooke, Dave Steinberg, Kate Weaver, and Jessica Weeks for sharing their insights on different parts of the project. I also presented findings from this research at the annual meetings of the American Political Science Association, the International Political Economy Society, and the Midwest Political Science Association; in addition to comments from the audience members and fellow panelists at these meetings, I am grateful for the conversations with Irfan Nooruddin, Stephen Kaplan, and Matthew Winters.

It was my good fortune that a towering figure in the fields of international economics and international political economy, Tom Willett, was interested enough in the project to read the entire manuscript and to provide illuminating comments.

This book would not have been possible without the patient advice and help offered by the IMF archivist, Premela Isaac. I thank Christian Brachet and Desmond Lachman for taking the time to share their personal reflections on the Fund programs in Argentina, and I am grateful to the numerous executive directors of the IMF who helped me better understand the work of the organization and how the organization works. I am grateful to Sergio Chodos for taking an interest in the work and for his insights on all things related to Argentina, the Fund, and the workings of the international economy.

My most recent (and rather sizable) debts are owed to the anonymous reviewers of the book for Cornell University Press, and to Roger Haydon and Eric Helleiner, who shepherded this book during its long journey with great care and patience.

Sections of the argument and evidence in chapters 1 and 3 draw on a previously published article, "Playing Favorites: How Shared Beliefs Shape the IMF's Lending Decisions" (Nelson 2014b). Some of the material in chapter 7 appeared in a volume edited by Manuela Moschella and Kate Weaver (Nelson 2014a).

Finally, I thank my family and friends for supporting me in endeavors personal and professional. Andy Engel and Jenna Feldman always asked, with sensitivity and genuine interest, about how the book was coming along. Elliott Feldman and Cindy Mogul offered support when we really needed it. Maeve

McGuire generously let me camp out in her beautiful home in Southport, Maine, while I worked on the first draft of the book.

My father- and mother-in-law, Gregg and Betsey Van Gundy, kept their faith in me and in this project as the years passed. My parents, Rick and Jan Nelson, and my sister Kelsey gave me the confidence to keep at the book and gracefully managed the challenge of having a son and brother whose time is often given to research and writing on obscure topics. I know they are proud of me, which means everything.

Kate has been my rock since we met all those years ago in Northfield, Minnesota. She has been a constant source of inspiration, strength, and joy. Life was good when it was just the two of us, but since we have added two incredible people, Siri and Greta, to our family our lives have become immeasurably richer and the work more meaningful. I thank Kate, Siri, and Greta for making it all worthwhile. This book is dedicated to the three of you. When I told Siri that I had finally finished writing it, she said, "Great! Can you retire now?" Not yet, honey. Not yet.

THE CURRENCY OF CONFIDENCE

UNDERSTANDING THE IMF AND ITS BORROWERS

We have been working quietly in the cool woods and mountains of
New Hampshire and I doubt if the world yet understands how big a
thing we are bringing to birth.

—John Maynard Keynes, 1944

In the final days before the 2007 presidential election in Argentina, television
viewers were treated to a new campaign advertisement. The first image in the ad
posed a question: "¿Qué es el FMI?" ("What is the IMF?"). The commercial then
cut to a nursery school classroom, where a series of precocious children gave
their answers. "I think the IMF is, like, a bunch of horses." "The IMF is a satellite
that crashed into the moon." "The IMF is a country where everything's upside
down." One young girl held up a picture of a duck while another said, "the IMF is
a place where there's lots of animals." While the schoolchildren giggled, a narrator
promised viewers that if they elected Cristina Fernández de Kirchner as president
of the Republic of Argentina, her government would ensure that "your children,
and your children's children, have no idea what the IMF is."[1]

Fernández won the 2007 election in a landslide. The campaign advertisement
mattered little for the electoral outcome, but it reveals a lot about our system of
global economic governance. In the seventy years since the end of the Second
World War, people residing far from each other have forged connections through
networks of market-based transactions. The internationalization of markets for
goods, services, and financial assets was accompanied by the development of a
"great, emerging global bureaucracy," consisting of transnational administrative
law, commercial and trade associations, and a panoply of international organiza-

---

1. Jude Webber and Richard Lapper, "It Won't Be Easy. . . . No Tears for the IMF as a Feisty Argentina Awaits Its Next Evita," *Financial Times*, October 25, 2007.

tions (IOs).[2] At the apex of the system of global economic governance stands the International Monetary Fund (IMF, or Fund), the "most powerful international institution in history."[3]

This book is about the most controversial of the activities of the Fund: conditional lending.[4] I develop an ideational approach to explain why each of the three core elements of the lending arrangements of the institution—the amount of credit granted to borrowers, the number of conditions attached to the loans, and the rigor with which the conditions are enforced—vary so much. In answer to the question, "Why does the Fund seem to systematically treat some borrowing members differently from others?" analysts have tended to focus on factors such as the varying interests and influence of the most powerful IMF member countries, the domestic political institutions and interest groups that structure bargaining between the two sides, and the incentives and constraints facing self-interested staff members working in a big bureaucratic IO. The degree to which the economic beliefs held by Fund officials and the top policymakers in the borrowing country clash or cohere plays little to no role in most explanations.[5] We lack a theory of the IMF-borrower relationship that links shared beliefs to the decisions that determine the generosity of access to Fund resources, the tightness of conditionality, and the laxity of enforcement.

The gap in our understanding of how economic ideas shape the relations of the IMF with its borrowers is surprising—and unfortunate—given that belief-

---

2. Graeber 2011, 368. On the bureaucratization of world politics, see, for example, Barnett and Finnemore 2004; Cohen and Sabel 2005; Mazower 2012.

3. Stone 2002, 1.

4. Throughout this book, I refer to the drawings made by IMF member states as *loans* and to the member states granted access to IMF credit as *borrowers*. Someone looking for references to *lending* or *borrowing* in the guiding document of the institution, the Articles of Agreement, will come up empty handed. The IMF legal department prefers to interpret the transactions between the institution and its member states as "sales" of the currency of one country and "purchases" of the currencies of other member countries. Likewise, the IMF avoids using language in the documents that set out the terms of the program that could be interpreted as a constituting a contract between a lender and a borrower (Gold 1988, 1130; Zamora 1989, 1017–18). That way, the IMF can cut off the flow of resources to a member that has fallen out of compliance with the conditions of the program without getting into a legal fight with the government about whether or not the contract was breached. The IMF prefers to interpret the interruption of an adjustment program as an instance in which the member state exercised its sovereign right to ignore IMF advice, with the full knowledge that the deviation would cost the country its access to further drawings from the credit tranches of the institution.

5. This is not to say that the institutionalization of neoliberal economic ideas within the Fund has gone unnoticed; a number of scholars have written on the ideas embedded in the culture of the organization (e.g., see Babb 2007; Barnett and Finnemore 2004; Chwieroth 2010; Stiglitz 2003; Woods 2006). Here I am making the more limited claim that the literature on IMF treatment has not systematically theorized and tested the relationship between shared beliefs and credit, conditions, and enforcement.

based disagreements have often driven wedges between the two sides. As Harold James, a historian, observes, "the attractions of an alternative theory of development to that involved in the Fund's analysis provided a constant siren song, an inducement to break with rather than cooperate in the international system."[6]

Examples abound. Michael Manley, the prime minister of Jamaica in the 1970s and a key figure in the demands of developing countries for a New International Economic Order (NIEO), remarked, "IMF prescriptions are designed by and for developed capitalist economies and are inappropriate for developing economies of any kind." That same year Julius Nyerere, the socialist leader of Tanzania, expelled the members of an IMF mission, explaining, "I do not know whether there are now people who honestly believe that the IMF is politically or ideologically neutral. It has an ideology of economic and social development which it is trying to impose on poor countries irrespective of their own clearly stated policies."[7] Two years later President José Lopez Portillo of Mexico gave a more florid depiction of the shortcomings of the IMF: "the remedy of the witch doctor is to deprive the patient of food and subject him to compulsory rest. Those who protest must be purged, and those who survive bear witness to their virtue before the doctors of obsolete and prepotent dogma and of blind hegemoniacal egoism."[8]

Anti-IMF sentiment was persistent in the 1990s, and especially vitriolic in the post-communist transition countries and the countries embroiled in the East Asian financial crisis. In East Asia, the bad feelings persist; during the height of the Global Financial Crisis in 2009, one finance minister told the *Financial Times* that "most Asian countries would rather be dead than turn to the IMF."[9] Kang Man-Soo, the finance minister of the Republic of Korea, explained that due to the strongly negative "sentiment" shared by many Koreans, his country would never again go to the Fund for credit.[10] Bad feelings have resurfaced in post-communist countries, too: Artis Kampers, the economic minister of Latvia, complained, "representatives sitting in Washington and educated at Yale do not fully understand what is going on in Latvia."[11] And distrust of IMF prescriptions remained potent in South America. In a 2004 meeting with clerics from the

---

6. James 1996, 142.

7. The Manley and Nyerere quotations are drawn from a collection of speeches made at a forum in Arusha, Tanzania, in June 1980 and published in *Development Dialogue* 2: 10–23.

8. Quoted in Helleiner 1994, 177; Mazower 2012, 356.

9. Quoted in Quentin Peel, "Political Will for Meaningful Reform of IMF Is Still Lacking," *Financial Times*, March 17, 2009.

10. Quoted in Helleiner 2014b, 36.

11. Quoted in Andrew Ward, "Latvia Warns IMF over Delayed Aid," *Financial Times*, June 22, 2009.

Catholic Church, Nestor Kirchner, the Peronist president of Argentina, told the assembled officials, "I have the honor of receiving you, who are envoys of God." His next meeting, Kirchner ominously warned the clerics, was with "the envoy of the devil"; the devilish figure to whom Kirchner referred was Rodrigo Rato, the managing director of the IMF.[12]

Political scientists are often skeptical of the meaningfulness of such rhetoric. The IMF is a convenient scapegoat, they argue; material interests, not ideas, drive policymakers' decisions, and the populist face presented to the public is very often different from what officials say and do when they are in private meetings with the IMF negotiating team.[13]

I do not dispute the possibility that the leadership of a country under an IMF arrangement can shunt some of the blame for its dire economic conditions onto the Fund. But, as the theory and evidence in this book reveals, shared economic beliefs exert powerful effects on the character of IMF-borrower relations. I show that, when borrowers' top officials and the IMF economists are working from the same basic set of shared (neoliberal) economic beliefs, the lending relationship looks different: programs are larger in size, have fewer conditions, and are less rigorously enforced. Put simply, the IMF has played favorites with its borrowers.

The Argument in Brief

I build my argument on a set of interlocking claims. First, I contend that key decision makers involved in program design and enforcement—the IMF staff and management—have significant autonomy from the member states of the organization. The wide leeway that the staff and management have for discretionary judgments is, in part, a consequence of another core claim underpinning my framework: key decisions facing actors involved in IMF adjustment programs are made in the presence of strong uncertainty. In highly fluid and uncertain situations, actors' interests are often unclear. Consider the IMF experience in Argentina. Reflecting on the role of powerful states in the decisions made by the Fund in the run up to the economic collapse of that country in December 2001, Claudio Loser (the former head of the Western Hemisphere Department of the Fund) said, "external pressures were less important to the staff than internal discussions. I believe that the G7 [Group of 7] did not know what to do."[14]

---

12. Quoted in "Devilish Design," *Financial Times*, September 1, 2004.
13. Lindert and Morton 1989, 74–75; Krasner 1968, 682; Remmer 1986, 21; Strange 1973, 280.
14. Quoted in Tenembaum 2004, 194 (my translation). Loser's surname is pronounced "LOH-ser."

In the next step, I argue that economic policymakers at both the international and domestic levels rely on shared economic beliefs for guidance in the presence of uncertainty. I characterize the beliefs that have shaped the IMF decision makers' views as neoliberal, and I contend that neoliberal economic ideas are deeply embedded in the organizational culture. The institutionalization of neoliberal beliefs within the Fund has much to do with the similarity of the staff members' educational backgrounds: a very large percentage of the officials of this multinational organization were trained in highly ranked U.S. economics departments.

The concept of uncertainty plays another important role in my theoretical framework: it helps us understand why IMF officials and national-level policymakers may have sincere (and durable) differences of opinion about managing an economy in crisis. In advancing this claim, I push against a stream of work in political science and economics resting on the assumption that, with the same information at hand, *all* actors will converge to the same view and, hence, that the only essential feature of the IMF-borrower interaction is the severity of conflicts of material interest (rather than contests of differing beliefs).

In the final step, I bring together the core claims to generate three testable mechanisms linking shared beliefs to variations in loan size, conditionality, and enforcement. When officials who share neoliberal economic ideas occupy top posts in the government, the IMF decision makers have greater confidence that the borrower will "do the right thing."[15] Greater confidence, flowing from the proximity of the economic beliefs held by the key players on both sides, leads to programs that are larger in (relative) size (because IMF officials are more confident that a program managed by neoliberals will succeed), that contain fewer conditions (because oversight is less stringent when the Fund decision makers believe that the policy team in charge of the program can be trusted), and that are more laxly enforced (because, from the IMF officials' perspective, waiving missed conditions is an important way that the organization can provide political support for like-minded policymakers).

Testable is a key word in the previous paragraph. Another major contribution I make in this book lies in the quantity and quality of the evidence I use to test the arguments. Some of the evidence comes from statistical analyses of the covariates of indicators of loan size, conditionality, and enforcement in a large sample of IMF programs signed by developing and emerging countries in the 1980s and

---

15. "Doing the right thing" is a trope that appears in IMF officials' depictions of the dealings of the organization with its borrowers. For example, in his farewell address to the institution, Stanley Fischer, the outgoing deputy managing director, observed, "often we do our job by reinforcing people struggling under enormous pressures to do the right thing." https://www.imf.org/external/np/speeches/2001/082901a.htm.

1990s. Other evidence is drawn from an in-depth case study, based on documents gathered from the IMF archives, interviews, news reports, and other scholars' investigations of the ebbs and flows of the relationship of Argentina with the IMF over a quarter century (1976–2002).

In addition to examining how economic beliefs shape the terms of the IMF engagement with its borrowers, I provide evidence showing that the power of the IMF extends beyond influencing how the economies of its borrowers are governed; I argue that the institution, through its conditional lending programs, also influences *who* governs the economy. In chapter 6, I build and systematically test an argument that confirms what many scholars of economic policymaking in developing and emerging countries have long suspected: the neoliberal-type policymakers in governments involved in IMF programs can parlay their cozier relationships with the Fund decision makers into political capital at home. Building on the finding that policy teams composed of neoliberal-oriented officials received larger loans with fewer binding conditions and benefited from more laxly enforced conditionality (a finding that I link to the greater confidence placed by the Fund in like-minded teams at the helm of the borrowing economies), I argue that the national leaders in countries participating in IMF lending arrangements have strong incentives to appoint and retain the neoliberal-type policymakers who can deliver tangible results while in office. Using the biographical data on policymakers, I statistically test two claims: (1) neoliberal economic policymakers in governments under IMF programs should survive in office longer than non-neoliberal policymakers in countries under IMF programs, and (2) neoliberals should be more common fixtures in government in the countries that had lengthier periods under IMF lending arrangements. The quantitative evidence presented in chapter 6 is consistent with these expectations.

In the main empirical analyses, I focus on the IMF-borrower relationship during the 1980s and 1990s—a period marked by extensive IMF involvement in the economic affairs of low- and middle-income countries and the solidification of the neoliberal orientation of the Fund. In addition, in chapter 7 I probe the plausibility of extending the argument to the context of the current, post–Global Financial Crisis era, and I provide some new statistical evidence suggesting that the IMF has continued to play favorites with its borrowers.

In exploring the ideational origins of the Fund pattern of playing favorites among its borrowers, I build on work that takes the cultures of IOs seriously.[16] But, rather than tracing a line between the economic beliefs embedded in IMF

---

16. Barnett and Finnemore 1999, 2004.

culture to dysfunctional organizational "pathologies," here I explore how officials at the IMF were predisposed to favor the national policy teams that they believed were more likely to the "do the right things." And the implication of my argument is rather different from the contention of many of the prominent critics of the Fund. Instead of leading to ever-greater standardization and uniformity in IMF-borrower relations, the embeddedness of neoliberal beliefs has been a powerful source of *variation* in the treatment by the IMF of its borrowers.

Conceptualizing Neoliberal Economic Beliefs

I argue that IMF officials share a set of neoliberal beliefs.[17] Although the neoliberal label has proliferated across the social sciences, the term is more often invoked than conceptualized.[18] Here, I use *neoliberal* to describe a bundle of theoretical principles and policy implications. My conceptualization of neoliberal economic ideas is neither expansive nor definitive. I simply try to distill the most basic principles and policies on which IMF officials and like-minded policymakers in borrowing countries would agree. During the time period on which the empirical analysis focuses (1980–2000), neoliberal ideas shaped the organizational culture of the Fund—and this neoliberal orientation sometimes put the organization at odds with officials of the borrowing country who hewed to different beliefs.

The neoliberal mental model is built on four main economic principles, which are each recognizable as being shared by many (although not all) neoclassical economists trained in the United States.

1. Economies (and the appropriate policies for their governance) are best represented and understood through the use of abstract, general (formal) models showing how competitive, decentralized market mechanisms bring about coherence (different spheres of economies settle into equilibrium).[19]

---

17. My conceptualization of *neoliberal* differs from how other scholars use the term. For critical social theorists, *neoliberalism* often denotes a hegemonic social order enveloping (and disciplining) everyone (Dardot and Laval 2013; Mirowski 2013). For others, the engine behind the rise of neoliberalism is class domination (neoliberal economic ideas are, in this framework, "the expression of class interests") (Duménil and Lévy 2011, 18 [quotation]; Harvey 2005).

18. See Boas and Gans-Morse 2009; Mudge 2008; Venugopal 2015.

19. Minsky 2008, 118–20; Mirowski 2013, 279.

2. In the possible set of arrangements for allocating the resources of a society, competitive markets are (usually) the most efficient.[20] The principle of the superior allocative efficiency of free markets does not imply the more extreme view that the market mechanism achieves efficiency always and everywhere—even though for many in the neoclassical tradition there is a relatively limited set of circumstances in which markets fail and nonmarket mechanisms for resource allocation are preferred.[21]

3. The free exchange of goods and services across national borders improves, on balance, the welfare of the countries whose residents are involved in the exchange.

4. Agents in the economy have rational beliefs.[22]

These principles can be linked to a broader neoliberal economic policy template involving three core elements.[23]

First, the neoliberal template suggests that governments should pursue, in general, fiscal and monetary policy discipline. Tight macroeconomic policy discipline, neoliberals argue, was particularly necessary to prevent developing countries from falling into inflationary spirals and balance of payments crises. And the recommendation fits well with the assumption of strong individual rationality— an assumption that, in elite U.S. economics departments, picked up steam in the early 1970s. "The so-called rational expectations revolution," argues Justin Yifu

---

20. Campbell and Pederson 2001; Mudge 2008.

21. Little 1982, 25–26. Market efficiency has, however, come under sustained criticism from economists who remained in the mainstream of the profession in the United States. Joseph Stiglitz's work on information economics, for example, led him to conclude, "markets by themselves do not produce efficient outcomes when information is imperfect and markets are incomplete" (2008, 42).

22. The concept of rational beliefs relates to a typology developed by John Maynard Keynes (1921). Keynes distinguishes three possible states that confront decision makers: (1) "knowledge," in which we can be certain that our choice will produce the desired outcome; (2) "rational belief," in which there are sufficient grounds to consider our prior beliefs to be probable; and (3) "uncertainty," in which probabilities are unknown, rational calculations cannot be made, and decisions are instead made on the basis of conventional (not rational) expectations (Arena 2010, 81, 84–85). Most neoclassical economists excise uncertainty (in the Keynesian sense) and assume that agents are always operating in decision settings characterized by calculable risks (Dequech 2007–2008; Minsky 2008, 5, 120; Nelson and Katzenstein 2014; Taylor 2004, 200–202; Zeckhauser 2014). Heterodox economists often reject the assumption of rational beliefs, arguing, for example, that "the assumption that individuals foresee the future perfectly with at most random error flies in the face of the rigidities and risks of the Third World, where consequences of political and economic change are largely unknown" (Shapiro and Taylor 1990, 867).

23. In highlighting these three elements, I draw on work by van de Walle (2001, 140) and Gore (2000, 789).

Lin, former World Bank chief economist, "refuted the structural foundation for the state's role in using fiscal and monetary policy for economic development."[24]

The second element of the neoliberal policy template holds that the free play of markets should be the primary mechanism for allocating the goods and resources of a society and for setting prices. Market-determined prices are, in this view, the "efficient instrument for determining resource allocation, while widespread administrative intervention is apt to lead to distortions and economic waste."[25]

And if prices can do a better job allocating resources within the borders of a country, why shouldn't governments make it easier for residents to conduct market-based transactions with people living beyond the borders? The neoliberal model thus generates a third core policy recommendation: the foreign economic policies of countries should promote—not inhibit via tariffs and administrative controls—cross-border trade.

It is widely accepted that market-oriented neoliberal ideas were well entrenched at the IMF by the late 1970s. "Running through the Fund's prescriptions," Richard Eckaus, economist at the Massachusetts Institute of Technology (MIT), observed, "is a faith in unimpeded market forces as the most effective means of achieving the desired levels of exchange reserves and a viable balance of payments."[26] Measuring the ideational distance between the IMF officials and the policy team in the borrowing country, however, poses a big challenge. In chapter 3 I describe an approach that uses biographical background information on the policymakers to indirectly measure their beliefs. The measure allows me to test my argument using a large sample of IMF lending programs.

The Politics of Conditional Lending

Membership in the IMF does not involve many obligations. One of the stronger membership requirements embedded in the Articles of Agreement (Article VIII)

---

24. Lin 2012, 19. Rational expectations, by assuming that people *at all times* and *in all places* understand the true underlying structure of the economy well enough to be able to formulate subjective probability assessments that, in the aggregate, match the *objective* probabilities, went a step even beyond the assumption of rational beliefs. The policy takeaway from this line of thinking, according to Mark Blyth, was clear: "government can't do much at all except screw things up by getting in the way. Left alone with common and accurate information, such [rational] individuals' expectations about possible future states of the economy will converge and promote a stable and self-enforcing equilibrium" (2013, 41).

25. Williamson 1980, 269–70.

26. Eckaus 1986, 240.

encourages members to abrogate a potentially useful foreign economic policy tool that nonmembers can retain.[27] Article VIII prevents members from restricting cross-border transactions that fall under the current account of the national balance of payments. In the 1930s, many countries ring-fenced their economies behind a wall of discriminatory policies. Regulations that prevented the residents of a country from or penalized them for trading with nonresidents (setting up multiple exchange rates, rationing access to foreign currency, forcing exporters to surrender some or all of their profits to the government, and so on) were linked in the minds of the Bretton Woods delegates to aggressive foreign policies. Article VIII, however, has been a rather weak obligation in practice.[28]

The conditional loans that the IMF makes to its members, then, are the primary levers by which the institution influences their policy choices. The practice of conditional lending is kick-started when the economic authorities of a member state notify the Fund that the country needs to draw on IMF resources. If the Fund management thinks that the request is credible (and it almost always does), a small group of staff members (the "mission"), drawn from the regional department and other specialized departments, is sent to meet with the policy team in the borrowing country. The mission works with the senior managers to sketch out the initial parameters for the program—the type of lending facility to be used, the total size of the loan and the disbursement schedule, the possible conditions to be included in the agreement, and so on—before it starts negotiations with the national policymakers. When the top officials in the borrowing country have signed off on the agreement, the staff and management present the program to the IMF Executive Board for a vote.[29] If the executive directors (EDs) approve the proposed program, the borrower gets its first infusion of hard currency.

---

27. Alongside the Article VIII commitments, the core membership obligations of the Fund pertain to oversight of exchange-rate practices (Article IV). The 1978 amendment of the Articles, in the wake of the decline of the "official" system of fixed exchange rates (a system, with the U.S. dollar at its core, that had been initially worked out at the Bretton Woods conference), weakened the control of the Fund in this domain but preserved its ability to surveil the exchange-rate practices of members to ensure that the policies foster domestic economic growth and price stability and to prevent the manipulation of "exchange rates or the international monetary system in order to prevent effective balance of payments adjustment or to gain an unfair competitive advantage over other members" (Article IV, sect. 1).

28. Members could appeal to the clause in Article XIV that allowed countries in their "transitional" phase to retain current account restrictions. And the transitional phase of some countries took a long time—the Philippines, for example, remained under Article XIV for over fifty years (Nelson 2010, 115).

29. Member states are represented through the twenty-four executive directors (EDs) who constitute the Executive Board. Voting on lending proposals from the staff is informal and recorded on an up-or-down basis, and the EDs almost always unanimously approve proposed loans.

The IMF, like all bureaucratic organizations, has evolved rules and routines that give its activities a degree of predictability.[30] The rules and routines associated with conditional lending should not, however, obscure an important fact about the relationship of the institution with its borrowers: at every step in the process, IMF decision making involves a good deal of subjective judgment. When the IMF staff members and management are setting the size of the program for a country, they are constrained by a rule that limits how much money a borrower can access.[31] But the access limit is not a hard-and-fast rule; in "exceptional circumstances" the top management can waive the ceiling on loan size. Some IMF programs are extremely large: the December 1997 Korean loan, for example, topped out at 1,939 percent of quota. The Korean program was the largest in Fund history until the May 2010 Greek standby arrangement, which, at $38 billion, amounted to nearly 3,300 percent of the quota for that country.

The wide dispersion in the relative size of IMF loans is mirrored by sizable variation, documented in several other studies by political scientists, in the second element of IMF lending activities: the extent of conditionality in the adjustment programs of the institution.[32] The data I collected on the content of IMF programs over a twenty-year period also reveal a high degree of variation in the number of binding conditions that appear in the lending agreements signed by the Fund borrowers. Like the decisions about the proper size of IMF loans, the process of settling on the proper scope of the conditionality included in lending programs is largely a matter of highly subjective judgments formed by the staff members and management.

The third element of conditional lending involves the monitoring and enforcement of the program. The work of the members of the IMF mission does not end with the approval of the program by the Executive Board. The Memorandum of Understanding that details the conditions of the program also specifies the "test" schedule of the country. At several points in the life of the program, the mission returns to the borrowing country to assess the progress of the country. If IMF officials find that the borrower has not lived up to the terms of the agreement, the program is suspended and funds are withheld—that is, unless staff members recommend waivers for the missed conditions. When evidence of noncompliance emerges, the staff and management can choose to recommend that the Executive

---

30. Barnett and Finnemore 1999, 718–19; 2004, 17–20.

31. The quotas are subscription fees that members pay for the right to make purchases from the general pool of Fund resources. For many years, IMF loans were capped at 300 percent of quota. The access limit was doubled (to 600 percent) in 2009.

32. See Copelovitch 2010; Dreher and Jensen 2007; Gould 2006; Pop-Eleches 2009a; Stone 2008, 2011.

Board approve waivers for the missed conditions (allowing the drawings to go forward as planned), or they can recommend that the program be suspended. The decision of the staff and management is, ultimately, based entirely on their subjective assessments of the situation. There is no formal rule to which the staff, management, and EDs of the Fund can appeal at this stage of the conditional lending process. They have to rely on their own judgment about the best course of action when a borrower has strayed from the strictures of the program. And IMF borrowers very often fall out of compliance with conditionality.[33]

How do IMF decision makers form their judgments about each of three elements of conditional lending (amount, conditionality, and enforcement)? The official line is that decisions about the design and monitoring of its programs are rooted in objective, technical (and, ostensibly, apolitical) analyses of the economic conditions facing its borrowers. The most recent edition of the *International Monetary Fund Handbook*, for example, refers to "the importance of maintaining the uniformity of treatment of member countries. This principle applies to all IMF activities. . . . It requires that members in similar circumstances be treated similarly."[34]

The IMF downplays the political nature of conditionality. The uniformity principle does not, after all, imply that the program for every borrower should look exactly the same. Uniformity simply means that the IMF decision makers use the same yardstick for all Fund members. It does not sort members into different classes and systematically treat members in one category differently. The principle of political neutrality—the IMF makes funds available to any kind of government, provided that the member can credibly demonstrate a financing need—is enshrined in the Articles of Agreement that define the mandate of the institution.[35] The Articles further prohibit "all attempts to influence any of the [Fund] staff in the discharge of functions."[36] Judgments are, in principle, made on the basis of well-established economic theory and the lessons that the institution has learned over seventy years of experience. The IMF tries to project a public image of technocratic, apolitical rationality.

The argument that design and enforcement decisions at the IMF are made solely on the basis of economic fundamentals is the null hypothesis in this and other

---

33. Programs were interrupted because of noncompliance in twenty-eight out of thirty-six developing countries that signed concessional loans between 1986 and 1994. Less than a quarter of the arrangements signed during the period were completed without significant deviations; Caraway, Rickard, and Anner 2012, 36.

34. International Monetary Fund (IMF) 2007, 9. On the origins of the principle of uniformity, see Gold 1975.

35. See Swedberg 1986 for a skeptical view.

36. Article XII, sect. IV.

studies of conditional lending—it is the baseline against which political explanations must be tested. But international relations scholars tend to be (justifiably) skeptical of the claim that politics have been purged from IMF decision making.

The role of subjective judgment in the design and enforcement of lending programs, as previously discussed, fuels international relations scholars' suspicions that IMF decisions are often the product of political wrangling. Suspicions are further stoked by policymakers' complaints about the excessively tough treatment by the IMF of their countries. In November 1997, Indonesia, struggling to control the financial fallout from a speculative attack on the rupiah, entered into an IMF arrangement. The autocratic leader of Indonesia, Suharto, told U.S. diplomats that the extensive conditionality attached to the loan was a sign that "the IMF didn't like him and wanted to overthrow him."[37] A blow-out argument in Athens in September 2012 over IMF insistence on additional spending cuts provides another example: in the midst of heated discussions between Poul Thomsen, the Fund mission head, and Finance Minister Yannis Stournaras, the Greek policymaker pointed to a hole in the window of the Finance Ministry and said, "you see this—this came from a bullet. Do you want to overthrow the government?"[38]

International relations scholars tend to agree that political factors are important for understanding conditional lending. How the politics of conditional lending plays out is a matter of much debate. What drives IMF judgments about its borrowers? What are the attributes of the types of borrowers that the IMF prefers? Existing research supplies several answers to these questions. Next, I situate my ideational argument alongside other prominent explanations for variation in the treatment by the IMF of its borrowers.

Political Explanations for Variation in IMF-Borrower Relations

One of the main lines of debate in the international relations scholarship on IOs concerns the extent of their discretion. Does their behavior reflect the preferences of their most powerful members, or do IOs "exercise power autonomously in ways unintended and unanticipated" by the foreign policy elites that enact the (perceived) national interests of their states?[39]

37. Blustein 2001, 231.

38. Liz Alderman and Landon Thomas Jr., "IMF's Call for More Cuts Irks Greece," *New York Times*, online ed., September 24, 2012, http://www.nytimes.com/2012/09/25/business/global/rift-with-imf-adds-to-greeces-tensions-in-pivotal-week.html.

39. Barnett and Finnemore 1999, 699.

For some realist international relations scholars, institutions such as the IMF—however high-minded and internationalist their mandates may be— are instruments that states will invariably use to ensure that their interests are served.[40] Keynes himself feared the possibility. He hoped the fact that "to the average Congressman [the IMF] is extremely boring" would shield the institution from political meddling, but in a provocative address to the delegates at the IMF inaugural meeting in Savannah, he cautioned against the "malicious fairy" that might twist the judgment of the institution so that its "every thought and act shall have an *arrière-pensée*; everything you determine shall not be for its own sake or on its own merits but because of something else."[41]

A widely held view of the IMF is that it violates the uniformity principle all the time because powerful actors in world politics intervene during the conditional lending process to shape the terms of access, conditionality, and enforcement of programs in ways that serve their own interests (but not necessarily serving the needs of the borrower).[42] In this approach, politicization of IMF decision making means that the most powerful members of the institution influence the lending process in ways that contravene the judgments made by staff members and management about the borrower. The perspective implies a counterfactual: if the borrower were less preferred (or less disliked) by a powerful member, its treatment would have been tougher (or easier).

Power-oriented explanations are differentiated by where they identify the locus of control over key decisions in the lending process. Realists expect pressure to come mainly from the foreign policy establishments in the powerful states. Others point to powerful private actors as the controllers of IOs such as the IMF. This is the view taken by many critical scholars, including Pierre Bourdieu, the late social theorist, who explicitly linked "the asymmetrical treatment granted by the global institutions to various nations" to the "position they occupy within the structure of the distribution of capital." Bourdieu observed, "The most striking example of this is no doubt the fact that requests by the International Monetary Fund that the United States reduce its persistent public deficit have long fallen on deaf ears, whereas the same body has forced many an African economy, already greatly at risk, to reduce its deficit at the cost of increasing levels of unemployment and poverty."[43]

---

40. Mearsheimer 1994 epitomizes the realist view of IOs as the handmaidens of powerful states.

41. Mikesell 1994, 445 (first quotation); James 1996, 71 (second quotation).

42. Dreher and Jensen 2007; Stone 2002, 2004, 2008, 2011; Thacker 1999; Oatley and Yackee 2004; Reynaud and Vauday 2009.

43. Bourdieu 2003, 94–95.

A recent turn in the power-oriented line of thinking about IMF program design and enforcement presents a more nuanced perspective on how control is asserted by powerful interests. Powerful countries such as the United States do not want to shape the terms of every decision that the IMF makes with respect to conditional loans.[44] Doing so would damage the credibility of the institution, thus making it less useful as a tool of foreign policymaking. During normal times, the principals (powerful member states) are content to let the agents (the IMF staff of highly trained economists) use the tools at their disposal to manage the problems that forced the borrowers to seek financing.

Discretion, however, is suspended when powerful members decide that the borrower requires special treatment. For Randall Stone, the United States mobilizes its extensive diplomatic resources to lobby for better terms when regimes in which it has a strategic interest get into trouble. Mark Copelovitch suggests that even more important are the interests of the financial communities of the major stakeholders; when big financial institutions are sucked into crises in the developing world, they lean on the representative of their country at the IMF to help arrange generous bailouts. Provided that the other powerful member states do not object, the bankers usually get their way.[45] The thread running through this line of research is that the discretion of an IO is always on loan from the member states because IOs in world politics depend on the material and symbolic resources that only states (and possibly some resource-rich private actors) can provide.[46]

Viewing the IMF as an organization that operates within a fairly narrow zone of discretion defined by its principals understates the power and autonomy of this institution. Michael Barnett and Martha Finnemore's signal contribution gives us a different lens through which to view IOs. They point out that IO autonomy comes in different forms. IOs may have wide discretion when states are relatively indifferent, but they also exercise discretion when they avoid following the directives of states, when they directly challenge the interests of powerful principals, and when they "change the broader normative environment and states' perceptions of their own preferences."[47] The discretion of the IMF, in this perspective, is a function of the dual roles of the institution: it is *in authority* because it has been formally delegated tasks by its members, and it became *an authority* in world politics thanks to its rational-legal bureaucratic procedures and the specialized

44. Copelovitch 2010; Stone 2008, 2011.

45. For other arguments and evidence on the influence of private financial interests on the design of programs, see Breen 2014; Broz and Hawes 2006; Gould 2003, 2006.

46. See Barnett and Finnemore 2004, 22; Barnett and Coleman 2005, 597–98.

47. Barnett and Finnemore 2004, 27–29.

knowledge possessed by its staff and management. The constructivist optic lets us see IOs as purposive actors in global governance using "their authority to expand their control over more and more of international life."[48]

One dimension along which explanations for the behavior of the IMF vary is the degree of the discretion accorded to the organization. The other dimension along which explanations differ is tied to a fundamental and enduring debate in the field of international relations between social constructivists and (generally materialist) rationalists.[49]

Rationalist explanations start by (implicitly or explicitly) assuming that individual agents in any choice setting seek to solve optimization problems. As Dani Rodrik explains, an optimization problem involves three components: (1) the thing that the agent wants to maximize (an "objective function," such as income, votes, and power), (2) the constraints under which the agent operates (the "rules of the game," constituted by, for example, budgets, technologies, and formal political institutions), and (3) the set of possible choices available to the agent.[50] Agents optimize by selecting the policy mix that maximizes an expected payoff function.[51] In this analytical mode, "people select certain actions as a rational response to their place in an environment implicitly characterized as an 'obstacle course,' in which payoffs may be opaque, but they are knowable."[52] Information is unevenly distributed among agents, but in the rationalist optic *all* agents have at least enough knowledge of their worlds to be able to attach payoffs to actions and assign probability distributions over the states of the world that might be brought about by different choices.

Decision makers live with risk—not uncertainty—in the rationalist approach.[53] Betting on a coin flip is a risky decision: you cannot be certain whether heads or tails will come up, but if the coin is a fair one you know the odds. Outside of casinos, decision makers rarely know the objective probabilities in a given choice setting, but in the rationalist optic, they behave *as if* they have a probability distribution in mind.

---

48. Ibid., 25, 44 (quotation).

49. For excellent discussions of the debate, see Abdelal, Blyth, and Parsons 2010; Fearon and Wendt 2002; Hurd 2008; Katzenstein, Keohane, and Krasner 1998.

50. Rodrik 2014, 190.

51. Page 2008, 123.

52. Abdelal, Blyth, and Parsons 2010, 3.

53. Knight (1921) and John Maynard Keynes (1921), working separately, formulated a conceptual distinction between risk and uncertainty ninety years ago that remains foundational in the analysis of individual and organizational decision making. Beckert's (1996, 2002) reintroduction of the distinction between risk and uncertainty in economic sociology and Blyth's (2002, 2006) use of the concept in political science has spurred a burst of interest in the role of uncertainty in economic life; see Abdelal, Blyth, and Parsons 2010; Nelson and Katzenstein 2014; Woll 2008; Rodrik 2014.

In the world characterized by risk and rational expectations, people have different objective functions and different information, but they do not disagree on what constitutes the "correct" model of reality.[54] The framework assumes "rational people responding to an obstacle course that any human being would perceive fairly similarly."[55]

A different research tradition questions the assumptions of risk and instrumental rationality. Agents' abilities to think probabilistically about economic problems are hampered by the incompleteness of our knowledge about the incredibly complex structure of the world (we cannot, in Mark Blyth's terms, always observe the "generators" that produce outcomes) and by paradigm-shifting transformations in the underlying economic structures.[56] In these kinds of environments, there is no basis for people to settle on what the objective probability distribution looks like. When faced with Knightian uncertainty, people depend on shared beliefs and social conventions to guide their decisions.[57] In a world of uncertainty, there is no reason why everyone's beliefs should converge into a single, shared model, and worldviews that are wrong "could remain so even in the face of new evidence if that evidence is just used to confirm past beliefs."[58]

Some international relations scholars have asserted that choice settings faced by IOs are often too ambiguous and uncertain to permit optimization by decision makers.[59] Instead of following decision rules that maximize expected payoffs, officials fall back on social scripts to guide their choices. Organizational culture supplies the rules that enable staff members to confront the problems they encounter as they try to carry out the organizational mandate. Rather than asking whether a policy mix is optimal, decision makers in an IO may ask (perhaps reflexively) whether, given their organizational identities, the action is appropriate in the sense of "matching the obligations of that identity or role to a specific situation."[60]

Comparing Political Explanations for the Variation

Two dimensions of variation help us make sense of the literature on the behavior of IOs. One dimension captures how scholars think about the autonomy of IOs. Both realists and liberal institutionalists regard IOs (and the IMF, more

54. Rodrik 2014, 193.
55. Abdelal, Blyth, and Parsons 2010, 4.
56. Blyth 2006; Meltzer 1982, 17.
57. Goldstein and Keohane 1993, 13–17.
58. Rodrik 2014, 194.
59. Barnett and Finnemore 1999, 2004; Haas 1990.
60. March and Olsen 1998, 951. See also Barnett and Coleman 2005, 600.

specifically) as operating within zones of discretion set by sovereign states (and possibly a few private actors with statelike power resources). Social constructivists think that this view dramatically understates the autonomous power of IOs, such as the IMF, that "constitute and construct the social world."[61] The second dimension distinguishes different models of individual and organizational decision making: rationalists assume that most decisions are made by optimizing agents in the presence of risk; constructivists argue that it is more realistic to acknowledge that many decisions are made by socially and culturally embedded actors operating in the presence of uncertainty.

Putting the two dimensions together yields a typology of explanations for variation in the IMF's relationships with its borrowers. In the power-oriented explanations that assert a low level of discretion (the top-left box in table 1.1), member states, acting out of their strategic interests or on behalf of powerful private economic interests, take (temporary) control of the institution, often through informal avenues (e.g., the lobbying of upper-level management), to influence the terms of treatment of the borrowers. Few scholars now would argue that the IMF is *always* under the thumb of its most powerful members. In Randall Stone's theory, for example, the zone of discretion is often quite wide, thanks to "the broad international consensus about its fundamental purpose."[62] But when the United States or other Great Powers have a pressing interest in the bailout program of a borrower, the zone of discretion collapses.[63] If a sizable number of observations lie in the top-left box of the table, we should observe negative associations between measures of the strategic and economic importance of borrowers to the Great Powers and indicators of the toughness of treatment by the

TABLE 1.1 Typology of political explanations of IMF-borrower relations

	RISK	UNCERTAINTY
LOW DISCRETION	I Great Power politics Private economic power	II
HIGH DISCRETION	IV Strategic design and enforcement Bureaucratic public choice	III Pathologies of IO culture Shared economic beliefs

61. Barnett and Finnemore 1999, 700.

62. Stone 2011, 31.

63. "The United States has drawn upon its influence at the Fund to attempt to induce recipient governments to support its foreign policy objectives, and at times it has pressured the Fund to be lenient because it has been reluctant to risk destabilizing friendly regimes" (ibid., 30).

IMF. In the top two cells in table 1.1 the predicted outcome—borrowers that are preferred (disliked) by influential external actors receive better (worse) terms from the IMF—is the same regardless of which logic of action dominates. But the top-right cell is left empty because the prominent power-oriented explanations are all lodged firmly in the world of risk.

The explanations in the two bottom cells of table 1.1 treat the institution as having a high degree of autonomy. How, in the context of conditional lending, does the IMF use its discretion? For some international relations scholars, the IMF is delegated discretion by member states because it helps solve otherwise intractable problems of international economic governance. The leading states want to prevent local economic crises from spiraling into regional and global conflagrations; hence, the IMF mandate is, in part, the preservation of global financial stability.[64] The task creates an incentive to favor some borrowers over others; specifically, "systemically important" borrowers should receive special treatment (they require especially large disbursements of currency, regardless of their level of compliance with the strictures of the program). This behavior violates the principle of uniformity of treatment but is consistent with a strategic, rational organization seeking to maximize its expected payoff. If the effort to save a systemically important country fails because the lending package was too small, then the IMF, too, has failed—and it can expect to be punished for its failure by some very powerful stakeholders.

The rationalist lens opened another line of thinking about the strategic logic of IMF conditionality. Borrowing governments have interests, too. They might, for example, want to maximize the chance of retaining power. IMF loans can be useful devices for diffusing some of the political heat generated by a program of reform and belt-tightening. Conditionality could also be used as a tool for reformers to pile another cost on obstructionist forces in the government (fighting against the plans of the leadership means making powerful enemies at home and in Washington, DC).[65]

But rational, survival-seeking governments do not want IMF conditions to harm the interests of their key bases of political support, lest those powerful supporters look elsewhere for parties and politicos more to their liking. Because "the IMF is interested in maximizing the success/implementation of its programs," the staff members and management, knowledgeable about the political constraints

---

64. Pop-Eleches 2009b; Vreeland 2003, 58. Susan Strange was the first international political economy scholar to observe the "highly political manner" in which "those members whose financial difficulties were most likely to jeopardize the stability of the international monetary system" were given preferential terms of treatment by the Fund (1973, 272).

65. Vreeland 2003, 14–16.

under which the borrowing government is operating, will soften the conditions in the program that reduce the likelihood of the success of the program.[66]

Scholars working in the bureaucratic public choice tradition also ascribe significant autonomy to the organization. Starting from the assumption that IO management and staff members' "preference for power, prestige and income leads them to favor more power and resources for 'their' international organization," explanations in this vein fixate on incentives and constraints facing individual bureaucrats who want to maximize their discretion and control (as well as their personal incomes). "Public choice theory suggests," according to Roland Vaubel, "that both lending and conditionality are arguments in the staff's objective function."[67] Credit and conditionality, in this approach, are used strategically by IMF officials. Vaubel's approach suggests that exogenous factors such as the demand for IMF credits and the timing of quota reviews create an incentive for staff members to either strengthen or loosen the programs they design. This explanation is perhaps better suited to explaining year-to-year variation in loan size and conditionality than variation in the treatment of individual borrowers, and it has been criticized for (among other things) failing to take the complexity and uncertainty of the IMF decision setting sufficiently seriously.[68]

Shared Economic Beliefs and IMF Decision Making

There are some obvious reasons for scholars to take the influence of powerful members on the design and enforcement of loan programs seriously. The ED from the United States, in control of just under 17 percent of the voting rights apportioned to Board members, has veto power in the institution. The United States and four other countries—the United Kingdom, Germany, France, and Japan—control nearly 35 percent of the total votes. And the home base of the IMF is, after all, six blocks from the U.S. Treasury Department and even closer to the U.S. State Department.

But there are also good reasons to be skeptical of the idea that the big, rich countries pull all the strings at the IMF. The process by which voting power on the Board is transformed into influence over the design and enforcement of conditional loans is not straightforward. The IMF staff members have carved out a sizable degree of independence from the directors.[69] The Board meeting in which

---

66. Caraway, Rickard, and Anner 2012, 36 (quotation); Rickard and Caraway 2014.
67. Vaubel 1991, 211 (first quotation), 232 (second quotation).
68. See, for example, Willett's (2002) perceptive critique of "hard-core" bureaucratic public-choice explanations.
69. Eckaus 1986, 248; Martin 2006, 164; Tirole 2002, 117.

the letter of intent is discussed may be the first time that directors have seen the content of the final version of the agreement.[70] The votes on proposed loans are recorded on an up-or-down basis, and there are strong norms of unanimity in support of staff proposals and deference to the judgment of the staff among EDs. The Board almost always approves the content of the programs devised by the staff and management and presented to the directors at the Board meetings.[71]

All IOs need material resources to stay in business—and resource dependence is a prime lever by which rich and powerful states can manipulate IOs. But the resource dependence of IOs varies a lot, and the IMF is far more self-sufficient than, say, the United Nations (which depends on annual dues payments). The IMF does not depend on contributions from member states to fund its operations. The administrative costs of running the institution are covered by interest payments from the borrowers. The currency that constitutes the lendable resources of the IMF comes from the quotas of the members—the one-time buy-in deposit that establishes the membership of a country in the Fund. To keep pace with the needs of borrowers, the members of the IMF have occasionally agreed to ad hoc increases in their quotas.[72] Setting aside the nine times in its history that the Fund has sought general quota increases from its members, the institution does not haggle with states over funding for its activities.[73]

The layers of insulation surrounding the IMF staff and management are thicker than many observers realize. And further, the strategic interests of powerful states in the countries involved in IMF-led adjustment programs are often neither very strong nor clear (nor are conditional loans particularly efficacious instruments of foreign policymaking).[74] In some high-profile cases (the Russian agreements in the mid-1990s and the 2005 Iraqi standby agreement come to

---

70. EDs have long complained about this issue. In a January 1987 memo from Yusuf Nimatallah, the Saudi ED, to Sterie Beza, associate director of the Western Hemisphere Department, Nimatallah worried that "members of the Board are put in an embarrassing position every time their authorities learn before them in detail about important country adjustment programs supported by the Fund." Referring to the withholding of information about lending arrangements with Mexico and Argentina, Nimatallah wrote, "I do not appreciate the Board to be perceived as a rubber stamp that learns about cases only after the whole world has learned there is an 'agreement' between the Fund and member countries." Office Memorandum from Yusuf A. Nimatallah to Sterie Beza (associate director, Western Hemisphere Department), "Argentina," January 16, 1987.

71. The only documented modification of a loan proposal by the EDs during a meeting occurred in 1979, when the Board reduced the size of the loan proposed by the staff for Sierra Leone (Gould 2006, 235).

72. The approval of quota revisions requires an 85 percent supermajority of Board votes. It is during these episodes (and in other instances in which supermajorities are required) that the veto power of the United States looms large.

73. Barnett and Finnemore 2004, 49–50.

74. Woods 2006, 35–38; Nelson 1992, 309–16.

mind), there is evidence that the U.S. government put pressure on the IMF to bend the rules.[75] But it is rarely the case that the economic health of a borrower matters enough to one of the Great Powers to merit an intense lobbying campaign over the design and enforcement of a lending program.

How much influence do powerful states have on the IMF treatment of its borrowers? This is a question that cannot be answered in the absence of data, and I test for the strength of the argument in the chapters that follow. My conclusion is that the U.S. and the other Great Powers set the broad parameters for the operations of the institution; within these borders, however, the IMF decision makers have accumulated a good deal of discretion over what goes into the conditional lending programs of the institution.[76]

The argument in this book bears a similarity to the explanations that I group under strategic design and enforcement in Table 1.1. That approach accords the IMF staff and management significant discretion and locates the politics of conditional lending at the level of the strategic interaction between the IMF decision makers and the policymakers in the borrowing country. Explanations in this vein are built from elements that are the stock in trade of rational choice institutionalism in political science: interactions are characterized chiefly by conflicts of interest, trust is lacking because of strong incentives to hide and manipulate information (particularly on the side of the borrowing government), both sides (but especially the IMF) are attuned to signals that credibly communicate information about the type of actor (committed or uncommitted, strong or weak) sitting on the other side of the bargaining table, the credibility of signals are related to their costliness, domestic political institutions that constrain governments by imposing costs are important for understanding the content and enforcement of bargained agreements, and so on.

The insights from the approach are important. The level of analysis in this book is influenced by the strategic design approach. My argument, too, explains variation in program design and enforcement by examining how the IMF perceives the key features of the political environment in the borrowing country. But my perspective deviates from the strategic design approach by taking the concept of Knightian uncertainty—and its implications—much more seriously.

Economic policymaking is a tricky business. Policymakers choose targets—such as output growth, price inflation, unemployment, the distribution of

---

75. On the Russian case, see Stone 2002. On the Iraqi case, see Momani and Garrib 2010.

76. Ngaire Woods, writing on the Fund and the World Bank, arrives at a similar conclusion: "powerful countries define the outer perimeter within which each organization works. . . . This sets down a general direction for the institution, but seldom defines the detail of what each of the IMF and World Bank do" (2006, 180).

income, and the balance of international payments and receipts—and use different instruments to achieve the targets. But experience suggests that once a policy instrument has been activated (or deactivated) the effect of the change on the target is hard to forecast because "unforeseen and unpredictable events can swamp the influence of the chosen instruments."[77] The risk-only world assumes that decision makers can compute probabilities based on frequency distributions; they (or their predecessors) have been in this situation many times before and know the likelihood that, for example, reducing the growth of the money supply by X percent will increase the level of foreign reserves to Z. In an uncertain world, by contrast, the parameters are both more numerous and more unstable over time.[78] At the extreme, "highly complex, unobservable generators produce patterns that shift in unexpected directions."[79]

Experienced IMF officials acknowledge the uncertainty and complexity with which they grapple. Claudio Loser, the former director of the Western Hemisphere Department who began his career at the IMF in 1972, told an interviewer that at the IMF "all decision analysis occurs in uncertain contexts."[80] After Stanley Fischer left the IMF (having served as the deputy managing director from 1994 to 2001), he gave his former student, Olivier Blanchard, this *bon mot* in a discussion of crisis management: "the difference between knowing something and realizing what it implies can be quite intense. There are 47 factors in the background. Always. The key to managing a crisis is to figure out which of them really matters."[81] Fischer's lesson was not lost on Blanchard, who became chief economist at the IMF two weeks before the September 2008 bankruptcy of Lehman Brothers. Uncertainty has played a central role in his analysis of the state of post–Global Financial Crisis economic policymaking: "Since it is nearly impossible to know what will make investors shift their beliefs, the situation policymakers face here is one of 'Knightian uncertainty.'"[82]

The idea that decision makers face Knightian uncertainty does not imply that anything goes. In fact, a key concern of economic sociologists and constructivist international political economy scholars has been identifying the "governing ideas, institutions, norms, and conventions" by which actors impose a sense

---

77. Spraos 1986, 12.

78. The first generation of Keynes's students and acolytes recognized this point well. Dudley Seers, British development economist, argued similarly in an article published in the early 1960s: "a developing economy alters beyond recognition in a few years, so that average coefficients derived from figures for a decade or more may have little meaning" (1962, 329).

79. Abdelal, Blyth, and Parsons 2010, 12.

80. Quoted in Tenembaum 2004, 116 (my translation).

81. Blanchard 2005, 18 (quotation).

82. Blanchard and Leigh 2013. See also Blanchard's January 2009 guest article in the *Economist*.

of stability in their worlds.[83] Organizational sociologists have long recognized that institutions (be they government agencies, corporations, universities, or IOs like the IMF) develop their own internal logics of appropriate conduct, "instantiated in and carried by individuals through their actions, tools, and technologies."[84]

In *Rules for the World*, Barnett and Finnemore remind the discipline of international relations that IOs are, at bottom, bureaucratic organizations that possess distinct cultures. For this study, the most important insight drawn from their framework is the notion that the organizational culture of an IO is constituted, in part, by elements drawn from the external environment—namely, the norms and beliefs inculcated by professional training.

The IMF is a global governance institution with a nearly universal membership; the tally of member states currently stands at 189. But the heterogeneity of the membership of the institution is not paralleled in its staffing. Many of the key IMF decision makers come to the organization after going through graduate training in highly ranked U.S. economics departments. To put some data behind that claim, I collected the curriculum vitas of 983 appointees to top-level positions in the Fund between 1980 and 2000.[85] Nearly half (47 percent) of the appointees in the data set received a graduate degree from a top-thirty-ranked U.S. economics department. The degree of similarity is further illustrated by the fact that a relatively small number of universities were the training grounds for the vast majority of the senior U.S.-educated economists at the IMF.[86]

The training of many of the institution officials imprinted a strong attachment to neoliberal economic beliefs; those beliefs, in turn, underpinned the financial programming models that the staff and management use to formulate (and justify) the content of conditional lending programs.[87] Two factors—(1) recruitment and promotion practices and (2) rigidly hierarchical authority relations—reinforced the institutionalization of neoliberal economic ideas at the

---

83. Abdelal, Blyth, and Parsons 2010, 12–13.

84. Powell and Colyvas 2008, 277.

85. Many officials cycled through several senior positions during their tenure at the IMF; consequently, the number of appointments (983) exceeds the number of individuals (467) that appears in the data set.

86. About 80 percent of the U.S.-trained senior officials in the appointee data set received their training from one of just thirteen universities. These supplier universities were the University of Chicago (11 percent), Harvard University and Columbia University (10 percent each), Yale University (8 percent), University of Pennsylvania (7 percent), George Washington University (6 percent), Johns Hopkins University (5 percent), University of Maryland and Stanford University (4 percent each), and MIT, University of California–Berkeley, University of Rochester, and Princeton University (3 percent each).

87. Pop-Eleches 2009a, 32; Taylor 1988, 3; Williamson 1980, 269–70.

Fund.[88] The pressure to toe the line can be intense; as Kenneth Rogoff, former head economist at the IMF, observes, "fundamentally most people in the Fund believe in markets and market-based solutions to problems."[89]

The Plan for the Next Chapters

In chapter 2, I lay out the currency of confidence framework. I start by fleshing out two theoretically and empirically informed observations about the IMF-borrower relationship: (1) that key decisions in the conditional lending process are necessarily informed by the subjective judgments of the staff and management and (2) that those judgments are often made in the presence of uncertainty. From there, I develop a set of mechanisms that link shared economic beliefs to the measurable outputs of the decisions about each element of the conditional lending process (access, conditionality, and enforcement).

I turn to testing the main argument in chapters 3–5. The evidence in chapter 3 is quantitative. Statistically testing an ideational argument such as the one in this book poses a serious measurement challenge. I collected information related to the generosity, conditionality, and enforcement of nearly five hundred IMF programs signed in the 1980s and 1990s for analysis. The key explanatory variable is the ideational distance between the IMF and the borrowing government; what I want to see is if, after conditioning on other important covariates of IMF treatment, borrowing countries with policymakers who shared beliefs with the IMF received bigger loans, fewer conditions, and easier enforcement of the conditions. Because it was not feasible to directly survey the 2,000 or so policymakers who held important positions in the ninety developing countries for which I was able to collect data, I turned to indirect indicators of economic beliefs. I used biographical information on the policymakers to help me decide whether they were likely (or not) to hold neoliberal beliefs. The quantitative evidence is consistent with my central argument.

In chapters 4 and 5, I present the case study of the relationship of Argentina and the IMF over a quarter century (1976–2002). The qualitative case study gives me more fine-grained evidence with which to test the argument. Argentina is an important case because it experiences variation in both the dependent variable

88. See Ahamed 2014, 27; Chwieroth 2010, 34–40; Vetterlein 2010; Woods 2006, 7.

89. Quoted in Alan Beattie, "IMF Succession: A Contested Quandary," *Financial Times* (online ed.), May 25, 2011, http://www.ft.com/intl/cms/s/0/07ca28e0–8702–11e0–92df–00144feabdc0.html. Lance Taylor observed, "socializing pressures are fierce along both sides of 19th street in Washington DC" (1988, 148).

(treatment by the IMF) and independent variable (the consonance of the economic beliefs of the national policymakers and the beliefs of IMF officials) over time. It is also a prominent case in the history of the organization.

The case study provides two types of confirmatory tests. In the same way that there should be statistically significant (and substantively important) correlations between the key explanatory variable and the indicators of IMF treatment in the quantitative analysis, the IMF treatment of Argentina should be different when the top economic policymaking positions in that country were occupied by people I call neoliberals. If I observe that governments dominated by neoliberal officials received tough treatment by the Fund, this forces me to ask whether the explanation needs to be refined. If the facts of the case broadly fit the explanation, this increases our confidence that the key explanatory variable is not a trivial cause. And if the argument works in the Argentine setting, we should observe references in the IMF archival documents to the confidence of the staff and management in like-minded officials or discussion among IMF officials of the uncertainties that they faced in designing IMF programs for various Argentine governments.

Note, however, that there should be a unified logic of inquiry in multimethod research. A research design that includes quantitative tests implies that the relationships between variables are probabilistic. If I thought that the variable measuring ideational proximity explained 100 percent of variation in IMF treatment, there would be no reason to include the kinds of quantitative tests that I use as evidence in chapter 3. It would be unfair, then, to hold the case study to deterministic standards of explanation. The large-N data analysis suggests that there is a substantively important relationship between the presence of neoliberal policymakers and the IMF treatment of the borrowing countries. Along with my explanation, other factors may influence aspects of the Fund relationship with Argentina. What the case study should do is to show that the explanation that focuses on shared economic ideas is analytically and empirically powerful. I do not (and cannot) show that it is the *sole* cause of variation in the IMF treatment of Argentina over time; rather, I use the case-level evidence to show that it is a very important source of variation in IMF-borrower relationships.

In chapter 6, I shift the analytical focus from the design and enforcement of the IMF lending arrangements to their effects on domestic economic policymaking. There is a large (and largely inconclusive) literature exploring the role of the coercive pressure applied by the IMF in the wave of liberalizing policy reform that swept the developing world after 1979.[90] Rather than examining policy out-

---

90. I review the empirical literature in Nelson 2016.

puts, I look at variation in the types of officials that occupied the top policymaking posts in developing countries. The evidence suggests that the power of the IMF extends beyond influencing *how* the borrowing economies are governed; I argue that the institution, through its conditional lending programs, also influences *who* governs the economy. In chapter 6, I provide systematic evidence of an association between participation in IMF lending arrangements and the presence of neoliberal economic policymakers in the government.

In chapter 7, I make the implications of the argument and findings for the study of international political economy and IOs explicit. I also discuss the context for the resurgence of the institution since 2008. To see whether the argument and evidence about ideational proximity extends to the most recent epoch in the history of the Fund, I analyze the covariates of the relative size of 104 lending arrangements signed by borrowers between 2008 and 2013. The results indicate that the positive association between my measure of neoliberal economic policymakers' influence in government and the relative generosity of IMF funding packages (established in the previous analysis of nearly five hundred programs signed between 1980 and 2000) also holds for the recent batch of conditional loans. I wrap up the book with reflections on implications for the future of the Fund. The IMF remains the most powerful of the international institutions dotting the landscape of world politics. International relations scholars need to better understand the empirics of the institution; we should firmly establish what it has done in the world and theorize why the organization behaves in the way that it does. But we should also be mindful of the policy implications of our research. I reflect on the lessons offered by this study for making the IMF, an IO that affects the life chances of hundreds of millions of people around the world through its lending programs, a more legitimate and efficacious element of the system of global economic governance in which we are all embedded.

HOW SHARED ECONOMIC BELIEFS SHAPE LOAN SIZE, CONDITIONALITY, AND ENFORCEMENT DECISIONS

We have agreed to disagree.

—Wolfgang Schäuble, German finance minister

We didn't even agree to disagree, from where I'm standing.

—Yanis Varoufakis, Greek finance minister

This is a world of unknown unknowns.

—An unnamed U.S. economic official on the Greek sovereign debt crisis, 2015

How does the distance between the economic beliefs held by the decision makers at the IMF and the beliefs of the officials at the helm of the borrowing economies affect the design and enforcement of conditional lending programs? In this chapter, I develop arguments to answer this question.

Subjective judgment necessarily informs the IMF decision makers at each stage in the lending process. Judgments by IMF officials, I argue, hinge on the beliefs of the elite national economic policymakers with whom the members of the Fund in-country mission and management interact. The unavoidable element of subjective political judgment in IMF decisions is related to the second component of the analytical framework laid out in the chapter: the high degree of uncertainty facing decision makers in both the IMF and the borrowing country.[1] IMF officials acknowledge that their judgments about borrowers are very often formed

---

Epigraphs 1 and 2: Quoted in Suzy Hansen, "A Finance Minister Fit for a Greek Tragedy?" *New York Times Magazine*, online ed., May 20, 2015, http://www.nytimes.com/2015/05/24/magazine/a-finance-minister-fit-for-a-greek-tragedy.html.

Epigraph 3: Quoted in Landon Thomas Jr., "Uncertainty over Impact of a Default by Greece," *New York Times*, online ed., April 27, 2015, http://www.nytimes.com/2015/04/28/business/dealbook/uncertainty-over-impact-of-a-default-by-greece.html.

1. See also Best 2012.

in the presence of strong (Knightian) uncertainty.[2] Bringing uncertainty into the framework shifts the analytical foci away from features that are central to the explanations in the strategic design and enforcement vein outlined in chapter 1 (strategic maneuvering by rational, materially oriented actors, unevenly distributed information, and formal domestic political organizations and institutions) and toward shared mental models that are often emphasized by social constructivists.[3] Facing uncertainty, economic policymakers at both the international and domestic levels fall back on shared economic beliefs for guidance.

Finally, I lay out mechanisms that connect shared beliefs to variation in the design and enforcement of IMF lending arrangements. The testable implications of the framework are then teased out so that they can be brought to the quantitative and qualitative evidence in the next chapters. I expect to observe that, as the beliefs of the top economic officials in the borrowing government came closer to the neoliberal economic beliefs that dominate within the IMF organizational culture, the character of the relationship changed: access became more generous, binding conditions less numerous, and enforcement of conditions more lenient.

Subjective Judgment in the IMF Decision-Making Processes

In focusing first on the crucial element of subjective judgment in the IMF decision-making processes, I deviate from the view that the organization is a highly technocratic agency, tightly bound (in its "normal" times, when the most powerful stakeholders are relatively disinterested in the content of loans) to well-defined sets of bureaucratic rules that govern the design of its programs.[4] Key decisions related to the terms of access to the pool of Fund resources are based partly on inflexible rules that have evolved over time, but there is a good deal of

---

2. Take, for example, a selection from the summing up by Anne Krueger, chief economist, of the Executive Board discussion of the staff report on the role of the Fund in the 2001 Argentine economic meltdown: a number of EDs "pointed to the difficulty of judging a country's prospects of success, and considered that the Fund will inevitably need to continue to make judgments in weighing the risks of failure against the high and immediate costs of withdrawing support in difficult circumstances." Minutes of the Meeting of the Executive Board, EBM/03/106, November 17, 2003, p. 137.

3. Interest in the role of differing mental models in decision making is not limited to constructivists; an interesting (although outside the mainstream) literature in economics also takes mental models seriously as an analytical concept (see Denzau and North 1994; Rodrik 2014; Van den Steen 2010a, 2010b).

4. Miles Kahler, for example, has called the IMF "quintessentially technocratic and apolitical" (1990, 92). See also Copelovitch 2010, 57; Stone 2011, 25–26.

ambiguity in how the rules are to be interpreted and applied in individual cases.[5] IMF lending programs are, in part, exercises in forecasting future states of the world subject to ex ante unknown (and unknowable) changes in key parameters. Organizational rules and macroeconomic models only partly inform judgments about the likely paths followed by borrowers undergoing adjustment programs.

Other observers of the institution have also raised this point. For example, Barry Eichengreen, an esteemed international economist, notes that in the course of bailing out a country suffering from a severe economic crisis, "the IMF will have to make a judgment not just about the evolution of economic conditions but also about the political and social constraints." Eichengreen connects the unavoidable element of political judgment to the mixed track record of the Fund in crisis prevention and resolution: "this is troubling, since social scientists in general, and macroeconomists like those who comprise the staff of the IMF in particular, are not especially skilled forecasters of political outcomes. . . . it is likely to be exceedingly hard for the Fund to say that it is reluctant to lend because a member country is incapable politically of implementing an IMF program."[6] IMF officials themselves do not deny that judgment heavily informs the decisions of the organization. Anne Krueger, former chief economist at the Fund, has made the argument to critics: "devising any stabilization program inevitably entailed judgment. . . . anticipating macroeconomic events is not a precise science. . . . evidently, judgment had to be used. . . . It is always a difficult judgment call as to how much fiscal and monetary tightening and how much exchange rate change is the minimum that would have a significant chance for successful outcomes. There is also a question as to the ability and willingness of the relevant government official in the program country to undertake the agreed-upon policies."[7] The internal staff report on the IMF role in the Argentine economic crisis of 2001 included a similar claim: "the Fund's decisions to continue or withdraw its support to a member country in particular circumstances are always decisions made under uncertainty, and it is more likely than not that the Fund will continue to make occasional judgment errors and take decisions that will prove wrong *ex post*."[8]

To say that IMF officials' judgments about its borrowers are informed by more than simply the dispassionate analysis of the macroeconomic data at hand and the application of technocratic rules should not be particularly surprising. As I note in chapter 1, there is by now a sizable set of studies linking variation in IMF

5. Best 2005.
6. Eichengreen 2002, 60.
7. Krueger 2003, 304, 306–7.
8. International Monetary Fund (IMF) 2003, 72.

treatment to domestic political factors.[9] Some of the work in this vein, however, assumes a degree of political knowledge, foresight, and analytical sophistication on the part of Fund staff members that is at odds with how the officials of the organization talk about politics. On this point, staff members' views can be illuminating.[10] Consider a typical remark from a former top official—in this case, Vito Tanzi (who joined the organization in 1974 and served as the director of the Fiscal Affairs Department)—on the dominant currents in the organizational culture of the Fund: "the economists working at the Fund were not encouraged to get involved in, or even to become knowledgeable about, political issues.... As long as a government was firmly in power, the Fund was expected to be indifferent to its political nature."[11] It would be unreasonable to insinuate that a powerful global governance institution, staffed with many experienced and well-connected international civil servants, is totally disengaged from important political events and dynamics in its member states. But there is no organizational routine for systematically incorporating a broad range of political factors into program designs, and the nature of IMF-borrower interactions produces a particular kind of political judgment, centered on the perceptions of the staff members and management of a relatively narrow slice of the policymaking elite in the country.

Historically, the engagement of the IMF with domestic politics comes mainly through its interactions with the handful of top-level officials in the finance ministry and central bank. "The IMF invariably negotiates with the executive branch, and mainly with a small part of the executive branch.... A small group of technocrats at the ministry of finance and at the central bank will typically negotiate the IMF agreement in private," observes Jeffrey Sachs.[12] In the early 2000s, the Fund began to reach out to groups beyond the top cabinet ministers and monetary authorities (such as employers' groups, labor union representatives, and nongovernmental organizations [NGOs]) in an effort to develop a greater sense of ownership of its adjustment programs.[13] The focal points for the negotiations on the content of the lending programs, however, remained the boardrooms and corridors of the central government ministries with the task of making economic policy.

---

9. See, for example, Caraway, Rickard, and Anner 2012; Chwieroth 2013; Pop-Eleches 2009a, 2009b; Rickard and Caraway 2014; Vreeland 2003.

10. Given the principle of uniformity in the treatment of its members, however, IMF officials' comments proclaiming political ignorance should be read with the appropriate dose of skepticism.

11. Quoted in Kedar 2013, 138.

12. Sachs 1989, 264. Sachs, having served as an interlocutor on behalf of Bolivia during its negotiations with the Fund in the 1980s, was a highly knowledgeable observer of the organization and its interactions with member states. For similar claims, see Barnett and Finnemore 2004, 56; Woods 2006, 77; Vetterlein 2010.

13. Barnett and Finnemore 2004, 61–63; Bird and Willett 2004; Woods 2006, 189–90.

Judgment in the Stages of Conditional Lending

The initial step in my framework builds from the observation that IMF officials' political judgments are shaped mainly through their perceptions of and interactions with elite policymakers in the borrowing countries. Judgment, in turn, is an ineluctable element of the decision making associated with each component (loan size, conditionality, and enforcement) in the relationship of the Fund with its borrowers.

ACCESS

The wide variation in the size of loans and the ambiguousness of the rules governing members' access to credit reflects the uncertain—and fundamentally political—nature of the problem with which the Fund and the borrower grapple. The borrowing country has obligations to creditors that it might not be able to honor (because the monetary authority of the country has run down its stock of reserves or because inflows of private credit have dried up), and thus it needs an infusion of money from outside to help it make its payments while it adjusts to its new, more difficult economic conditions. But how much of the IMF credit will the borrower need to access to (temporarily) fill the financing gap? The IMF cannot mechanically derive the optimal size of a lending program by looking only at the numbers on the national balance sheet of the country. The current state of the balance of payments is of rather limited use when staff members and policymakers are settling on the proper size of a lending program. As Benjamin Cohen pointed out many years ago, "the accounting balance can do little more than indicate . . . the extent of balance or imbalance of *past* transactions."[14] The IMF and the national economic authorities have to forecast the size of the gap between the domestic consumption and investment requirements of a country, on the one hand, and the expected amounts of foreign exchange that the country will attract from various sources (exports, foreign investment, aid, etc.), on the other. Cohen nicely captured the uncertainty involved in forecasting the future borrowing requirements of a country: "the prognosis is a highly subjective one. . . . financing requirements are projected . . . in relation to certain levels of domestic consumption and certain rates of domestic investment which, in this context, *are matters of political judgment*."[15]

In line with Cohen's view, IMF officials acknowledge that decisions about the appropriate amounts of access for member states are, to a large degree, exercises in guesswork. Organizational rules mattered in the process: programs were for many years limited to 300 percent of quota (a cap on total program size that was

---

14. Cohen 1969, 51.
15. Ibid., 52–53 (emphasis added). See also Buira 1983, 126; Helleiner 1983, 353.

raised to 600 percent during the Global Financial Crisis of 2008), and members with patchy repayment records were restricted in the amount of credit that they could access. But those rules are often cast off when circumstances require. When asked by a number of EDs to justify an unusually large program proposed for Argentina in March 2000, the representative from the Fund Policy Development and Review Department (PDR; the unit charged with ensuring that the staff proposals and reports are consistent with the overarching goals of the organization[16]) responded by pointing out that "there were no hard and fast rules to determine access. The staff exercised a measure of judgment."[17]

CONDITIONALITY

Conditionality, too, involves a significant degree of subjective judgment on the part of IMF officials. The conditions in IMF loans serve multiple purposes. They limit the policy discretion of the borrower to ensure "full and expeditious repayment" of the loan.[18] In the view of the IMF, giving a member a loan without narrowing the range of policy actions available to the government risks feeding a permanent payments crisis (or, worse, rewarding failed policies). A second-order goal of conditional lending is to improve overall economic performance. Conditionality is a way to ensure that the borrower follows a consistent, comprehensive reform program because unfettered governments that institute effective reforms in one area of the economy often let policies deteriorate in another.[19] Conditionality can play a role in catalyzing inflows of private capital as well, by signaling that the borrower is serious about stabilizing and reforming the economy.[20]

The practice of conditionality evolved without any precise rules to guide staff members and management on how best to apply the policy tool. An institution-wide review of conditionality in 1978 produced guidelines intended to make the IMF treatment of its borrowers more consistent.[21] But by the mid-1980s,

---

16. The staff and management in the PDR exerted a heavy hand in its dealings with officials on missions from the regional units; some went so far as to call PDR the IMF "thought police" (Momani 2007, 48).

17. Minutes of the Meeting of the Executive Board, March 10, 2000, EBM/00/24, p. 147.

18. Polak 1991, 8. Sticking to the pre-arranged repayment schedule is a more pressing concern for the IMF than the risk that a country will default on its loans because "official" IMF debt is, by custom, senior to privately held debt and the nonrepayment of credit owed to the IMF is exceptionally rare (Bulow 2002, 239). Although some countries have missed a scheduled repayment, only a handful of very poor member countries have fallen into long-term arrears to the Fund.

19. Acemoglu et al. 2003, 50–51, 63.

20. Copelovitch 2010.

21. The policy, approved in March 1979, reads, "while no general rule as to the number and content of performance criteria can be adopted in view of the diversity of problems and institutional arrangements of members, only in special circumstances will performance criteria relate to other than macroeconomic variables" (IMF 1978, 2).

those guidelines were thrown out as the scope of conditions expanded to include "structural" distortions in the borrowing economies (eliminating subsidies, freeing prices of goods, liberalizing trade, privatizing state-owned assets, etc.). The expansion of Fund conditionality into the microstructures of the economies of countries was not accompanied by the creation of clearer rules to guide staff members involved in program design. The IMF mandate in tying access to structural reforms remained extremely ambiguous.[22] Ultimately, there is no limit on the number of conditions that can be attached to a loan, aside from what is judged to be economically salubrious and politically feasible.

ENFORCEMENT

The scope for discretion and political judgment is widest when it comes to decisions by staff and management to recommend waivers or to suspend a program because of noncompliance with binding conditions.[23] Whereas rules exist (albeit in ambiguous and evadable forms) to guide decisions about the amount of access to credit and the conditions that end up in the Fund adjustment programs, there are no formal rules to which the staff, management, and EDs of the Fund can appeal in the enforcement stage of the conditional lending process. In 2004, the Independent Evaluation Office floated the idea of instituting inflexible stop-loss rules that would lead to the automatic suspension of lending programs that had gone off track; the Fund staff members rejected the proposal, arguing that the "discretionary elements" of conditionality (more specifically, the ability "to grant waivers for missed performance criteria" and to push through program reviews so the borrower can access the next tranche of the program) "are necessary in view of the imperfect nature of any objective measure of policy performance and moreover provide an opportunity to reassess policies in relation to the overall program objectives and strategy." "No quantitative indicator," the staff report continued, "is likely to provide a one-dimensional test of viability" of the lending programs of the organization.[24] Subjective judgments about the commitment of the political authorities responsible for carrying out the dictates of the adjustment program continue to drive decision making at the enforcement stage.

---

22. Goldstein 2003, 379.

23. John Spraos notes the wide berth for discretion in the Fund enforcement activities in a critical review of conditionality: "targets are often missed by a substantial margin, despite the best endeavors of the powers that be. . . . the Fund recognizes this and departs from automaticity and thus objectivity by using its discretion in condoning breaches of targets *ex post*" (1986, 20).

24. "Staff Response to the Evaluation by the Independent Evaluation Office of the Role of the Fund in Argentina, 1991–2001," presented to the Executive Board, July 26, 2004, p. 112, http://www.ieo-imf.org/ieo/files/completedevaluations/072920046-staff.pdf.

Judgment in the Presence of Uncertainty

The decision-making contexts on both the borrower and the Fund sides are often highly unique, always complex, and (most important) suffused with a high degree of uncertainty. Uncertainty (in the Knightian sense) implies that policymakers' knowledge of the underlying parameters shaping economic and social life is too limited, too incomplete, or too fragmented to allow them to attach credible probabilities to future states of the world that might be brought about by their decisions (see chapter 1).

As an illustration, consider the September 2001 discussion of a proposed $8 billion augmentation for the loan to Argentina. A week before the Executive Board meeting to discuss the proposal, the Managing Director Horst Kohler called a meeting with the senior officials, the purpose of which was to gather the range of views on the chances of the program. The participants' estimates varied widely: guesses ranged from just above zero (expressed by Kenneth Rogoff, the new chief economist and head of the Research Department) to, at best, around 50 percent probability of success. Stanley Fischer, the second in command at the Fund, noted at the end of the meeting that none of the people in the room could know with any certainty that the augmentation of the standby arrangement would or would not work. In his view, the Fund had to give the benefit of the doubt to the Argentine policy team. Others agreed with Fischer's view that "precise quantification was not really meaningful."[25]

Other evidence for the role of uncertainty in Fund decision making comes from the record of IMF projections, which have often wildly deviated from the realized values of the forecasted variables.[26] The 2010 standby arrangement for Greece provides a stark example of how forecasting can go awry. The IMF staff predictions for Greek debt dynamics in 2010 suggested that the burden for the country was manageable; the debt/gross domestic product (GDP) ratio would peak in 2013 at 155 percent before falling toward the target of 120 percent in 2020. A program of economic austerity and structural reform—without any serious effort to get private bondholders to consider reducing their claims on the Greek government—went forward on the basis of staff projections. The depth of the downturn in the next two years far exceeded the IMF projections: the staff expected a 5.5 percent decline in real GDP, but the actual decline turned out to be 17 percent; unemployment was 10 percentage points higher than the staff

---

25. The meeting is described in two different sources: Blustein 2005, 140–42; Independent Evaluation Office of the IMF 2004, 53.

26. On the forecasting record of the IMF, see Conway 2006, 130–31; Easterly 2006.

projections; and the debt/GDP ratio in 2012 was 30 percentage points higher than the predicted path.[27]

Alongside point predictions for key variables that miss the realized values by wide margins, the forecasting abilities of the organization failed in the run up to some of the biggest market crises in the past forty years. Before Mexico suspended interest payments in 1982, kicking off the sovereign debt crisis that swept the developing world over the next decade, there was little concern among the Fund economists about the sustainability of the debt buildups of the low- and middle-income countries. In the months and weeks before the outbreak of the East Asian Financial Crisis in 1997, the IMF issued clean bills of health for several of the countries at the center of the crisis.[28] And the eruption of the crisis in the U.S. financial system and its transmission to the rest of the world in 2008 caught the officials of the organization by surprise; in fact, as the U.S. residential housing market cratered and the downward pressure on the value of mortgage-backed securities emerged in summer 2007, the IMF presented an optimistic assessment in its *World Economic Outlook*: "core commercial and investment banks are in a sound financial position, and systemic risks appear low."[29]

Uncertainty and the Autonomy of the Fund Staff and Management

Uncertainty plays two important roles in my argument. First, it helps us understand the wide scope for discretionary judgment granted by member states to the Fund staff and management. The irreducible uncertainty of the tasks at hand—managing global financial stability and shepherding borrowers through the straits of severe economic crises—is one reason why member states have been so willing to delegate authority to the staff and management of the organization.[30]

The tilting of authority toward the Fund staff and management is reflected in their peculiar relationship with the putative representatives of state interests within the institution, the EDs. All conditional lending arrangements are subject to approval by the EDs, and directors sometimes vigorously debate the staff proposals at Board meetings. But, in practice, the EDs do not tamper with the content of the proposals at the Board meeting. By the time the program is brought before the Board, the content of the agreement has been, for all intents and purposes, decided. The weakness of the EDs' oversight is a long-standing concern.

27. International Monetary Fund (IMF) 2013.
28. Kirshner 1999, 315.
29. Quoted in Joyce 2013, 163.
30. Barnett and Finnemore 2004.

During the 1978 Fund review of conditionality, the Dutch ED worried about the "too limited" involvement of the Board in the details of ex ante program design and ex post evaluation, noting, "We discuss at length a proposed stand-by and its conditions, ex ante, at the moment of concluding the arrangement but do not evaluate the final outcome of the stand-by and in particular whether the conditionality, considered in retrospect, was too harsh or too lenient."[31]

The EDs have not fully ceded authority to the staff and management; as Bessma Momani argues, their preferences may be reflected in efforts "by IMF staff to design agreements and reports that meet the interests of powerful Executive Board members to avoid stonewalling and expedite the approval process."[32] When powerful member states are uncertain about what to do, however, the message communicated from the home governments to their representatives on the Board will not be clear and consistent.

And an individual ED may not be a perfect agent for getting the interests of her principal into the design features of the lending program either. Because (unlike staff and top management) EDs are political appointees who tend to stay with the organization for a shorter duration than regular staff members, they may be less fully immersed in the neoliberal economic beliefs that predominate in the organization. But the claim about the cohesiveness of the IMF intellectual culture extends to the EDs, as well. Even when the home government would very much like to tamper with a staff proposal, the ED may resist because she has come to agree with the thrust of the program or because she does not want to pay the reputational cost incurred by bucking the organizational norm of cohesiveness.

Uncertainty and Shared Beliefs

The second role of uncertainty in my framework relates to the durability of differing views held by the policymakers involved in conditional lending programs. With Knightian uncertainty in the picture, there is no reason why differences in peoples' "priors" (their subjective beliefs about how the future course of events will play out) should collapse to a singly shared model—and this is the case even if more information becomes available to the decision makers. Information added to an environment rife with uncertainty is usually not assimilated by

---

31. "Intervention by Mr. H.O. Ruding at the Meeting of the Executive Board of the IMF on June 2, 1978 on 'Conditionality in the Upper Tranches,'" mimeograph found in the IMF Archives. For an insider's account of how the struggle between the EDs and the management and staff played out in the early years of the Fund (with "a strong Management/staff and an Executive Board that acted largely on Management recommendations" as the eventual outcome), see Southard 1979, 6–11 (quotation on p. 7).

32. Momani 2007, 41.

people in an unbiased fashion. As Dani Rodrik, a famously perceptive scholar of economic policymaking in developing countries, observes, "people often downplay evidence that seems inconsistent with their model of the world. Anomalous outcomes are dismissed as a fluke or as the result of insufficiently vigorous application of their preferred policy."[33]

Shared systems of economic beliefs—the mental models by which policymakers understand their worlds—always matter, but they become particularly important in conditions of uncertainty when material interests (and the routes by which those interests can be realized) are less clear.[34] Adding uncertainty to the analytical framework also helps clarify why people hewing to different beliefs in the realm of economic policymaking can remain at odds even when information is common and plentiful. Microeconomic models show how information on its own is not sufficient to generate convergence to a singly shared model of the world when agents' prior beliefs differ.[35]

Economic beliefs can drive apart policymakers' prior beliefs about, for example, the likelihood that the package of policy changes in an IMF-designed adjustment program will work. Someone hewing to the neoliberal policy template is likelier to believe that imposing strict limits on credit expansion, eliminating the government budget deficit, and removing price supports for agriculturalists and other producer groups will yield a sustainable balance of payments and (simultaneously) promote output growth than someone whose beliefs are informed by structuralist economics.[36] And because economic policymaking in difficult times is not a very good laboratory for learning—governments typically do not rapidly cycle through a series of alternatives to see which produces the best results, and the lessons from previous crises are contested, forgotten, or filtered through ideological lenses—the different and sometimes competing mental models held by policymakers tend to endure.[37] As a result, sincere, belief-driven disagreements

33. Rodrik 2014, 193. The claim is buttressed (indirectly) by the rich and deep vein in the psychology literature on how information is used by individual decision makers. In a highly influential (and extraordinarily widely cited) article, psychologist Robert B. Zajonc argues, "Most of the time, information collected about alternatives serves us less for making a decision than for justifying it afterward. Dissonance is prevalent just because complete and thorough computation is not performed before the decision" (1980, 155).

34. On this point, see Abdelal, Blyth, and Parsons 2010; Blyth 2002; McNamara 1998; Goldstein and Keohane 1993; Rodrik 2014.

35. Dixit and Weibull 2007, 7353; Van den Steen 2010a, 2010b.

36. There are large literatures on structuralist economic ideas; good starting points are Dosman 2008; Leiva 2008; Toye and Toye 2004. I discuss the content of structuralist beliefs in more detail in chapter 4.

37. van de Walle 2001, 43–44. For a similar claim about learning (and the lack thereof) in the context of armed interstate conflict, see Kirshner 2015, 173, 175.

over whether or not the set of policy changes recommended in the IMF adjustment programs will work have been a consistent feature of the interactions of the organization with its borrowers.

Birds of a Feather: The Rise of Neoliberal Policymakers in Developing Countries

In some settings, however, there was significant overlap between the views of top policymakers and visiting IMF officials. In the policy-reform literature of the 1980s and 1990s, these particular policymakers were often called neoliberals.[38] Some of the neoliberals were members of national (or transnational) groups of economic reformers. Research on the South American policy-reform experience supplies several examples—the Chicago Boys in post-Allende Chile,[39] Club Suizo in Colombia, the MIT/Stanford group in Mexico, the IESA (Instituto de Estudios Superiores de Administración) Boys in Venezuela, and the Fundación Mediterránea group in Argentina (among others in the region)—but the phenomenon was observed outside of South and Central America as well (with the Berkeley Mafia in Indonesia as perhaps the best-known example).[40]

Most neoliberal policymakers identified in the policy-reform literature were not members of well-known groups and did not possess much of an international profile. There were, however, several distinguishing and commonly shared characteristics that suggest they can, notwithstanding particularities ranging from the type of political regime in which they were embedded to their personal

---

38. Some scholars prefer to call the policymakers described in this section *technocrats* rather than *neoliberals* (e.g., Centeno 1993; Silva 2008). The *technocrat* label is often imprecisely defined. But for most analysts employing the term, it describes an official whose authority is derived from her expertise (which, in the words of Cohen and Sabel 2005, 777, lies well "beyond the grasp of laypersons"), who is motivated primarily by achieving objectively "correct" (and thus politically neutral) policy goals, and who is not closely tied to any particularistic interest group (be it political party, patron, or sectoral group). It is hard to think of many policymakers in developing countries who can check off all three items on this list of traits; perhaps as a consequence, the scholars employing the *technocrat* descriptor either emphasize only one of the traits or add an adjective, such as "market-friendly technocrats" (Centeno and Cohen 2012, 324). I prefer *neoliberal* because it effectively distinguishes the group of economic policymakers who had educational and professional experiences prior to entering their positions (which perhaps make them appear more technocratic than other kinds of officials), but who also (and more important) hold economic beliefs that are closer to those at the heart of the IMF approach.

39. The Chicago Boys, who did graduate work (although few finished their PhDs) in the Economics Department at the University of Chicago (most of them working with Milton Friedman and Arnold Harberger), were brought into policymaking in Chile under the autocratic rule of Augusto Pinochet in the mid-1970s; Silva 2008; Valdes 1995; Dosman 2008, 464–65.

40. On these groups (and others), see Corrales 2002; Dominguez 1997; Edwards 2014, 132–33; Edwards and Steiner 2000; Markoff and Montecinos 1993; Pepinsky 2009, 43–44; Amir 2008.

temperaments and other personality traits, be usefully grouped together under the same conceptual category. Neoliberal policymakers in developing countries had their training and professional backgrounds in the field of economics; they had gained significant exposure to the dominant economic ideas of the elite departments in the United States through either their formal education or through work experience in the IMF and/or the World Bank; and, by dint of their socializing experiences (both educational and professional), they were skeptical of (and in some cases outright hostile to) the alternative, non- or anti-neoliberal economic belief systems.

The policy-reform literature debated whether teams of neoliberal economic officials could engineer significant and durable market-oriented policy changes (an agenda that yielded rather mixed conclusions). But there was another important—yet largely overlooked—consequence of the presence of neoliberals in top-level positions in governments: the role that these individuals could play in reshaping the relationships of their countries with the IMF.

Why Neoliberal Policymakers Get Less Demanding (and More Generous) Programs

Policy teams composed partly (or wholly) of neoliberal-oriented officials share more common beliefs (and a similar analytical language) with the staff members and key decision makers at the Fund. The degree of similarity of the beliefs held by the policy team and the IMF management and mission members is linked to the judgments that inform IMF decisions governing conditionality, amounts of credit, and enforcement of the conditions in the programs of the organization.

SHARED BELIEFS, CONFIDENCE, AND MONITORING

In the context of conditional lending, IMF officials work from analytical models, rooted in neoliberal economic principles, that are deeply embedded in the institution. As the mandate of the Fund has expanded over time and more areas of the borrowing economies have come under its purview, the expansionist tendency of the organization has not been accompanied by a stronger commitment to mutual learning.[41] Negotiations with member states, as a consequence, tend to run in one direction. IMF officials have strong prior beliefs about the optimal mix of policy changes that will produce a successful adjustment program, and

---

41. Barnett and Finnemore 2004.

their efforts are aimed at getting the borrowing government to accept the key elements of the program.

When IMF officials and the top policymakers in the borrowing government have similar beliefs about what should be done to handle the crisis that brought the country to the Fund, negotiations are easier. The management and staff at the IMF have confidence that the policy team in charge of the program will "do the right thing." And when confidence in the policy team is high, owing in large part to the proximity of the beliefs held by the two sides, IMF decision makers are less concerned about the program going off track. As a result, they will not feel the need to use the main monitoring technology at their disposal (the binding conditions that are built into the program) as vigorously as usual.[42]

In this framework, the conditionality in the IMF programs is a form of oversight. Conditions are a way of exerting a measure of control over governments that, were it not for the constraints imposed by the agreement, would make the wrong choices from the staff members' perspective. Some of the top officials of the Fund have made just this kind of claim. Morris Goldstein, who started his career at the organization in 1970, argues that following the advice of anti-conditionality voices such as the members of the Meltzer Commission (the U.S. congressional advisory group chaired by Allan Meltzer, economist, that encouraged the Fund to drop all conditionality from its programs) "would require *more faith that the crisis country would want on its own to 'do the right thing.'*"[43] When the IMF decision makers have confidence that the borrowing government will do the "right" things—a perception that, in my argument, is strongly shaped by the presence of like-minded neoliberals in the top rungs of the policymaking institutions of the country—there is less need to use numerous conditions to hem in the borrower.

The main empirical implication of the mechanism relating monitoring effort to shared beliefs is illustrated in figure 2.1, which depicts the impact of common beliefs on the range of the bargaining between the IMF and its borrowers over conditionality in the loan agreements. There are two vertical axes in the figure: the axis on the left side represents the desirability (or utility) of the IMF program from the perspective of the borrowing government; the axis on the right side captures the (subjective) prior belief that the program will succeed from the perspective of the Fund staff and management. The curves in the figure depict

---

42. The mechanism linking common beliefs to monitoring effort operates in other environments as well. In corporate settings, managers are more comfortable delegating decisions, without much oversight, to workers who share the managers' beliefs (and thus are more likely to make the "right" decisions from the perspective of the management) (Van den Steen 2010a, 2010b).

43. Goldstein 2003, 415 (emphasis added).

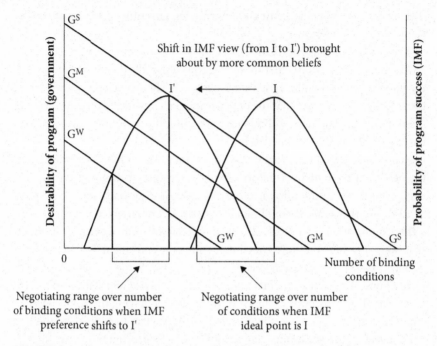

FIGURE 2.1 Shared beliefs reduce the preferred number of IMF conditions in lending program negotiations. G^M, moderately strong governments; G^S, strong governments; G^W, weak governments; I, IMF ideal point.

the government and the IMF preferences on the extensiveness of conditionality; the shapes of the curves reflect some simplifying assumptions, but those assumptions are not unrealistic. For the IMF, I depict the "ideal point" of the organization (with respect to the optimal level of conditionality) as the peak point on the inverted-U-shaped curve (I), which captures the idea that for the members of the IMF in-country mission and the management there is a point at which adding additional conditions to the program becomes counterproductive (but up to that peak point on the curve adding more conditions increases the likelihood that the adjustment program will succeed).

The assumption that there is a negative (but linear) relationship between the number of conditions attached to the loan and the perceived value of the program from the perspective of borrowing government requires more justification because, in drawing downward-sloping curves extending from the left vertical axis, I deviate from work in the strategic design and enforcement tradition (see chapter 1) that posits precisely the opposite relationship between conditionality and the desirability of the program. That is, in the framework developed by James Vreeland, officials in reformist governments may prefer *more* conditions in the agreements they sign with the IMF; in his argument, conditions serve as commitment devices for the borrower, and piling on more conditions increases commitment by raising the costs paid by the antireform opposition forces bent on blocking the program from going forward.[44] In contrast, I contend that the relationship laid out in figure 2.1 more closely reflects the actual preferences of most of the Fund members. In making this assumption, I draw on the observations of senior IMF officials, such as Michael Mussa (who moved to the IMF in 1980 and rose through the ranks of the organization to become its chief economist in 1991, a position he held for a decade). In Mussa's experience, borrowers almost always prefer weaker programs over tougher programs (in his words, "the choice of members understandably tends toward the high-disbursement, weak-conditionality facility").[45] Binding conditions may well serve as commitment devices for borrowing governments, but the rational-strategic interpretation ignores the other dimensions that make more extensive conditionality unattractive to borrowers: aside from making the program more difficult to administer and presenting more opportunities for slippage (and thus a greater risk of suspension or cancelation), conditions are meaningful. They signal a (partial) surrender of government control over some key areas of economic governance—and top policymakers in a country are generally disinclined to invite outside forces in to more closely dictate and monitor their decisions.[46]

Almost every government that approaches the Fund for a conditional lending program faces resistance (from, among other forces, nationalists in and outside the government who dislike ceding control to an IO and from the organized groups that stand to lose from the adjustment and reform efforts). Borrowing governments vary in their susceptibility to political backlash against conditionality; to capture the idea I include three downward-sloping curves in figure 2.1, with the highest conditionality schedule depicting governments that have reason to believe they are relatively insulated from resistance and that thus find IMF programs tolerable ("strong" governments, denoted by G^S in the figure); the two other curves denote moderately strong (G^M) and weak (G^W) governments (the

---

44. Vreeland 2003.

45. Mussa 2006, 19. Mussa also observes that "virtually all members prefer to deal with the sympathetic social worker rather than the tough cop" (2002, 68).

46. An observation from Kaushik Basu, writing during his time as a senior advisor in the Indian Ministry of Finance, illustrates this point: "One fear that all our political parties have is of foreign powers. Is the International Monetary Fund (IMF) infiltrating our polity too much through the sherpas of the ministry of finance?" (2011, 73).

weakest governments will find even IMF programs with low conditionality difficult to survive). The space between the IMF ideal point on the horizontal axis and the point at which the weakest government curve intersects with the IMF schedule defines, in this simplified heuristic model, the range of the number of conditions over which the IMF and governments will negotiate.[47]

In this framework, when there are shared beliefs IMF decision makers have greater confidence that the borrowing government will "do the right thing" and that the program, in turn, will succeed; as a consequence, there is less need to use extensive conditions to monitor the borrower. The effect of more closely shared beliefs (and greater confidence) is captured by the leftward shift in the number of conditions preferred by the IMF in the negotiations (from point I to I'). The observable implications of the positional shift in the IMF curve engendered by common economic beliefs are clear: the number of binding conditions in lending programs will (on average) be lower in the settings in which neoliberals are at the helm of the policy team, and given the wider negotiating space when the IMF ideal point is further to the right along the horizontal axis, the negotiations over conditionality will be lengthier and more difficult.

Two questions arise. First, why do the decision makers at the IMF choose to build more conditions into programs when there is disagreement rather than just devoting extra effort to persuading the borrowing government to come closer to the staff and management views? Negotiations are, after all, partly about the transmission of the beliefs of the Fund about adjustment to the prospective borrower (and vice versa)—and the organization devotes substantial resources, via its training programs and technical assistance missions, to persuading members that its policy recommendations are the right ones. But the scope for communication and persuasion is limited in the harried, time-constrained conditions under which the IMF mission and the crisis-stricken member governments enter negotiations.[48] There is a stark time-and-cost trade-off facing the IMF negotiators, and as in other settings when hard decisions have to be made, "in many cases persuasion is just not the right option."[49] Further, persuasion is unlikely to bring two sides with divergent sets of prior beliefs together—particularly when uncertainty is a key feature of the decision setting.

Second, why would programs include *any* binding conditions when the beliefs of the Fund and the domestic policy team completely overlap? Even though, as

---

47. The argument pertains to the *number* of binding conditions in IMF agreements, not to any specific *kinds* of conditions. The kinds of conditions that generate the most societal and political resistance (and thus might be omitted from programs) vary by national context.

48. Barnett and Finnemore 2004, 188n. 49.

49. Van den Steen 2010b, 624.

I show in the following chapters, the IMF principle of uniform treatment does not fit the data (because some borrowers systematically receive better deals), the organization has learned that its legitimacy would be put at stake if its members perceived that it had blatantly different rules for different classes of countries.[50] Omitting any hint of conditionality for one country using the same lending facility as other countries laboring under a high number of conditions would be unacceptable to a broad swath of the membership. IMF decision makers also understand that the policy team in place at the time of the negotiations might not be the same one at the helm of the economy three months later and that the new policymakers may not share the views of the IMF. Hence, even policy teams composed entirely of neoliberal officials have to deal with some binding conditions in the agreements that they negotiate with the IMF.

SHARED BELIEFS AND ACCESS TO IMF CREDIT

The logic of the argument about the link among shared beliefs, confidence, and conditionality extends to the relative generosity of lending programs, as well. Deciding on the appropriate amount of credit to grant to a member state is an exercise suffused with highly subjective judgment. The financing gap that the borrower needs to fill (in the case of a current account crisis) is the amount of credit that can fully cover the import bill of the country and enable it to pay off the maturing debt in the near term—but, as Stanley Fischer notes, estimates of the financing gaps of countries are "bound to be inaccurate."[51] In crises generated by panics in the financial markets that result in sharp cutoffs of inflows of financial capital (and, in capital account crises, large and rapid outflows from national financial systems), estimating the financing gap that needs to be filled using official sources is even more difficult.[52] There are rules in place to cap the access of borrowers to IMF credit, but those rules can be bent when governments face exceptional circumstances.

---

50. The perception of unequal treatment has long been a sensitive issue for developing countries, triggered by the 1967 UK standby agreement, which was a relatively large drawing that did not include any binding conditions. Much later, in a statement before the managing director, long-time Brazilian Executive Director Alexandre Kafka called that agreement a "watershed," noting "that [the British] standby brought the Fund holdings of the member's currency practically to the 200 percent mark, which was then considered the effective maximum available. Nevertheless, the staff proposed neither phasing nor performance criteria. While their proposal was supported by the Executive Board, it was also noted that a similar absence of conditionality had not been available to most other members." Minutes of Executive Board Meeting, EBM/86/190, December 3, 1986.

51. Fischer 2001, 39.

52. The modal IMF adjustment program deals with a crisis springing from an imbalance in the current account; in Ghosh et al.'s (2008) record of 236 IMF programs (1972–2005), just 16 were set up to deal primarily with capital account crises.

Judgments about the appropriate amount of access to Fund resources are influenced by how much confidence the Fund decision makers have in the policymakers overseeing the adjustment program. When there are disagreements between the IMF mission members and the top officials in the borrowing government about what to do, there is good reason (from the perspective of IMF officials) to use conditions to more closely monitor the borrower. Likewise, when there is disagreement and confidence in the policy team is low, the IMF will want to limit the amount of credit that the borrowing government can access. When the staff and management working with the domestic policymakers have a high degree of confidence in them (and thus believe that the program has a good chance of succeeding), they are more inclined to support requests for large disbursements. In the contexts in which the Fund staff and economic officials in the government share neoliberal economic beliefs, convincing the management and EDs to sign off on larger-than-average programs is easier because there is a clearer case to be made that the relatively generous program will succeed and thus IMF resources have not been put in jeopardy of being misused (or, in the extreme case, of nonrepayment).

FRIENDS IN NEED: SUPPORTING FRIENDLY
(BUT FRAGILE) POLICY TEAMS

To this point, I have derived two central testable implications from my argument. When the IMF is dealing with policy teams containing individuals who share the cluster of beliefs that underpin the Fund approach, disagreement is less common and the level of mutual confidence is higher; as a result, IMF officials (1) feel more comfortable letting the program go forward with fewer conditions in place and (2) are more willing to grant greater access to the resources of the organization.

Another mechanism, also related to the degree to which the two sides share economic beliefs, may have an important effect on the character of IMF-borrower relations. This mechanism links, in a more straightforward way, the political judgments made by IMF decision makers to the design and (especially) the enforcement of its conditional lending programs.

To start, consider the difference between the relationship of the IMF management with member governments and the relationship of management with workers in a firm. In corporate settings, managers try to hire employees who share the "correct" beliefs and who, from the perspective of the management, will then go on to make good choices (and managers can try to drive out the employees who do not share those beliefs). The laws, norms, and practices of self-determination in world politics, by contrast, preclude the IMF from intervening in the politics of its members by handpicking the individuals who are put in charge of managing the economy of a member.[53] Given that the relationship between the IMF and its borrowers is smoother when the domestic policy team shares the views of the organization, and with the understanding that economic policymakers are always at risk of being jettisoned by the leadership (and the heirs apparent may be far less sympathetic to the Fund views), IMF decision makers are motivated to support like-minded neoliberals in top-level policy positions. But the organization cannot (in all but the most unusual cases) directly intervene in the political decisions to select, retain, or replace top government officials. Are there any other (less direct) means by which the IMF can provide political support for friendly but fragile policy teams?

The stringency of program enforcement is the main lever by which IMF officials can try to shore up like-minded policymakers under pressure. When a borrower has fallen out of compliance with one or more of the binding conditions attached to a conditional lending program (as borrowers very often do), the staff and management can deliver one of two possible recommendations to the Executive Board: suspend the scheduled drawings until the program is back on track (thereby cutting the country off from much-needed infusions of hard currency) or waive the missed conditions (allowing the borrower to continue to access tranches of credit in spite of its noncompliant status). Policymakers presiding over lending programs that are suspended due to noncompliance face an elevated risk of being removed from office; for example, the withdrawal by the IMF of support for the first economic policy team under democratically elected Argentine President Raúl Alfonsín in February 1985 led directly to the removal of the team and its replacement with a new team (composed, not coincidentally, of officials whose views were closer to those held by IMF staff and management). IMF in-country officials prefer to work with policy teams containing individuals who share their economic beliefs; when teams dominated by neoliberal policymakers fall out of compliance with the conditions attached to the adjustment program, I contend that frequently the Fund decision makers judge it to be excessively risky to pull the support for the government by suspending the program. The cost of, in essence, sanctioning noncompliance is lower than the perceived benefit to the organization of doing what it can to support the like-minded officials under pressure—which, in this case, means recommending waivers to enable the borrower to continue accessing Fund resources rather than suspending the program.

---

53. The IMF was constitutionally mandated, in the wake of the Dayton Accords that marked the end of the brutal civil war, to select and appoint the central bank governor for Bosnia and Herzegovina for the first six years after the ratification of the Constitution—but I am not aware of any other case in which a country handed over appointment power to Fund officials.

Theorizing about the IMF-Borrower Relationship

The arguments I develop in this chapter yield one general expectation—the character of the IMF relationships with its borrowers is strongly shaped by the proximity of the economic beliefs of the two sides. They also yield three specific hypotheses that I take to the data in the next chapters: when the top national economic policymakers and the decision makers at the IMF share common beliefs, I expect to find that the number of binding conditions in loans is fewer, the amount of access granted to the borrower is larger, and the enforcement of the conditions is laxer.

The focal objects of inquiry in this study are the decisions that define the contours of the relationship of a borrower with the IMF, the most powerful IO in world politics. These decisions are the products of collective, group-level deliberations. The primary level of analysis is what sociologists call the meso level. Meso explanations lie at a level of granularity below the macro-level concepts and mechanisms that define the broadest contexts in which collective decisions are formulated and at a level above the micro mechanisms that focus on individual processes, attributes, and traits (emotional, cognitive, and genetic).[54] For example, research that situates outcomes in the very broad context of a hegemonic global culture of neoliberalism privileges the macro level of analysis. Because my interest lies in explaining the surprising degree of variation in the IMF treatment of its borrowers, macro-level theoretical constructs (such as global neoliberalism) cannot do much to help me understand the problem.

The key role played by shared economic beliefs in my argument invites thinking about micro-level mechanisms that might be important for understanding the IMF-borrower relationship. Two possibilities stand out. First, the commonly shared beliefs that in my approach are integral to group-level decisions about monitoring, access, and enforcement may have an effect on individual affective judgments. People are likelier to become friends if their beliefs overlap. But the fact that, say, the head of the IMF mission and the finance minister of a country have personal affection for each other is unlikely to be a satisfactory explanation for outcomes such as the extent of conditionality and the relative size of the disbursement, which are, as I have noted, the product of collective decisions involving many people.

A second possible micro-level mechanism involves social networks that tie individuals together. Networks seem to matter for a range of outcomes. Economists have shown, for example, that congressional representatives who are part

---

54. See Hackman 2003 for an illuminating discussion of different levels of analysis in social scientific research.

of the same alumni network are more likely to vote together and that firms with board members and managers who have tight political connections to the ruling regime are treated differently by the markets than firms lacking such political connections.[55] We could try to make the case that the neoliberal policymakers and IMF officials are members of a loosely defined social network, constituted by exposure (primarily via education in U.S. economics departments) to a set of economic ideas.[56] The issue for the network-based mechanism, similar to the emotional-affective mechanism, is how network membership (even if we accept my very loose conceptualization) can be used to explain the variation in program design and enforcement. Alumni networks among legislators or business associates can promote quid pro quo deals (e.g., two legislators connected to each other through a social network might trust that the other is more likely to honor the deal to vote for one another's pet projects than someone who is not part of the network), but it is hard to see how that logic extends to the IMF-borrower setting. IMF officials are well compensated, unelected, bureaucratically insulated international civil servants; there is not much that a domestic policymaker, part of the IMF officials' social network or not, can credibly deliver to Fund decision makers in exchange for preferential treatment.

In the next chapters I turn to testing the mechanisms, starting with statistical tests using quantitative data drawn from a large sample of IMF conditional lending programs. From there, I move to more fine-grained qualitative evidence drawn from the important case of Argentina. The evidence strongly suggests that systematic differences in judgments by the IMF about its borrowers are rooted in the perceived beliefs of the policymakers at the helm of the economies of the borrowing countries.

---

55. Cohen and Malloy 2014; Fisman 2001; Faccio 2006.

56. The circulation of IMF officials within the departments of the organization makes it highly unlikely that multiple members of the in-country mission or departmental management will be tightly connected (sharing membership in the same cohort in the same economics graduate program, for example) to top policymakers in the borrowing government.

PLAYING FAVORITES

Quantitative Evidence Linking Shared Economic
Beliefs to Variation in IMF Treatment

In this chapter, I statistically test the argument linking shared economic beliefs to
the treatment by the IMF of its borrowers—that is, that the makeup of domestic
policy teams systematically affected the decisions taken by the IMF about the
design and enforcement of its programs. I begin by describing the measures of
IMF treatment before turning to the (indirect) indicators of policymakers' economic beliefs that I used to construct the key variable in the analysis.

Measuring the IMF Treatment of Its Borrowers

For most of the history of the IMF, the granular details of lending arrangements were inaccessible to outsiders. Occasionally, financial journalists obtained
leaked copies of IMF documents; otherwise, the Fund and its negotiating partners closely guarded the information contained in the documents signed by the
member governments. The thick fog of secrecy that enveloped the negotiations
between the Fund and its members hobbled research on IMF-borrower relations.
"A proper audit of IMF conditions," fretted Ian Little, a development economist,
"is not possible. No full comparative account of them, how they vary from case to
case, how they have evolved, has been made. The exact role of the IMF will never
be known because the degree of agreement and disagreement between it and the
government is secret at the time."[1]

---

1. Little 1982, 316.

The IMF went through something of a transparency revolution in the early 2000s. The Meltzer Commission, convened in 1999 by a Congress disinclined to raise the U.S. quota contributions after the East Asian Financial Crisis, lambasted the IMF for its secrecy and opacity. Making the Fund archives available was an important step to opening the Fund to the scrutiny of outsiders. With access to the archives, I was able to collect the documents that outline the terms of IMF agreements, including the size of the loan, phasing of disbursements, binding and nonbinding conditions, and policy commitments and goals set out by the economic authorities of the country involved.[2] The data set I put together includes nearly all of the high-conditionality agreements signed between 1980 and 2000.[3]

Measuring the relative generosity of the IMF programs is straightforward. I calculated the amount granted to the recipient country as a percentage of the annual quota contribution of the country. To illustrate the wide variation in relative loan size, in figure 3.1 I plot the indicator for each of the nearly five hundred lending arrangements included in the data set. Because the raw loan-size-to-quota data are so heavily skewed (the measure ranges from 14 to 1,939 percent of the country quota), I log-transformed the indicator, which makes a visual comparison of the measure more legible (and makes the statistical estimates of the covariates of relative loan size more reliable).[4]

I visualize the loan size information using a strip plot. The plot allows me to display the interquartile range of variation in the measure for each year (captured by the boxes in the figure), the median size of loans in each year (denoted by the horizontal line inside the boxes), and the (logged) loan-to-quota values for each individual observation in the data set (displayed as the short vertical

---

2. When an agreement is reached, officials produce two documents (the Letter of Intent and Memorandum of Understanding) that are submitted to the Executive Board for approval. These documents outline the terms of the agreement. The data set includes each of the conditional lending facilities: standby arrangements (SBA), extended fund facilities (EFFs), Structural Adjustment Fund (SAF), Enhanced Structural Adjustment Fund (ESAF), and Poverty Reduction And Growth Facility (PRGF).

3. *High-conditionality agreements* are loans that are (generally) larger than 25 percent of the quota of a country. Agreements within the first credit tranche (smaller than 25 percent of the quota) typically do not include performance criteria. I picked the decades between 1980 and 2000 as the time frame for the empirical analysis for two primary reasons: (1) the general approach of the IMF to conditional lending in the developing world was solidified after the 1979 review of conditionality, and (2) the period between the debt crises of the early 1980s and financial crises of the late 1990s marks the era of the most sustained and active IMF involvement in developing countries through its lending facilities.

4. Exponentiating will restore the log-transformed value to its original (pretransformation) value. Applying the formula for the largest program (relative to the quota) in the data set shows that the 1997 Korean arrangement was 7.57 in log points, or 1,939 percent of quota ($e^{7.57} = 1,939.14$).

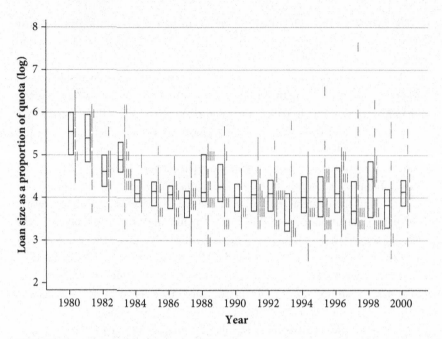

FIGURE 3.1 The (relative) size of IMF programs over time

"pipes" next to the boxes).[5] The variation in the relative size of conditional IMF loans between 1980 and 2000 was large; moreover, for much of the time window there is no clear upward or downward trend in the average (logged) loan size. The first three years of the 1980s are exceptional; the median values of the loans negotiated in that period were significantly larger than the loans that came after 1984. There is a simple reason for the break in the loan-to-quota data: at the moment when the developing-world sovereign debt crisis erupted, driving up demand for Fund resources, the quota contributions of the members lagged far behind their financing requirements. The IMF member quotas had not been significantly revised since 1963.[6] A revised quota system, intended to bring the contributions of the members in line with their greater financing needs, came into effect on November 30, 1983. As a consequence, in the main statistical analysis of the covariates of relative loan size I include only the programs signed in the years between 1984 and 2000.

---

5. When there were multiple loans in a year that had the same value, the pipes are stacked on top of each other.
6. IMF 2000.

Measuring the extent of the conditionality in the IMF lending programs is more challenging. Typically, IMF programs include several different kinds of conditions. Performance criteria, whose violation triggers the suspension of the program, are more binding than other kinds of conditions, such as benchmarks and indicative targets (on which the viability of a program rarely hinges). Most conditions are specified in the documents that lay out the details of the arrangement, although some policy changes (called prior actions) must be satisfied before the agreement can even come up for Executive Board approval.

In the statistical tests that follow, I report only the results of the analysis of the covariates of the performance criteria in the IMF conditional lending programs. There are two good reasons to regard performance criteria as the most important and informative measure of the stringency of programs: they are, after all, the conditions with the sharpest teeth (in that their violation triggers a suspension of the next tranche of the loan in the absence of a Board-approved waiver or modification to the program), and given their centrality to the programs, they are (unlike some of the other types of conditions) almost always unambiguously spelled out in the texts containing the terms of the IMF arrangements.

Zeroing in on the performance criteria as the main indicators of conditionality is the first step; the next step requires a rule for comparing the extent of conditionality in different programs. I opted for a simple and imperfect—but nonetheless highly informative—measure of conditionality: I counted up the number of performance criteria attached to the agreements.[7]

There is a trade-off in using this coding rule. I sacrifice potentially interesting information about the particularities of the individual conditions in arrangements between countries and the Fund to develop an indicator that lets me compare, on a single dimension, *all* of the programs for which I was able to find the texts in the IMF archives that described the performance criteria. The counting approach is, in any case, consistent with the mechanism laid out in chapter 2. (Recall that the main observable implication is that the comprehensiveness of conditionality is decreasing in the increasing ideational proximity of the domestic policy teams to the IMF.)

Beyond the pragmatic reasons for using the measure, counting up the number of binding conditions in programs does tell us something important about how

---

7. I record the loan size and conditionality in the agreement as initially agreed on and approved—the method is akin to taking a snapshot of the content of the program when it was formulated, and it is the most common way to organize data on IMF treatment. See Copelovitch 2010; Gould 2006. But see also Stone 2008, 2011 for an alternative approach that counts the number of *categories* of conditions at each of the test dates for a sizable sample of IMF loans.

the IMF makes decisions about how tough it should treat borrowers. Programs with many performance criteria are comparatively more onerous than programs with few binding conditions. They are administratively (and politically) more demanding for governments to carry out; increasing the number of performance criteria means there are more opportunities for slippage and, in turn, an elevated risk that a program will go off track and face suspension. And even though the counting approach cannot account for the variation in the relative toughness of *specific* conditions that appear in Fund agreements, the number of conditions included in an agreement is frequently the major point of contention in loan negotiations. As Graham Bird observes, developing countries "themselves insist on the use of only a limited number of performance criteria in an attempt to maximize their own degree of policy discretion," whereas the Fund staff and management often prefer to add more conditions to constrain member states (particularly those governments that are less likely, from the IMF perspective, to "do the right things").[8]

I visualize the variation in the extensiveness of conditionality over time in IMF programs using (as I did for the loan-size indicator) a strip plot. The boxes in figure 3.2 denote the interquartile range of binding conditionality in 486 loans signed the years between 1980 and 2000; the horizontal line inside the boxes denotes the median number of performance criteria in the programs concluded each year; and the short vertical lines next to the boxes display the values for each of the individual loans in the data set.

Two patterns are notable in the raw data. First, the average number of performance criteria in IMF programs increased over time (the median number of performance criteria climbed from eight to fourteen during the time window); second, in every year the scope of the conditionality in the Fund loans varied widely. Some borrowers agreed to relatively narrow programs with a small number of conditions, whereas others received expansive agreements with numerous binding conditions.

I also collected data on the enforcement of conditionality. A government that misses the targets spelled out in performance criteria may find that its program has been suspended and, as a result, that it has been cut off from access to the next tranches of the program until the IMF mission can report that the program has been brought back in line with the targets (or the original criteria are modified). If the deviations from the program are severe, the agreement might be cancelled. Enforcement of binding conditions is uneven, however, because governments

---

8. Bird 1983, 172.

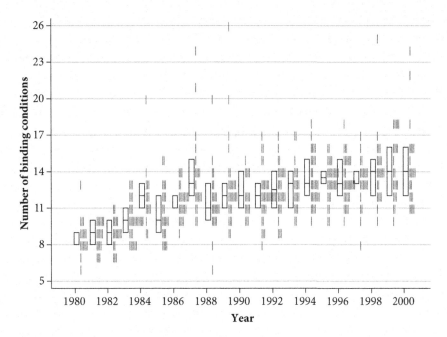

FIGURE 3.2 Performance criteria in IMF programs

can obtain waivers for missed targets that allow drawings to continue without interruption.[9]

The records of waivers were unavailable to external researchers prior to the opening of the Fund archives. Consequently, scholars relied on two indirect measures of enforcement. First, by comparing the proportion of funding actually drawn to the amount agreed on at the outset of the program, investigators indirectly inferred whether Fund decision makers had cut off the borrower.[10] This approach assumes that any country that did not draw 100 percent of the loan was punished for noncompliance. The second approach compares the schedule

---

9. The staff, management, and country representatives in the IMF rely on subjective judgments in supporting and approving requests for waivers. My interviews with EDs indicated that they do not take waivers lightly. One European ED emphasized the reputational risks he took by backing waivers recommended by the staff. Supporting a program that ultimately proves untenable would, he said, erode his credibility with other members of the Executive Board and, most important, with the upper-level management at the organization; in his words, "the most important role of the Executive Director is to be credible for the Managing Director . . . to be able to say 'yes, you can take that risk, these people are serious.'" Author's interview with an ED (name withheld per the interviewee's request), February 7, 2008.

10. Killick 1995 pioneered this approach, which is critically examined in Vreeland 2006, 364–65.

of planned disbursements to the observed pattern of disbursements and assumes that gaps indicate punishment intervals by the IMF for noncompliance.[11]

Both measures are problematic because they cannot differentiate between programs that were legitimately suspended for noncompliance and programs that were concluded early by governments that simply did not want or need the program.[12] I avoid this problem in my construction of a measure of enforcement by relying on newly available records of the issuance of waivers. I recovered from the Fund archives a complete record of the decisions by the Executive Board to approve waivers for borrowers that had fallen out of compliance with programs in the years between 1980 and 1997.

I use two different indicators of enforcement in the statistical analysis. The first measure of enforcement is a dichotomous variable that takes a value of 1 when a waiver is approved by the Executive Board and 0 for years when a program is active and a waiver has not been issued. This measure of enforcement, however, has some shortcomings. Ideally, we could assemble a sample consisting of borrowers that sought and received a waiver to compare with a sample of borrowers that also needed—but were denied—waivers. Countries under IMF programs that had no need for a waiver (and thus did not receive one) could be omitted from the analysis. The problem is that we observe the staff decision to recommend a waiver only—and the Executive Board always approves the staff recommendation, even when the discussion of the proposal is contentious.[13] The staff members are given the discretion to recommend a waiver, but we cannot feasibly observe (in a large sample of countries over two decades) the cases in which the staff privately considered and ultimately rejected recommending a waiver for a borrower. Given the shortcoming of the dichotomous indicator for waivers, I examined a second measure of enforcement stringency: the number of waivers approved by the Board.

To summarize, with access to the Fund's archives I collected three main measures of variation in the IMF-borrower relationship. My indicator of the

---

11. Edwards 2005; Stone 2002, 2004.

12. Randall Stone tries to avoid this problem by using evidence from interviews and press reports to confirm that programs were suspended for noncompliance. Stone did not have access to archival materials for his work and thus admits that "a considerable amount of uncertainty remains in the measurement" of punishment intervals (2002, 51–52). (In his 2011 book, however, Stone was able to analyze the covariates of the number of waivers issued during program reviews for the years between 1992 and 2002.)

13. Even in the rare cases when the representatives from the most powerful member states dispute the staff recommendation, the waiver is ultimately approved. This is not to say that the Executive Board is powerless (it can discourage staff members from even proposing a waiver), but it does suggest that by the time proposals reach the Board they are take-it-or-leave-it offers that the EDs always accept (Martin 2006, 143).

generosity of access granted to the borrower is the size of the loan relative to the quota of the country, the measure of the extensiveness of conditionality in the statistical tests is the number of performance criteria set out in the loan agreement, and my preferred indicator for the stringency of enforcement is the Executive Board decision to approve a waiver requested by the staff for a borrowing country that has missed one (or more) of the binding conditions in the agreement. I turn now to the challenge of constructing the measure of a key concept in the book—the degree to which the members of the economic policy team share some core economic beliefs with the decision makers at the Fund.

Identifying the Key Members of the Policy Team and Measuring Their Economic Beliefs

Who are the top economic policymakers that drive the adjustment program of a country? We know from a number of previous studies of IMF-borrower interactions that the IMF mission and management tend to fixate on the individuals at the top of two bureaucratic arms in most governments: the finance ministry (which is typically charged with managing fiscal policy) and the central bank (in charge of the monetary policies).

But the approach I take in this chapter does not just assume that the finance minister and central banker are the officials at the apex of the national policy-making team. I use the documentation of the IMF itself to identify the key policymakers in a country. The major national economic officials always sign the Letter of Intent specifying the terms of the agreement; the signatories of the Letter of Intent are, in this approach, then recorded as the key economic policymakers of the country.[14] Because the leader of the country preserves final authority over economic policymaking, the economic policy team in this analysis consists of the signatories to the agreement plus the chief of government.[15]

To test the argument, I need some method for tapping into individual policymakers' beliefs. Surveys and survey experiments are tools that social scientists commonly use when they want to directly measure nonmaterial, individual-level concepts such as beliefs, identities, attitudes, and preferences. By dint of the scope

---

14. The finance minister and central bank governor sign the Letter of Intent for the majority of IMF programs; however, in other countries the planning minister, prime minister, or special economic advisor is a signatory.

15. I used the *Archigos* (version 2.8) global database of leaders, compiled by Hein Goemans, Kristian Skrede Gleditsch, and Giacomo Chiozza, three political scientists; http://www.rochester.edu/college/faculty/hgoemans/data.htm (last accessed June 24, 2015).

of the analysis—over eighty low- and middle-income countries made use of IMF resources in the 1980s and 1990s, and I seek to test the argument on the broadest possible sample of countries—directly querying a huge number of policymakers to try to uncover their beliefs is impossible. The enormous costs and complexities involved in surveying the beliefs of many hundreds of policymakers in the developing world during the period of my study required an alternative approach.

I turned instead to biographical information as an indirect way of distinguishing neoliberal economic policymakers from other types. I combed through individuals' backgrounds looking for experiences that are highly likely to transmit (via the powerful force of socialization) the suite of neoliberal beliefs (see chapter 1). I settled on two background experiences that distinguish the officials that, from the perspective of the IMF, are likely to "do the right things" when they manage an adjustment program: educational background and previous employment.

The first is the educational background of policymakers. A number of researchers provide evidence that graduate training in economics "is a transformative experience for doctoral students that creates strong professional identities."[16] It is widely recognized that mainstream U.S. economics departments were hubs for neoliberal economic ideas, and I focused on the top departments.[17] Consequently, I code policymakers as being of the neoliberal type if they earned a master's degree or above from a highly ranked U.S. economics department.[18]

---

16. Kogut and Macpherson 2008, 114. See also Chwieroth 2007a, 2007b, 2013; Fourcade 2006, 2009. Reflecting on this line of research, David Colander, an economist, writes, "the replicator dynamics of graduate school play a larger role in determining economists' methodology and approach than all the myriad papers written about methodology" (2005, 175). See also Colander and Klamer 1987; Colander and Brenner 1992; Klamer and Colander 1990.

17. My strategy for selecting the top departments was to compare a large number of different rankings of economics programs in the United States over the past thirty years. The approach showed that, although the rankings of the different departments can vary widely in terms of placement on the list, there is consistency in terms of the universities that are ranked in the top thirty over time and across rankings. I surveyed several rankings of economics departments in the United States: Davis and Papanek 1984; Dusansky and Vernon 1998; Graves, Marchand, and Thompson 1982; Hirsch et al. 1984; Hogan 1984; Scott and Mitias 1996

18. I am aware of only a handful of other efforts to code the educational backgrounds of a large sample of policymakers in developing countries. Adolph (2013) gathered complete career histories (including educational backgrounds) for central bankers in 31 developing countries (he has less complete records of central banker backgrounds for 110 countries from 1973 to 2003). Adolph did not, however, collect data on policymakers other than central bankers (his illuminating book focuses on the link between different career trajectories and central bankers' preferences on inflation). Jeffrey Chwieroth (2007a) looks at the backgrounds of policymakers in twenty-nine developing countries between 1977 and 1999, which is a considerably smaller sample than the one I collected for this study. Chwieroth also makes some questionable coding choices. He records finance ministers and central bank chiefs as neoliberal if they earned a PhD from one of the top ten economics departments, defined in terms of publication frequency in the *American Economic Review* (a choice that oddly excludes the University of Minnesota, regarded as a leader in the rational expectations revolution that

The second socializing experience involves policymakers' previous employment histories. In addition to the officials that were educated in highly ranked U.S. economics departments, I code policymakers who had significant, sustained work experience in the IMF and the World Bank as being in the group of neoliberal officials.[19] The reason for selecting the IMF as a professional environment conducive to the transmission of neoliberal beliefs should not require much explanation.[20] The World Bank, although offering a perhaps more heterogeneous intellectual culture than the Fund (owing largely to its more expansive mandate in developing countries), nonetheless also remained an incubator for neoliberal economic beliefs.[21] The neoliberal orientation of the World Bank in 1980s and 1990s becomes even clearer when contrasted with the UN economic agencies, whose policy advice was built largely on a non-neoliberal framework. As Richard Jolly, at the time one of the prominent UN economic officials, later recalled, "we looked at the Bank with a great deal of suspicion. . . . We, with our own structuralist, multidisciplinary, more radical stance on many issues, particularly international trade issues, tended to see the Bank as more of a bastion of neoclassical, somewhat conservative analysis. . . . I believe that over the 1980s, the Bank did not change very much. It continued mainstream adjustment policies with a certain amount of change in rhetoric."[22]

My data set includes the dates of entry into and exit from office and accessible biographical information for more than 2,000 economic policymakers and

---

swept the field of macroeconomics in the 1970s and 1980s). Chwieroth's restrictive approach excludes some well-known neoliberal officials. For example, Miguel Mancera, the central bank governor of Mexico between 1982 and 1997, obtained an MA in economics from Yale—in Chwieroth's approach, Mancera would not be coded as a neoliberal. Similarly, Leslie Delatour, a Haitian finance minister whose "radical 'free-market' economic policies helped transform him into a national demon soon after his appointment in April 1986" started but did not complete his doctoral program in economics at the University of Chicago (Danner 1987, 59) and, according to Chwieroth's restrictive coding rule, would also not be considered a neoliberal official.

19. By *significant, sustained work experience* I refer to employment in a position involved in the day-to-day operations of the institution. It is important to make this distinction because many policymakers are appointed as the representative of their country on the IMF Board of Governors, which meets only once per year. These fleeting, mainly symbolic experiences with the institutions are unlikely to have the kind of socializing effect that deep involvement in the institution as a staff member, advisor, or ED imparts.

20. Well before the onset of the developing-world debt crisis, Susan Strange, the gimlet-eyed analyst of world politics (and progenitor of the field of international political economy) identified "the habit of poor countries of recalling staff members from the Fund after a few years to take key posts at home in the finance ministry or the central bank. The Fund thus functions at times as a nursery for monetary managers, producing a worldwide 'old boy network' of officials susceptible to its influence" (1973, 269).

21. Sarfaty 2012; Woods 2006.

22. Quoted in Weiss 2005, 48–49, 113.

leaders in 90 low- and middle-income countries observed between 1980 and 2000. I used a wide variety of sources to construct the policymaker data series; an overview of the main sources I consulted during the data-collection process appears in the appendix that follows this chapter. I used the information I collected on economic officials and heads of state to create the main variable of interest in the analyses, which I refer to in the book as proportion neoliberal.

My aim with this variable is to capture the degree of ideational coherence among the members of the domestic economic policy team (plus the head of the government). Some policy teams are, after all, divided. To cite one example, Richard Webb, the Peruvian Harvard-trained central bank chief (having survived the transition to the Alan Garcia administration in his post thanks to Article 151 of the Constitution of Peru, which specified that the central bank governor could be removed before the end of his or her five-year term only by impeachment initiated by the Peruvian Senate), constantly battled with the more left-leaning structuralists in the finance and planning ministries.[23] Similarly, Sylvia Maxfield describes the divisions within the Mexican policy team during the run up to the 1982 Mexican debt crisis, in which Carlos Tello, the heterodox central banker who had studied economics in an East German university, rejected the proposals coming from the "neoliberals" in the Finance Ministry.[24]

The index is constructed by calculating the proportion of the key policymakers who had one (or both) of the socializing experiences that are likely to transmit the set of neoliberal beliefs (see chapter 1) to individuals:

$$\text{Proportion neoliberal} = \frac{\text{Number of neoliberals in top policymaking positions}}{\text{Total number of important economic policymakers}}$$

The proportion neoliberal indicator ranges in value between 0 (no neoliberals in important economic policy positions) and 1 (a fully unified policy team in which neoliberal officials occupy each of the top policy positions, including the office of the head of state).

In table 3.1, I use a hypothetical example to illustrate how the proportion neoliberal measure is constructed (and how the indicator might change in a country over time). In the example, the policy team is identified as the finance minister and central bank governor (both of whom were, in this illustrative case, the signatories on an IMF agreement) plus the country leader. In the first time period (t), only the central banker among the top policymakers had the kind of

---

23. Lago 1991, 251.
24. Maxfield 1990, 11, 123–24.

TABLE 3.1 Construction of the proportion neoliberal variable over time

TIME PERIOD	FINANCE MINISTER	CENTRAL BANK GOVERNOR	COUNTRY LEADER	VALUE OF PROPORTION NEOLIBERAL
t	0	1	0	0.33
$t + 1$	1	1	0	0.67
$t + 2$	1	0	0	0.33
$t + 3$	0	0	0	0

educational and/or work experience that, according to my coding rules, distinguishes her as a likely holder of neoliberal economic beliefs. If in the next period ($t + 1$), a new finance minister with graduate training from a top-ranked U.S. economics department was brought into the government, that change is reflected in the uptick in the index (from 0.33 to 0.67). In the last time period ($t + 3$) in this example, a new government enters and none of the officials in the top policy posts had the experiences that are likely to confer familiarity with and acceptance of neoliberal ideas, and the value of the indicator drops to 0.

This is an admittedly blunt indicator for the ideational makeup of a government. I have a coding rule that attempts to transform a theoretically important but difficult-to-measure concept (neoliberal policymakers) into a categorical variable on the basis of socializing experiences in individuals' educational and career backgrounds prior to ascending to office. I do not weigh (based on my own subjective judgments) any of the socializing experiences more heavily than others, either on the basis of the site for the experience (a Chicago-trained official is not recorded as being more neoliberal than someone educated in the MIT economics department), the duration of the experience, or the degree of achievement in that socializing environment (i.e., above the threshold of graduate coursework in U.S. economics departments, I do not distinguish in the coding between those who earned a masters degree and officials who completed their PhDs). Nor do I weigh one policymaking position more heavily than the others in the construction of the proportion neoliberal indicator.

The goal of the exercise is not to construct the perfect indicator but, rather, to develop one that captures—albeit imperfectly—the proximity of the beliefs of the two sides when the Fund decision makers are formulating the details of lending programs. I show empirically in this chapter that the rough-and-ready measure of shared beliefs is a powerful explanatory variable. The granular details of the ideational compositions of the policy teams and their varied relationships with the IMF can be fully captured only in primarily qualitative, historically oriented case studies—an approach that I deploy in chapters 4 and 5 using evidence from Argentina.

There is solid evidence behind the claim that the recipients of graduate train-ing in highly ranked U.S. economics departments are much more likely to hew to neoliberal beliefs (see chapter 1). But that does not necessarily imply that depart-ments in the U.S. reproduced automatons. When, in the process of assembling the biographical data, I found convincing evidence in secondary sources that someone unexpectedly espoused non- (or even anti-) neoliberal beliefs, I did not record that official as being of the neoliberal type. Kighoma Malima, an impor-tant Tanzanian economic official during President Julius Nyerere's tense negotia-tions with the IMF in the 1980s, is a case in point. Malima completed his PhD in the Princeton University economics department as a student of Arthur Lewis, the Nobel laureate. (Malima's dissertation emphasized the responsiveness of Tanza-nian peasant farmers to market-based price signals, in fact.) But as a policymaker, Malima was obstinately opposed to the IMF orthodoxy. "Affected by structuralist views," Malima and his fellow Tanzanian policy-team members "didn't like the institution, its officials, or its policies."[25] Against the IMF approach, he contended that "planning, rather than leaving everything to the whims of the free market, is the only effective means of solving our economic difficulties."[26] In my research for this book, I found very few individuals like Malima—but the example suggests that a dose of subjective judgment in coding policymakers' beliefs is necessary. When the narratives in secondary sources reveal that officials' views were at odds with what we would expect based purely on their biographical information, the coding rules have to be adjusted so that those officials (like Malima) are not dubi-ously recorded as being of the neoliberal type.

The top-level economic policymakers who fit the neoliberal criteria were a surprisingly rare breed: out of the entire sample of finance ministers and central bankers (in total, around 2,000 officials from 90 developing countries observed between 1980 and 2000), my coding procedure identified just over two hundred episodes in which the position was held by an official with neoliberal credentials (although in some of those episodes the neoliberal official remained in office for a lengthy period).

The bulk of the policymakers who I identified as likely holders of neoliberal beliefs—77 percent, to be precise—had educational experiences before ascend-ing to office that met my coding criteria (i.e., they earned advanced degrees from top-ranked U.S. economics department). Among the officials who were coded on the basis of their educational background as being of the neoliberal type, there was a sizable degree of concentration in their training grounds; 44 percent of the

---

25. Edwards 2014, 100.
26. Quoted ibid., 133.

neoliberal policymakers studied economics in one of five U.S. universities (in descending order of commonness: Yale University, Harvard University, and the universities of Chicago, Pennsylvania, and Wisconsin). In the sample, 20 percent of the neoliberal officials had significant work experience in the IMF, and 17 percent of the neoliberals identified in the data-collection process had worked at the World Bank at some point before they took the policy post.[27] And it is worth noting that, out of a total of 462 country leaders for whom I have data, only 14 were coded as neoliberal using the criteria I developed in the project (and half of the neoliberal leaders headed governments in Latin American countries).

Other Covariates in the Statistical Analyses

In addition to the main explanatory variable, I include a set of other covariates of IMF treatment in the statistical tests. The idea is to subject the hypothesis linking the ideational makeup of the policy team to variation in IMF treatment to the toughest possible tests. To that end, I include variables that correlate with aspects of IMF treatment in other studies or were suggested by the alternative explanations for variation in IMF-borrower relations.

Economic Covariates

The "uniformity of treatment" principle of the Fund (that any variation in treatment of borrowers reflects differences in their economic "fundamentals") is the baseline hypothesis against which political explanations must be tested.

To capture the possibility that tighter, tougher programs reflect severer economic problems, I use several covariates in the models to measure relevant features of the economic landscape of the borrower. I use two main indicators to measure the severity of the external economic constraints of countries: international reserves as a percentage of external debt (reserves) and debt as a percentage of gross national income (GNI) (debt/GNI).[28] I also include the growth rate of GDP per capita (economic growth rate) in the models as an indicator of the macroeconomic performance.

---

27. The socializing experiences—educational background and work experience at the Fund and World Bank—are not mutually exclusive, and some officials in the data set had both kinds of experiences in their biographies. Relatively few officials were coded as being neoliberals because they had *only* IMF work experience (12 percent) or *only* World Bank experience (9 percent) in their backgrounds prior to joining the policy teams of their countries.

28. The two indicators of indebtedness are drawn from the World Bank Global Development Finance database, http://data.worldbank.org/data-catalog/global-financial-development.

It is essential to include an indicator for policy liberalization in the analysis. If neoliberal officials are more likely to be observed in countries that have pursued market liberalization *and* the IMF decision makers are less likely to include binding conditions in programs undertaken by countries that have liberalized their foreign economic policies, failing to control for the degree of economic reform would then overstate the impact of ideational proximity (measured by the proportion neoliberal variable), particularly when the outcome of interest is the number of conditions. In the main set of statistical tests, I include a dichotomous measure of trade liberalization (liberalized trade).[29] But I also try a different specification with an index variable that combines information about market openness from several different policy areas (trade, capital and current accounts, domestic financial market regulation, agricultural policy, and product market regulation) to see if the results change.[30]

Because I have three different elements of conditional lending as the outcomes of interest in this chapter, each with its own particular features, not all the statistical models include exactly the same covariates. In the model of the correlates of the size of IMF loans, for example, I include an indicator for the current account balances of the countries (current account balance).[31] Countries with larger current account balances may have larger financing gaps and, as a result, require more access to the pool of Fund resources. Previous research has linked compliance with binding conditions to levels of inflation and government consumption in borrowing countries; consequently, these measures (inflation and government consumption) are included in the models of waivers.[32]

Intra-Organizational (Bureaucratic) Covariates

Some scholars emphasize incentives and routines at the bureaucratic level as keys to making sense of variation in the outputs of the decision making of the Fund.

---

29. The indicator comes from Wacziarg and Welch (2008), who updated and improved the variable originally collected by Sachs and Warner (1995). It is worth noting that the liberalized trade indicator is robustly correlated with international investors' evaluations of the creditworthiness of developing countries; see Nelson 2010 for statistical evidence.

30. I constructed the alternative, broader index of policy liberalization from the data set collected by Giuliano, Mishra, and Spilimbergo (2013). I do not use this as my main measure of policy liberalization in the statistical models (I prefer, instead, to use liberalized trade from Wacziarg and Welch 2008) because of a significant number of missing observations in the components of the broader liberalization index.

31. The current account balance comes from the IMF World Economic Outlook database, https://www.imf.org/external/ns/cs.aspx?id=28.

32. Stone 2002. Both variables are drawn from the World Bank World Development Indicators, http://data.worldbank.org/data-catalog/world-development-indicators.

Barnett and Finnemore's framework, oriented around organizational cultures (and positioned in the bottom right-hand corner of table 1.1, my typological mapping of explanations of IMF-borrower relations), implies that, as a consequence of the IMF expansionist drive "to incorporate more and more aspects of domestic life into its stabilization programs," there was an expansion of conditionality over time.[33] To account for organizational mission creep, I include a variable (time counter) that starts at 0 in 1980 as one of the covariates in the model of the correlates of performance criteria.[34]

I include two other variables to account for the possibility that bureaucrats in the organization used the scope for discretion in program design and enforcement as opportunities for institutional, departmental, or even personal aggrandizement.[35] As global financial conditions worsen, the interest rate subsidy provided by the IMF (because interest on its loans is for most borrowers well below market rates) becomes more attractive, enabling the staff to increase lending and to expand conditionality. The IMF should, in this line of thinking, also be tougher in enforcing conditions when alternative sources of funding for borrowers are scarce. As a measure of global financial conditions, I include the annual nominal U.S. Treasury bill rate. I also include a measure of the total annual use of IMF credit and administrative resources as a percentage of the total quota of the IMF provided by the members (use of quota). This indicator captures the annual level of demand for IMF resources by member states and should (if we take the public-choice view of organizational decision making) be positively correlated with conditionality and negatively correlated with the amount of funding disbursed.[36]

Strategic Design and Enforcement Covariates

Among the alternative frameworks to the one developed in this book, the approach I term strategic design and enforcement (see chapter 1) fixes attention most closely on the constellations of materially oriented interests that can affect the terms of IMF-borrower relations. One variant of this framework highlights the special treatment that the IMF, responding rationally to its incentive

---

33. Barnett and Finnemore 2004, 71.

34. To account for time dependence in the logit model of the determinants of waivers, I include three natural cubic splines (Beck, Katz, and Tucker 1998).

35. Both covariates come from the data collected by Dreher and Vaubel (2004).

36. The logic of the public choice view is as follows. During periods when the demand for IMF credit is lower, the staff reduces the number of conditions in programs to make borrowing less costly for governments, and when demand spikes and there is little unused lending capacity, the staff increases the number of conditions to exert more control over borrowers (Vaubel 1991, 232–35).

structure, doles out to "systemically important" member states.[37] I use the natural log of GDP (log(GDP)) as a standard way to measure the size of the economy of a country (and hence the risks posed by its collapse for the economic performance of its neighbors and, potentially, for the global economy as a whole).[38]

Other work in this vein focuses on the role of organized domestic political actors and formal political institutions. Randall Stone and Grigore Pop-Eleches, for example, highlight the partisanship of the government in office in their (separate) work on IMF-borrower relations. Some readers may ask why, if economic beliefs play such an important role in the theory developed in the book, I devote rather little attention to governmental partisan orientations—after all, political parties on the left in historically rich Northern countries are less friendly to neoliberal beliefs than parties and politicians on the right. I do include in all the models an indicator for government partisanship (left-wing government) to see whether the ideational composition of the policy team mattered for program design and enforcement, even after conditioning for the partisan character of the government.[39] But there are some clear limits to how much we can learn about shared beliefs and, in turn, variation in the IMF treatment of its borrowers from an indicator of government partisanship. In some settings in the developing world, politics is dominated by catchall, nonprogrammatic parties led by charismatic personalities. Often there is little connection between the kinds of economic beliefs that bring the government closer to the IMF (or drive the two sides apart) and the electoral party platform (or the label attached to the party). Further, in some cases a party from the left wing of the political spectrum took power and quickly appointed neoliberal-type policy elites to implement a very different agenda than the one on which the party leader had campaigned. (We see a stark example of this phenomenon in the case study of Argentina.) In such a case, the types of individuals on the policy team are much more informative about the likely character of the government interactions with the Fund staff and management than the putative ideological position of the ruling party. Thus, the models include an indicator for the partisanship of the government, but I contend that competing ideas about economic policy may not always line up along partisan lines.

---

37. Pop-Eleches 2009a.

38. Pop-Eleches (ibid., 89–102) includes GDP per capita (but not GDP) in his statistical tests; however, he treats indicators of the debt load and country reserves as the measures of systemic importance of borrowers in his statistical models of loan size in Latin America and post-communist Europe (his data for the analysis of the number of conditions cover only post-communist countries from 1993 to 1998).

39. The Database of Political Institutions (Beck et al. 2001) records the political party of the chief of government and the largest party in government. I code the variable as 1 when either the executive or the largest party in the governing coalition is recorded as a left-wing party.

The models include a handful of other measures of domestic political factors. Two of those measures—the electoral cycle and the level of democracy—appear in other work on the correlates of IMF treatment, but neither variable has an a priori unambiguous relationship with the outcomes examined in this chapter. The literature on the economic effects of the electoral cycle suggests that governments are more prone to adopt "irresponsible" macroeconomic policies in the period just preceding competitive elections. An internal review by the IMF staff, for example, identifies preelection dynamics as an important cause of deviations from binding conditions in at least six major programs in the 1980s and 1990s.[40] In this case, the IMF should be tougher on countries before elections.[41] On the other hand, in the honeymoon period following an election the IMF might be more lenient on the new government. To measure the electoral cycle, I used the World Bank Database of Political Institutions (DPI) to gather the dates of elections in countries in the sample. Because political business cycles should be present in competitive elections only, I included elections with multiple candidates and/or parties only (denoted by a score of 5 or above in the DPI electoral competitiveness index). Two dichotomous variables were generated from this process: an indicator that takes a value of 1 if a legislative or executive election is scheduled in the next six months (preelection period) and an indicator for elections that occurred in the previous six months (post-election period).[42] In the model of waivers, the election indicator takes a value of 1 if there was a competitive election in year t.

The effect of regime type on IMF treatment is controversial. James Vreeland suggests that the IMF might prefer negotiations with dictatorships, which are more insulated from societal forces and can thus more readily commit to and carry out tough conditions.[43] Others argue instead that democracies, not autocracies, can more credibly commit to policy courses.[44] Regime type is measured continuously via the widely used Polity2 score.[45]

Vreeland argues that executives might seek to bring in the IMF when there are many veto players in place that can prevent the executive from pursuing her preferred policy changes; in contrast, the IMF might be tougher on countries with

40. IMF 1997.
41. Dreher (2004) provides evidence that program interruptions are more frequent around elections.
42. Beck et al. 2001. I ran analyses using separate indicators for legislative and executive elections, and experimented with different lengths of time for pre- and post-election variables; the results did not change significantly in the alternative specifications.
43. Vreeland 2003, 88.
44. For example, Schultz and Weingast 2003.
45. Marshall and Jaggers 2007.

many veto players because ambitious reforms are less likely to be carried out in these cases.[46] I include a veto points indicator in the statistical models.

I also include indicators for political instability. "Violent political instability," argues Christopher Adolph, "is likely to increase inflation by reducing the ability and incentives of politicians to commit to low inflation."[47] The IMF may be tougher with countries in the midst of upheaval (and hence prone to more erratic macroeconomic policymaking); to account for this possibility, I include a political violence index in the model of conditionality.[48] And to account for the possibility that the IMF is more likely to issue a waiver for countries experiencing political instability, I include a variable (political instability) that equals 1 if the Polity2 score (regime type) changes (in either direction) by at least three points during a three-year period.[49]

Covariates of Powerful Principals

I include a handful of variables to account for explanations that focus on how borrowers of particular strategic and economic importance receive special treatment from the Fund. I add two measures to control for the strategic importance of a borrower to the most materially powerful member of the IMF—the United States. First, Stone argues that political significance is indicated by the flows of foreign aid.[50] I include a variable that records annual (logged) U.S. military aid and grants (log(U.S. military aid)).[51] Dreher and Jensen suggest that voting in the UN General Assembly is a better variable to measure the effect of geopolitical interests on the behavior of the IMF.[52] The similarity of voting profiles in the UN General Assembly is used as an indicator of the closeness of a borrower and powerful state in a number of studies of the IMF.[53] The measure I use captures the similarity of the voting decisions of a borrower and the United States on UN General Assembly resolutions. The variable (U.S. affinity score) ranges from −1 to 1, with higher values indicating closer relations.[54] If the United States intervenes in the lending behavior of the IMF, we should observe that friendly, politically influential countries received bigger loans with fewer conditions and were more frequent recipients of waivers.

---

46. Vreeland 2003. The veto points indicator is drawn from Keefer and Stasavage 2003.
47. Adolph 2013, 159.
48. The political violence indicator records the intensity of annual episodes of intra- and interstate conflict (Marshall 2010). The index ranges in value from 0 to 13.
49. Fearon and Laitin 2003.
50. See Stone 2002, 2004, 2008, 2011.
51. U.S. Agency for International Development (USAID) 2012.
52. Dreher and Jensen 2007.
53. See Barro and Lee 2005; Oatley and Yackee 2004; Thacker 1999.
54. Gartzke 2006.

Finally, to capture the impact of private financial interests on IMF treatment, I create a dichotomous variable (Paris Club) that is coded positive when a Paris Club debt restructuring agreement was reached in the six months preceding or following the initiation of an IMF program.[55] I expect that these are periods in which creditors are both more interested in the content of IMF programs and better organized than usual.[56] Many, but not most, IMF loans are accompanied by freshly negotiated Paris Club debt agreements.[57]

Methods of Analysis

Because the data on IMF treatment have very different properties—two indicators are count variables (I recorded the numbers of performance criteria in programs and the numbers of waivers in Executive Board decisions to extend a program for a noncompliant country), another is a continuous indicator of loan size (relative to the country quota, and log-transformed to reduce skewness in the data), and the remaining measure of IMF treatment is a dichotomous variable (the decision by the IMF to issue a waiver or not)—I specify several different kinds of statistical models. To test the correlates of the relative size of loans, I estimate Prais-Winsten regressions with panel-corrected standard errors and an AR(1) correction.[58] When the outcome is the total number of binding conditions, I fit Poisson models with robust standard errors clustered by country. When the dependent variable measures whether a country under an IMF program receives a waiver, I estimate logistic regressions with robust standard errors clustered by country. And finally, when the number of waivers is the dependent variable, I estimate negative binomial count models.[59] Most of the explanatory variables are lagged by one year to reduce simultaneity bias.[60]

---

55. Creditor countries organize Paris Club negotiations, but the comparability of treatment clause extends the terms of restructurings to outstanding private debt.

56. Gould 2006. I also ran the models of conditionality and loan size with a measure of G5 bank exposure (drawn from Copelovitch 2010) as a covariate (see the robustness checks later in the chapter).

57. Van der Veer and de Jung (2006) report that Paris Club debt agreements accompanied 45 percent of loans signed between 1987 and 2004.

58. Beck 2001.

59. This follows Stone (2011, 191–93), who analyzes the covariates of the number of waivers granted by the Board between 1992 and 2002.

60. Because I have the date of approval for all the programs signed by the IMF and a borrower, I can identify the period of the year in which the program was concluded. For more accurate estimates, when a program was signed in December I include data for the year of the observation; otherwise, covariates (save for proportion neoliberal) are lagged by one year.

Discussion of the Statistical Results

Correlates of Loan Size

I start the discussion with the results from the model of the covariates of the (logged) size of the IMF loans (1984–2000). Throughout the chapter I use dot-plots to visualize the findings from the statistical analyses. The figures show, for each covariate in the analysis, the estimated coefficient and the 95 percent confidence interval around the estimate.

The results from the baseline loan size regression ($N = 373$) are displayed in figure 3.3.

The findings in figure 3.3 conform to one of the central implications of the argument: conditioning on a set of other factors thought to affect the amount of access granted to borrowers, there is a statistically significant and substantively large correlation between the proportion neoliberal variable and the loan/quota ratio. Based on the results from the baseline model reported in figure 3.3, a 1 standard deviation increase in the measure is associated with an increase in the

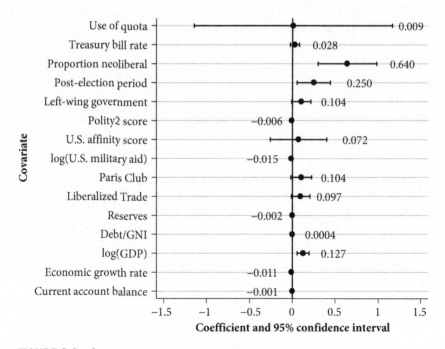

FIGURE 3.3   Covariates of relative loan size

relative loan size of 11.5 percent [5.4, 17.6].[61] Holding all the other variables constant, a completely transformed the policy team (marked by a shift in proportion neoliberal from a value of 0 to 1) received loans that were 64 percent larger (with confidence intervals around that point estimate ranging from 30 percent at the bottom to 98 percent at the high end). To put this finding in context, the average size of loans for the sample used in the baseline model in this chapter was 78 percent of the country quota. Augmenting the size of the average loan by 64 percent would drive it up to 128 percent of the quota.

My interest lies in statistically estimating the effect of the proximity of the economic beliefs of the policy team and the IMF on three measures of IMF treatment, drawing on a large sample of programs from two decades (and controlling for a range of alternative explanations for variation in Fund-borrower relations). Hence, I do not devote very much discussion in this chapter to the estimates for the other covariates in the models—although I do pause to (briefly) remark on particularly notable or surprising findings. When it comes to the correlates of the relative generosity of agreements set out between 1984 and 2000, the analysis shows that only a few macroeconomic features had sizable effects: countries with larger economies (as measured by log(GDP)) received, on average, larger loans (consistent with the claim that systemically important members can expect preferential treatment). The debt burdens of countries, however, had no statistically detectable correlation with loan size. The Fund was somewhat sensitive to the financing needs of countries when it set the terms of access. There is a statistically significant negative correlation between the reserves variable and the loan size measure; on average, a 1 standard deviation increase in the level of foreign currency reserves (as a proportion of the external debt load) was associated with 6 percent smaller loans (with uncertainty around that estimate ranging from –11 to –2 percent). The current account balance was not a significant correlate of loan size. Nor did the indicators of foreign policy affinity (as measured by voting patterns in the UN General Assembly) or the strategic importance of borrowers to the most powerful IMF member (indicated by the amount of military aid given by the United States) explain much of the variation in the loan size measure. The domestic political factors (aside from the ideational composition of the policy team) that mattered most were, first, the electoral cycle (the point estimate for the post-election period indicator shows that borrowers in the honeymoon period just after a reasonably competitive election received loans that were 25

61. The estimated effect is calculated by multiplying the point estimate (0.6401) and the standard deviation of the proportion neoliberal variable (0.180). The numbers in the brackets reflect the statistical uncertainty around the point estimate (based on the 95 percent confidence interval captured by the whiskers on each side of the point estimates).

log points, or 29 percent, larger on average), and, second, the partisanship of the government (the estimated coefficient on the left-wing government indicator was, surprisingly, positive, although not quite statistically significant).

ROBUSTNESS OF THE RELATIONSHIP BETWEEN THE PROPORTION NEOLIBERAL AND LOAN SIZE VARIABLES

The evidence is consistent with the mechanism laid out in chapter 2: on average, policy teams dominated by individuals with the markers of neoliberal economic beliefs obtained larger (relative) disbursements. The association between the two variables is positive, highly statistically significant, and substantively large.

How durable are the findings? Most analysts report the robustness of their main statistical findings (if they do so at all) in a series of results tables, typically inserted in a data appendix buried at the back of the book chapter or article. Results tables, however, are a very inefficient way to show how key findings look under different model specifications. Instead, I use a ropeladder plot to visualize the robustness of the association between proportion neoliberal and (logged) loan size when I changed the specification (by removing and adding covariates, altering the measurement of key variables, or adjusting the estimation technique).[62]

The ropeladder plot (figure 3.4) shows the point estimate for the key covariate (proportion neoliberal) and the 95 percent confidence interval around the estimate. I start at the top of the graphical display by showing the coefficient and confidence interval from the baseline model (whose full results are reported in figure 3.3). The results from the alternative specifications follow. The more durable the statistical relationship between two variables, the more that the plot will resemble a very stable ropeladder. (The dots denoting the coefficient and the whiskers capturing the uncertainty of the point estimate should not swing wildly from one specification to another.)

Figure 3.4 shows results from the baseline model plus twelve other specifications (estimates for the control variables are omitted). In each of the alternative models (save for one specification, which is likely to produce unreliable estimates given the properties of my data), the coefficient on the key covariate in the analysis remains statistically significant. When I roll back the start of the time window from 1984 to 1980 (ignoring the break marked by the 1983 quota reform), the relationship holds. Adding additional covariates to the baseline model does not change the conclusion I have drawn from the initial analysis. I reran the baseline

---

62. Adolph 2013, 90.

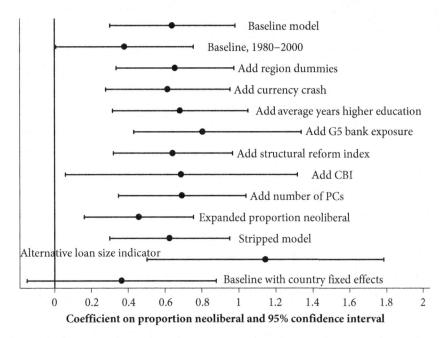

FIGURE 3.4 Correlation of proportion neoliberal with the loan size indicator under different model specifications (CBI, central bank independence; PCs, performance criteria)

model with separate indicators for different world regions,[63] with an indicator for the presence/absence of a currency crisis,[64] with a measure of the average level of educational attainment in borrowing countries,[65] with a variable capturing the exposure of private banks headquartered in the G5 group of countries

---

63. The dichotomous region variables (for sub-Saharan Africa, Latin America and the Caribbean, Eastern Europe and Central Asia, and the Middle East and North Africa; South Asia is the omitted reference category) may pick up any region-specific variation in IMF program design (which may itself be correlated with the key covariate). See Copelovitch (2010) and Stone (2011), who also use region dummies in their statistical analyses of the covariates of IMF treatment.

64. The currency crash variable comes from the data set compiled by Laeven and Valencia 2008.

65. It is, of course, possible that the appointment of neoliberal-type policymakers is simply an artifact of the quality of the bureaucracy of a country and/or a marker of a generally well-educated population; hence, it might be important to control in the regressions for the quality of the policy environment and the general level of educational attainment. Well-governed countries would presumably be given more discretion by the IMF. The inclusion of the Polity2 score, which is highly correlated with existing measures of bureaucratic quality and is positively correlated with the education level of leaders, should allay this concern (Besley and Reynal-Querol 2011). But I also ran the baseline model using Morrison and Murtin's (2009) measures of country-level education attainment as additional controls; the results remained essentially unchanged.

(United States, United Kingdom, Japan, Germany, and France) to borrowers,[66] with a much more expansive indicator of the degree of market-oriented policy liberalization in borrowing countries than the one used in the baseline model,[67] with an indicator for the degree of central bank independence,[68] and with the number of performance criteria in the agreement included as a right-hand-side variable.[69] The main finding held in each of these alternative specifications.

Nor was the main finding affected when I removed all the covariates from the statistical analysis, save for proportion neoliberal and the substantively strongest of the control variables (log(GDP)), for the stripped model specification ($N = 392$). In fact, the estimated effect of the key covariate on the size of loans ($\beta = 0.623$) was slightly larger in the stripped-down model than in the baseline model.

I also ran the baseline model with an indicator of the log of the loan size collected independently by Mark Copelovitch. My data set covers a much larger sample of programs (Copelovitch's sample includes 197 nonconcessional programs in the years between 1984 and 2003);[70] nonetheless, the two loan size variables are very highly correlated ($\rho = 0.96$) and the positive partial correlation between the alternative loan size indicator (available for a subset of the countries in my data set) and the proportion neoliberal indicator is strong and highly significant.

My measure of the ideational composition of policy teams, based on socializing experiences in individual policymakers' backgrounds, is admittedly an

---

66. The G5 bank exposure variable is drawn from Copelovitch 2010.

67. I constructed the alternative index of policy liberalization from the data set compiled by Giuliano, Mishra, and Spilimbergo 2013. The data set includes separate indicators for liberalization in six areas (trade, domestic financial sector, capital account, current account, product markets, and agriculture); I combined the six indicators into a super-index of policy reform.

68. Bodea and Hicks 2015.

69. The fact that the IMF makes decisions about conditionality and loan size jointly suggests that the number of conditions should be a covariate in the loan size model, and vice versa. Ray (2003) warns, however, that the inclusion of a covariate that intervenes between the key explanatory variable and the outcome can generate misleading estimates (and the results reported in this chapter indicate that some of the impact of the key variable will be channeled through the measures of loan size and conditionality). Yet the size of the proportion neoliberal coefficient is slightly larger when loan size is included as a covariate of loan size (relative to the quota).

70. The concessional facilities of the Fund are multiyear programs offering a lower repayment cost, reserved for the least-developed member countries and funded from a different pool of resources than the facilities provided on nonconcessional terms by the organization. Copelovitch's (2010) analysis is limited to the subset of nonconcessional lending arrangements (hence, he looks at only the covariates of loans to middle-income borrowers). Much of the lending activities of the Fund, however, were in low-income countries, many of which made use of the concessional facilities of the organization (e.g., almost half of all IMF programs went to low-income countries in sub-Saharan African between 1980 and 2000, and most of those were concessional programs).

imperfect way of capturing individuals' economic beliefs. How do the results change if I broaden the criteria denoting the neoliberal policymakers to include other socializing experiences (aside from graduate training in highly ranked U.S. economics departments and/or significant work experience in the IMF and the World Bank)? Another follow-on question immediately leaps out: What are other socializing experiences that might confer neoliberal beliefs—and, perhaps even more important, which of those additional experiences turn up in the sources I can find to reconstruct policymakers' biographical histories?

While working through the IMF archives, I stumbled on a resource that enabled me to add another criterion to the operationalization of the neoliberal policymaker concept: lists of individuals who had completed IMF-offered train-ing coursework. In 1964, the IMF Institute opened its doors to domestic policy-makers from member countries. The Institute offered courses of study (ranging from six to twenty weeks) for its participants, covering topics related to macro-economic policymaking. The participants in the Institute courses (given in mul-tiple languages) were mostly from developing countries and were at the time of training all working in mid-level positions in the macroeconomic and financial policymaking institutions of their countries. The socializing mission of the IMF Institute—to correct "the lack of proper training and education" among civil ser-vants in national economic policymaking bureaucracies, a "deficiency" hamper-ing the relations of the Fund with its members—was explicit.[71] IMF economists led the courses, and the content reflected the dominant organizational beliefs about macroeconomic policymaking and structural adjustment.

I used the Institute directories and quarterly reports to the EDs to compile a complete record of the names, countries of residence, and job titles of the more than 6,000 participants in the Institute courses between 1964 and 1988.[72] I then matched the records of training-program participants to the data I collected on the backgrounds of top economic policymakers. I identified seventy-four eco-nomic policymakers from forty developing countries who, prior to entering office, had completed coursework at the IMF Institute. Some of those individu-als were, by dint of their educational backgrounds, already recorded in the data

---

71. "IMF Institute Program for 1971–72," Secretary's Circular No. 70/153, November 30, 1970.

72. In my scouring of the archives I could find directories and reports to the Executive Board that covered only the years between 1964 and 1988—hence, the early cut-off date. In 1992, in the face of a huge increase in the number of applications from policy officials from the post-communist, transition countries, the Institute was shut down and the IMF, working with other IOs, including the Organization for Economic Cooperation and Development (OECD) and the World Trade Organi-zation (WTO; then the General Agreement on Tariffs and Trade [GATT]) opened the Joint Vienna Institute (JVI) for training mid-level policymakers. The JVI has not (to the best of my knowledge) opened its files on trainees for inspection by outsiders.

set as being of the neoliberal type—but many were not. I recoded the individuals who were in the list of IMF Institute participants (and had not been identified in the first round of coding as neoliberals) and recalculated the proportion neoliberal indicator with this new information at hand. I then regressed the Loan size variable on the battery of controls plus the recoded measure of the ideational composition of the policy team. As the ropeladder plot in figure 3.4 shows, the more expansive indicator remained positively and significantly correlated with loan size.

Finally, I tested the relationship in a model that included country-level fixed effects. Fixed-effects models are, by definition, within-estimators; by adding a dichotomous indicator for each country in the sample, to account for the possibility that some unmeasured country-specific characteristic(s) causes the country to have its own (otherwise unexplained) base level of access to the IMF's resources, all the cross-sectional variation in the outcome is washed out. Thus, the estimate describes only the average impact of a change in the covariates on the outcome over time in each country in the sample. The model with country fixed effects was the single specification among the alternatives reported in figure 3.4 for which the 95 percent confidence interval around the (positive) point estimate extended across the value of 0 (and hence fell just below the standard level of statistical significance). But the point estimate from this model is unlikely to be very reliable; fixed-effect models are not well suited to estimating covariates that change slowly over time in many of the units in the analysis. In a number of countries, the proportion neoliberal variable does not change—in these cases, no neoliberals have ever held prominent positions in the government. In addition, fixed-effects models may return inconsistent estimates when the structure of the data includes many units (countries) and relatively few time periods per unit.[73]

Correlates of Performance Criteria in IMF Programs

The next set of statistical tests examined the covariates of the number of binding conditions in IMF agreements between 1980 and 2000 ($N = 436$). The results of the regression are reported in figure 3.5.

The transformative impact of having neoliberals in prominent decision-making positions in the government should be observed, according to the theory sketched in chapter 2, in fewer performance criteria. The statistical evidence

---

73. See Abrevaya 1997. This is certainly the case for my data. For example, in the comprehensive model of loan size (which includes each of the covariates described in the chapter), there are seventy-eight countries with an average of 4.8 observations per country and several countries appear only once in the data set because they signed just a single program during the two decades of the analysis.

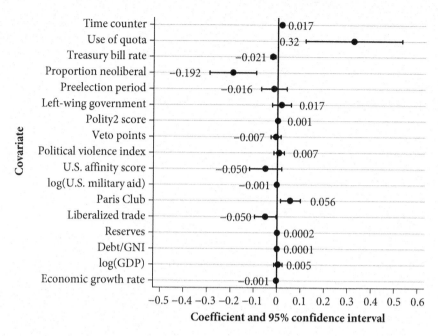

FIGURE 3.5 Covariates of performance criteria in IMF programs

conforms to the argument: higher proportion neoliberal values led to less oner-ous programs for borrowers (as measured by the number of performance crite-ria). The results show that, controlling for a range of other plausible explanations for variation in the treatment by the IMF of its borrowers, an increase in the proportion neoliberal variable is negatively associated with the number of bind-ing conditions in IMF programs—and that the negative estimate of the (average) relationship between the two variables is highly statistically significant.

To produce the results in figure 3.5, I estimated a kind of model that is well suited to handle count data but that makes the interpretation of the substantive impact of changes in the value of the key covariate on the number of perfor-mance criteria (holding the other covariates constant) less straightforward than it was for the previous linear regression.

I show the substantive effect graphically in figure 3.6. The figure shows the predicted number of binding conditions in IMF programs (tracked with the solid line) when the other covariates are held constant and proportion neoliberal moves from its minimum (0) to its maximum possible value (1). The uncertainty of the estimated effect is captured by the dotted lines (denoting the 95 percent confidence interval) on either side of the point estimates. All the other covariates in the model are held constant at their mean values.

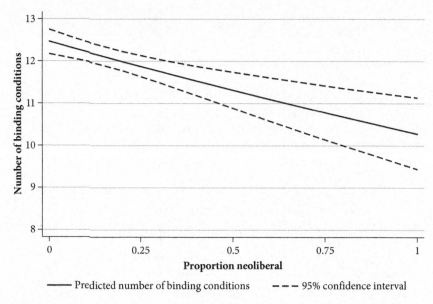

FIGURE 3.6   Effect of proportion neoliberal on predicted number of conditions

The substantive impact of the composition of the policy team of the borrowing country, revealed in the statistical analysis of the covariates of binding conditions in a large number of IMF agreements, is sizable; all else remaining equal, moving from a policy team without any individuals identified as neoliberals to a team composed entirely of neoliberal policymakers shaved about two performance criteria off the program.

There is, by contrast, little evidence that domestic political institutions, the strategic importance and foreign policy friendliness of borrowers to the most powerful IMF member state, or the importance of the economy of the borrower to regional (and possibly global) market stability (measured by log(GDP)) were systematically driving the design of IMF agreements during the period examined in this analysis. Neither of the two indicators of the strategic importance of the borrowers to the United States significantly correlates with the number of performance criteria; the level of democracy, number of veto players in the government, and the extent of political violence in the borrowing country are each insignificant correlates of the outcome of interest. The macroeconomic and indebtedness variables have little effect. The liberalized trade indicator is negatively and significantly correlated with conditionality, but the substantive effect was quite small. Borrowers that were also engaged in (or had just wrapped up) Paris Club debt negotiations received, on average, slightly more conditions in their programs, as did borrowers during periods in which the resources of the organization were in demand (increasing the value of the total use of IMF resources from its minimum to maximum value is associated with an increase of one binding condition).

ROBUSTNESS OF THE RELATIONSHIP BETWEEN PROPORTION NEOLIBERAL AND THE NUMBER OF PERFORMANCE CRITERIA

How durable is the estimate of the direction, strength, and statistical significance of the relationship between the indicator of the economic beliefs of the policy team and the measure of conditionality? Here I took the same tack as in the discussion of the robustness of the correlation between proportion neoliberal and the loan size indicator: I tried a suite of alternative model specifications and visualized the results using another ropeladder plot.

Recall that the ropeladder plot is a way to track how the point estimate (and confidence interval around that estimate) from the baseline model compares to estimates when the model is altered in some way. The more durable the statistical relationship between the variables, the more stable the ropeladder appears. The partial correlation between the proportion neoliberal measure and the number of performance conditions appears to be very robust; as shown in figure 3.7, it remains negative and significant when several other covariates are added to the

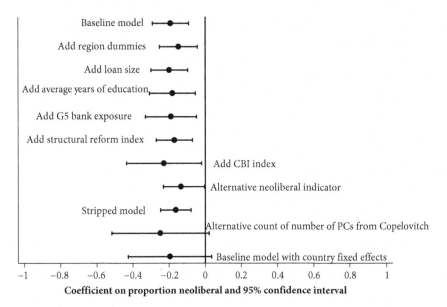

FIGURE 3.7 Correlation of proportion neoliberal with the number of binding conditions in IMF agreements under different model specifications (CBI, central bank independence; PCs, performance criteria)

right-hand side of the equation (including regional dummies, the size of the loan, the average years of education in the borrowing country, the exposure of private banks in the G5 countries to the borrower, central bank independence, and the more expansive index of the level of market openness). The finding stands when the covariates are reduced to just two (proportion neoliberal and the time counter) and when the key covariate is recoded to add the individuals who went through IMF Institute courses to the pool of neoliberal policymakers, as well.

The coefficient estimate for the proportion neoliberal variable falls below the level of statistical significance (and just barely) in only two of the ten additional specifications reported in figure 3.7. In one of the specifications, I used a different dependent variable: the number of performance criteria collected by Copelovitch (for a smaller sample of programs than in the set I collected).[74] The point estimate is actually slightly larger when I use this alternative measure of conditionality, but there is more uncertainty around that estimate (hence, the upper bound of the 95 percent confidence interval spills across the 0 threshold). The other model uses country fixed effects, and as I explained previously, there is good reason to suspect that the fixed-effects estimator is not well suited for data sets with this kind of structure.

Correlates of Waivers for IMF Program Countries

The analysis of the determinants of the third aspect of conditional lending—the issuance of waivers to allow a borrower that missed conditions to access the next tranche of the program—yields the strongest substantive (and most robustly significant) relationship between the proportion neoliberal measure and the outcome variable. In figure 3.8, I visualize the results from a logistic regression in which the dependent variable is the issuance of a waiver ($N = 682$). Because the waivers data set includes not just the year in which a program was signed but all years in which a program was active, I measured the index annually.[75]

Relatively few variables proved to be statistically significant determinants of waivers.[76] Countries with better Polity2 scores and higher inflation were more

---

74. Copelovitch 2010.

75. Because I recorded the dates of entry into and exit from office for the policymakers in the data set, I was able to reconstruct the makeup of the policy team (plus the executive) in each year for each country in the sample. If, for example, the finance minister, central banker, and planning minister signed an agreement in 1980, the policy team for that country consisted of the occupants of those three positions (plus the national executive) for all years during which that program remained active, unless one of the positions was eliminated.

76. The coefficients for the regional dummies (not shown) indicated that waivers were significantly more common for borrowers that were post-communist countries and Middle Eastern and North African countries.

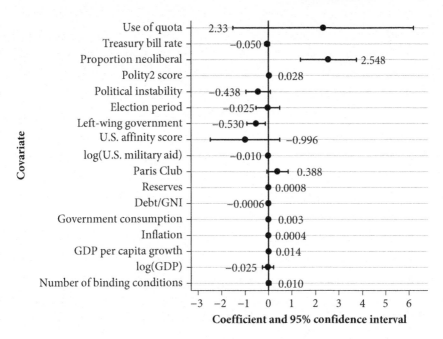

FIGURE 3.8 Covariates of issuance of waivers in IMF programs

likely to secure waivers, whereas left-wing governments were less likely to receive one or more waivers. But neither of these variables, although significant, are very strongly correlated with the decision by the Executive Board to issue a (or several) waiver(s).

The correlation between the proportion neoliberal indicator and waivers, on the other hand, is very large and robustly significant (the estimated relationship changes so little in the alternative specifications that I do not report those results to save space). The strength of that relationship is displayed in figure 3.9, which, holding all other covariates in the model at their mean values, tracks the effect of the increase in the proportion neoliberal variable on the predicted probability that a country under an active IMF program received a waiver. The effect of the composition of the policy team in borrowing countries on the decision to issue a waiver is large: fully unified neoliberal policy teams were approximately 50 percent more likely to receive at least one waiver at some point in the program than policy teams that contained no individuals with the socializing experiences that confer neoliberal beliefs in their backgrounds.

I describe one final statistical test of the argument in this chapter. Recall from the previous discussion that there is a problem with the dichotomous waivers measure: I observed only whether a waiver was granted by the Executive Board

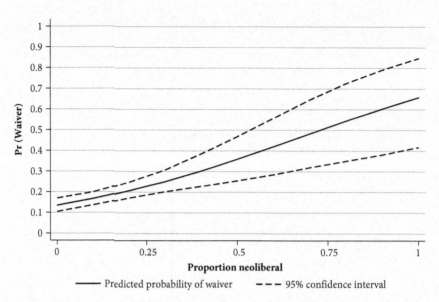

FIGURE 3.9 Effect of proportion neoliberal on the predicted probability of receiving a waiver

(which always approves the IMF staff recommendation to go forward with the program), and I could not observe the cases in which the staff members privately considered and ultimately dismissed an appeal by a borrowing government for a waiver to let the program continue despite the missed performance criteria. Hence, I cannot easily distinguish in this quantitative analysis between the subset of countries that did not need (and thus did not receive) waivers from those that needed a waiver to continue drawing down the loan but were not supported in their plea for relief by the IMF staff members and management.

I also asked whether, conditional on receiving a waiver, the proportion neoliberal indicator correlated with the number of waivers granted by the Executive Board. The average number of waivers approved in Executive Board decisions was two; the variable ranged from a minimum of one to a maximum value of seven waivers in a single approval decision by the IMF Board. The results of the model of the determinants of the number of waivers are given in figure 3.10. In line with the other findings from the analyses in this chapter, I find that, conditional on getting a waiver, policy teams with more neoliberals in top positions received more waivers (although the substantive effect of the variable, shown in the plot in figure 3.11, was rather small).

The findings about the impact of the composition of the policy team on the enforcement of the terms of the IMF agreements, when put together with the

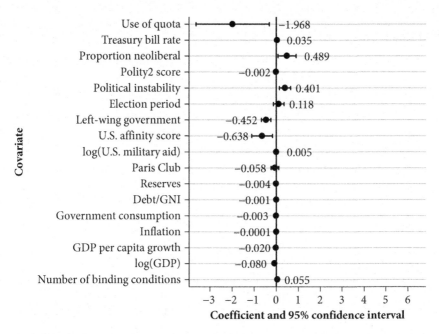

FIGURE 3.10 Covariates of the number of waivers for borrowing countries

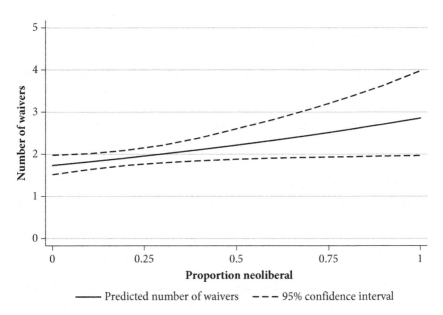

FIGURE 3.11 Effect of proportion neoliberal on predicted number of waivers

other evidence that the IMF has played favorites with its borrowers, suggests that the individuals that I identified as neoliberals may have been closer in their views to the beliefs that dominated at the IMF but were not necessarily more capable governors of the economies of their countries. The evidence showed that neoliberal-heavy governments, on average, received larger loans with fewer conditions attached. Highly competent policy teams should have found successfully completing such programs to be (comparatively) an easy task. Yet one of the strongest findings from the data analysis in this chapter is that these kinds of policy teams were much likelier to obtain waivers (and to obtain more waivers) to continue to draw on IMF resources despite evident noncompliance with the conditions in the agreements.

Conclusion

The statistical evidence amassed in this chapter demonstrates that IMF decisions were strongly influenced by the ideational makeup of the policy team overseeing the implementation of the adjustment program. The evidence points to a pattern of systematic bias in the treatment by the Fund of its members: teams composed of officials likely to share the neoliberal economic beliefs that predominated in the organizational culture during the time period (1980–2000) were able to secure, on average, larger loans with fewer conditions—and the conditions that were in those agreements were more lightly enforced.

The quantitative evidence reveals a pattern of favoritism in a large sample of the Fund programs. But setting up the kinds of tests conducted in this chapter means that the granular details (e.g., concerning the content of individual IMF programs and the dynamics in the policy teams at the helm of the adjustment program) of IMF-borrower relations have been put in the background so that the statistical relationship between my measure of the ideational composition of the economic policymaking corps of the borrowers and the indicators of treatment by the Fund could be established. For the kind of fine-grained, processual, mechanismic evidence that I need to fully establish the consistency of my theory with the evidence, historically oriented case studies are necessary. I turn in the next two chapters to just that kind of approach; using newly available archival materials, copious secondary sources, and interviews, I reconstruct the relationship of the IMF with Argentina over a quarter century, focusing on the ways in which the makeup of the policy team at the helm of the Argentine economy affected the interactions of the country with an IO that became deeply involved in its economic governance.

DATA APPENDIX TO CHAPTER 3

Sources of Data on Economic Policymakers

Some countries maintain historical records on the occupants of the top policymaking positions on the websites of their ministries; those records were the starting point for the data-collection effort, but for most of the countries in the analysis, the dates of economic policymakers' entry and exit from office had to be collected by hand. Two sources—the CIA *Chiefs of State and Cabinet Members of Foreign Governments* and *Keesings Record of World Events*—proved to be particularly useful for this effort. These sources were supplemented (and the precise dates were confirmed) using additional information on entry and exit dates contained in the online archives of the *BBC Summary of World Broadcasts, Financial Times,* and *New York Times* and, in some cases, from correspondence with archivists and administrators in finance ministries, central banks, and other relevant national economic policymaking institutions of the countries. The dates of entry and exit for national leaders were drawn from the *Archigos* (version 2.8) database.[77]

Biographical data on the national leaders was not particularly difficult to find. Collecting the relevant biographical information for often-obscure (and sometimes short-lived) economic officials, however, meant delving into an even broader set of sources. From the IMF archives I collected the records of all post-1979 appointments to positions above the entry level in the organization as well as the names of all of the more than 6,000 individuals who went through the IMF Institute training programs between its founding in 1964 and 1988. The voluminous histories of the IMF written by Margaret Garritsen de Vries (covering the 1950s and 1960s) and James Boughton (who produced two mammoth volumes surveying the activities of the IMF from the 1970s to the end of the 1990s) were essential.[78] I consulted a number of sources to identify individuals' educational backgrounds and work experience: Proquest's *Digital Dissertations* database, Gale's *Biography Resource Center, International Who's Who, The Statesman's Yearbook, Who's Who in International Organizations,* and numerous country- and region-specific editions of *Who's Who*. I obtained the digital records of the membership survey of the American Economics Association, which confirmed some of the educational information I had found. I also consulted as many books and articles on the policy-reform experiences of individual countries as I could identify to extract details on the top officials involved in crafting economic policy.

---

77. *Archigos* data, http://www.rochester.edu/college/faculty/hgoemans/data.htm (last accessed June 24, 2015).

78. de Vries 1985, 1987; Boughton 2001, 2012.

ARGENTINA AND THE IMF IN TURBULENT TIMES, 1976–1984

> **The Fund clearly must undertake a good deal of soul-searching when it comes to Argentina, for it has played a significant role in the country's affairs for a very long time.**
>
> —Mike Callaghan, Australian executive director at the IMF, 2003

In this and the next chapter, I delve into the case of Argentina and its relationship with the IMF. I track the engagement of the country with the IMF from the arrival of a Fund mission soon after the military junta took power in 1976 through the economic meltdown in the last months of 2001, which culminated in the withdrawal of IMF support for the country and the largest sovereign default in history to that point.

I selected the Argentina-IMF case primarily for three reasons. First, the case provides a rich repository of evidence that I can use to test the argument linking treatment to shared economic beliefs. The Argentine economic policymaking pendulum swung in different directions several times during the period I investigate, and in each episode, the swing was marked by the arrival a new corps of economic officials with different beliefs from those of the members of the previous team. During the decades covered in the case study, Argentina was frequently under conditional lending arrangements. And the treatment of the country by the IMF varied over time. The case thus provides a very good testing ground for assessing how well my argument about the effects of shared beliefs on the interactions of the Fund with its borrowers fits with the evidence.

The second reason for a close study of the Argentine case is more general. For an argument built on shared economic beliefs to be more fully convincing,

---

Epigraph: Minutes of the Meeting of the Executive Board, EBM/03/106, November 17, 2003, p. 32.

we should see evidence from the decision-making *processes* of the organization—in addition to the observed (and quantifiable) *outcomes* of those decisions—that the makeup of the policymaking team was a highly consequential factor in IMF judgments and that the confidence of the Fund in the policy team flowed largely from the degree to which beliefs were shared by the two sides. And even more important, we should find evidence that greater confidence led IMF decision makers to support a more generous treatment of the country.

The third reason to look closely at Argentina is the prominence of the case. Few would disagree with the claim that several of the lending programs of the country were among the most important in IMF history. Good theoretical frameworks for understanding the interactions of the IMF with its borrowers should, I contend, shed light on novel and analytically valuable features of the most prominent cases of the organization. Argentina is an exceptional country in many ways (starting with its century-long tumble from near the top to the middle rungs of the global distribution of wealth), and some readers may wonder why I devote so much effort to examining a single (possibly aberrant) country case over a number of years rather than working through a larger, more representative set of IMF program case studies.

The prominence rationale for the case study puts me closer to the qualitative research culture sketched by Gary Goertz and James Mahoney in their illuminating treatise on different methodological traditions in the social sciences.[1] In the quantitative research culture, the best cases are the ones that provide the most inferential leverage. Determining whether the case lies "on or off the regression line," for example, is often thought to be a better criterion for selection than the prominence or importance of the case. This case merits close investigation for reasons beyond providing the raw material for testing the argument; the Argentine programs were crucibles for the organization, shaping and reshaping outsiders' views of the role of the Fund in the world and, especially after the crisis of 2001–2002, serving as flashpoints for moments of intra-organizational soul-searching (as referenced by the Australian ED in the epigraph that opens this chapter).

Preview of the Case Study of Argentina

I develop the case study chronologically. The Argentine case is bookended by two periods in which neoliberal policymakers were ascendant. Economic policy

---

1. Goertz and Mahoney 2012, 184–85.

under General Jorge Videla's repressive military regime (1976–1981) was guided by a group of economic policymakers, led by the José Martínez de Hoz, the economy minister, and Adolfo Diz, the central banker, that shared the IMF worldview. A decade after the Martínez de Hoz–Diz policy team lost power, another group of U.S.-trained economists consolidated its hold on the top policymaking positions in Argentina. Neoliberals dominated economic policymaking in Argentina between 1991 and 2001.

In the years between 1981 and 1984, which spans the disastrous war with Britain in the South Atlantic and the democratic transition under President Raúl Alfonsín, the control of economic policymaking oscillated among teams that varied in their friendliness toward neoliberal economic beliefs; during the two episodes of IMF-program participation during this period, however, the pendulum swung away from the neoliberal officials and toward a group of policymakers who were steeped in the structuralist economic ideas that also influenced economic policy in many other developing countries. The end of this period, not coincidentally, marked a nadir in IMF-Argentine relations (until the breakdown of the relations at the end of the fourth and final episode in the case study).

If the first and final episodes account for periods in which neoliberal influence in the economic policymaking institutions of Argentina peaked and the period between 1981 and 1984 was a low-water mark for neoliberals in Argentina, the 1985–1989 period sits somewhere in the middle. A handful of U.S.-trained economists were able to gain access to power, but their influence over policy was circumscribed in important ways. Table 4.1 gives an overview of the four periods that form the basis of comparison in the chapter, along with expectations about the character of the IMF treatment of Argentina in each period.

TABLE 4.1 Organization of the case study

TIME PERIOD	INFLUENCE OF NEOLIBERAL-ORIENTED OFFICIALS OVER POLICYMAKING	EXPECTED CHARACTER OF THE FUND LENDING PROGRAMS IN ARGENTINA DURING THE EPISODE
1976–1981	High	Generous/lenient
1981–1985	Low (in the periods when the country was under IMF programs; control of policymaking oscillated during the episode)	Stingy/tough
1985–1990	Medium-low	Variable
1991–2001	High	Generous/lenient

Episode 1: Neoliberals to the Rescue, 1976–1981

The trajectory of the relationship of the Fund with the Argentine military government in the years between 1976 and 1981 followed the predicted pattern: the presence of neoliberal economists in top policymaking positions reassured the IMF staff and management that the country was serious about reform. In turn, the government was rewarded with lenient treatment. Here I discuss the two lending arrangements that the Fund negotiated with the military regime during the period. I also devote some attention to the historical position of neoliberal economic ideas in Argentina. Not only was 1976–1981 the first era in which neoliberals exerted significant influence over economic policymaking, but the openness of the military regime to the propagators of neoliberal economic ideas set the path for a second generation of U.S.-trained economists to gain a foothold on policy and reshape the relationship of the country with the Fund a decade after this period came to its conclusion.

The Proceso Takes Power

When IMF officials arrived in Buenos Aires two months after the March 24, 1976, coup that swept Isabel Peron from the presidency, they were immediately confronted with the fact that Argentina was a country mired in deep political and economic crisis. Members of the IMF mission team received word that they were possible targets for assassination by the leftist guerrilla organization Ejercito Revolucionario del Pueblo (ERP), and they were forced to conduct the negotiations with the new military government in secret.[2] The briefing for the members of the IMF mission that arrived in Buenos Aires on May 26 cautioned that "few Fund members have experienced financial deterioration to the extent now present in Argentina and neither the Argentine authorities nor the Fund staff have had much experience in dealing with such situations."[3]

The new military regime (Proceso de Reorganización Nacional), headed by General Jorge Rafael Videla, envisioned a reconstruction of Argentine society to purge the corruption, subversion, and moral degradation that they saw as endemic to the Peronist movement. IMF officials had no apparent qualms about

---

2. Interview with Christian Brachet, Washington DC, May 31, 2009. Brachet was an economist in the River Plate Division in 1976; later, he became the deputy division chief of the Western Hemisphere Department, a position he held between 1981 and 1984. See also Tanzi 2007, 24–25; Kedar 2013, 138.

3. "Briefing for Mission to Argentina," prepared by the IMF Western Hemisphere Department, May 20, 1976.

working with the economic policymakers in Videla's military government. The terrible human toll that the regime would exact over the next four years—estimates of the number of murdered "subversives" range as high as 25,000—casts the eagerness of IMF officials to get involved in the economic reconstruction of the country in a very harsh light. Proclaiming ignorance of the aims and methods of the regime rings hollow—the strategy of the junta, as Jonathan Kirshner notes, "was not subtle." (One of the top military brass announced that to defeat left-wing forces in Argentina, the regime would "have to kill 50,000 people: 25,000 subversives, 20,000 sympathizers, and we will make 5,000 mistakes.")[4]

Fund officials invoked the principle of uniformity of treatment as the justification for the evident lack of IMF concern about the behavior of the regime with which it was working.[5] But in taking a pro-Argentina position, the IMF swam against the tide. The United States cut off all bilateral military and economic aid to Argentina as the evidence of state-led violence against "subversives" mounted. A new bureaucratic body, the Interagency Group on Human Rights and Foreign Assistance (informally known as the Christopher Group after its chairman, Deputy Secretary of State Warren Christopher), was convened with a mandate (as described by Zbigniew Brzezinski, national security advisor) "to examine our bilateral and multilateral aid decisions as they relate to human rights." The IMF sought and successfully received an exemption from the purview of the Christopher Group (the lobbying effort to exempt the organization was led by Fred Bergsten, the assistant secretary of the treasury).[6] U.S. foreign policymakers clearly did not dictate the decisions taken by the Fund with respect to Argentina. If anything, the behavior of the IMF contravened the espoused preferences of the U.S. government during the episode. The degree to which Fund officials and their negotiating partners on the Argentine side shared economic beliefs was the far more consequential factor.

The Neoliberal Orientation of the New Argentine Economic Policy Team

In a briefing from May 20, 1976, the leaders of the IMF mission to Argentina noted, with approval, "the new economic team, headed by Minister of Economy

---

4. Kirshner 2007, 174.

5. "How could an international organization that in 1947 became a specialized agency of the United Nations have had such close relationships with governments that systematically violated human rights?" asks Claudia Kedar, a historian. Kedar notes that in her archival research she "found no evidence of any discussion of the political and moral implications of collaborating with that dictatorship [the Videla regime]. And even if such a discussion ever did take place, it is clear that the IMF ultimately prioritized economic over moral and political considerations" (2013, 150).

6. Schmidli 2013, 110–11.

Martínez de Hoz and Central Bank Governor Diz, has *espoused an economic philosophy radically different from that of the previous government.*[7]

Adolfo Diz, the new central bank governor, held a PhD in economics from the University of Chicago. Diz had also served as an ED at the IMF from 1966 to 1968.[8] Diz retained Ricardo Arriazu, a University of Minnesota–trained economist and holdover from the final months of the Peronist period, as his top deputy. The planning ministry went to the new finance minister, Martínez de Hoz's "close friend and right hand" Guillermo Walter Klein Jr., who held a master's degree from Harvard and was closely involved with Fundación Mediterránea, a neoliberal-friendly economic think tank.[9]

The key appointee, "superminister" José Martínez de Hoz, was neither a U.S.-trained economist nor affiliated with either of the Washington-based international financial institutions. He did, however, possess strong international ties and a preference for economic policies that were closely aligned with IMF views on stabilization.[10] Tall, impeccably dressed, and aristocratic in manner (he was on safari in Kenya when the coup occurred), Martínez de Hoz hailed from a wealthy landowning family and had served as economy minister for six months in 1963. Trained in law at Universidad de Buenos Aires in 1949, Martínez de Hoz "was deeply influenced by anti-Keynesian, libertarian thinking," particularly through the work of Friedrich von Hayek, Austrian economist.[11] His closest links were with the Argentine and international business communities, forged through his role as the chairman of Acindar, the largest Argentine steel company, and his leadership of a major Argentine business association (Consejo Empresario Argentino, CEA). When Walter Robichek, the director of the Western Hemisphere Department of the Fund, related the news of the coup to the Executive Board, he reported that "he had learned that the Government was trying to co-opt Mr. José Martínez de Hoz, a civilian who had already been Minister of Finance, and *who was well-known not only to the Fund but throughout the Western world.*"[12]

---

7. IMF Western Hemisphere Department, "Briefing for Mission to Argentina," May 20, 1976 (emphasis added).

8. Veigel 2009, 50, 53.

9. *Cronista Commercial*, April 9, 1976; Bonelli 2004, 239; Kedar 2013, 136 (quotation). His father, Guillermo Walter Klein Sr. had served as an ED at the IMF from 1960 to 1964.

10. Martinez de Hoz denied that he followed any particular "academic" theory; the *New York Times* reported that "he describes himself as a 'pragmatist,' rather than an economic liberal in the sense of 19th century capitalism" (Juan de Onis, "Argentina's Planner," *New York Times*, April 1, 1976, p. 2). See also Manzetti 1991, 94.

11. Veigel 2009, 50 (quotation). It has been mistakenly reported that Martínez de Hoz was a Harvard graduate; for example, the *Economist* referred to him as "a graduate of the Harvard Business School" ("Argentina, Brains—and Brawn," July 10, 1976, p. 84).

12. Minutes of the meeting of the Executive Board, EBM/76/52, March 26, 1976 (emphasis added).

Neoliberals and Structuralists

"La teoría ricardiana de las 'ventajas comparativas,'" ("the Ricardian theory of comparative advantage") argues Marcelo Bonelli, esteemed Argentine financial journalist, lay at the core of the market-oriented policy agenda of the new team.[13] The neoliberal orientation of the Videla team stood in stark contrast to the set of structuralist beliefs to which many, in Argentina and elsewhere, hewed.[14]

Albert Hirschman distills the essence of the structuralist framework: "without a judiciously interventionist state in the periphery, the cards were inevitably stacked in favor of the center."[15] Raúl Prebisch, Argentine-born economist, developed and tirelessly promoted a central structuralist idea—that the persistently negative external balances of peripheral countries were due in large part to "a secular downward trend in the prices of primary goods relative to the prices of manufactured goods" and other malfunctioning elements of the global goods markets—through his leadership in the 1950s and early 1960s of the Economic Commission for Latin America (ECLA; one of the UN regional economic agencies) and, starting in 1964, as the secretariat of the UN Conference on Trade and Development (UNCTAD).[16] Structuralists following Prebisch's lead advocated a development strategy of import-substitution industrialization (ISI).[17] In the ISI model, the policies at the disposal of the government—the exchange rate, selective tariffs, credit creation, and subsidies—were used to protect the domestic manufacturing sector by driving out consumer goods that were previously imported from abroad in exchange for goods produced by domestic firms.[18]

---

13. Bonelli 2004, 32.

14. As one historian of the region observes, "economic structuralism was embraced as virtual official ideology by many governments" (Gootenberg 2004, 241).

15. Hirschman 1981, 15–16. Assar Lindbeck, Swedish economist, observes similarly that structuralist beliefs invoked "strong distrust of the price mechanism and . . . considerable enthusiasm for government regulation . . . as well as economy-wide central planning" (1991, 103).

16. Dosman 2008, 242–43; Sikkink 1991; Toye and Toye 2003, 449.

17. Neoliberal economists in the United States opposed the recommendations made by Prebisch and ECLA at every turn. Arnold Harberger, at the University of Chicago (and later the University of California–Los Angeles, UCLA), was a leading opponent; his depiction of the regional policy orientation in the 1970s and 1980s is that "There was also a sort of chronic protectionism, pursued actively by policymakers. The intellectual father of that protectionism was Raúl Prebisch, an Argentine economist and long-time head of the United Nations' Economic Commission for Latin America, whose experts actually 'helped' countries design protectionist schemes of 'import-substituting industrialization.' Thus we had a sort of permanent protectionism, motivated by a desire for self-sufficiency and a very suspicious and defensive attitude toward world markets, side by side with an ad hoc protectionism motivated primarily by balance-of-payments considerations in the face of inflationary monetary and fiscal policies" (2003, vii).

18. For example, Frieden 1991, 46–51.

Structuralist and neoliberal views also diverged on the issue of price stability. In the IMF monetary approach, inflation was a consequence of excessively large expansions of credit, which spilled over into disequilibrium in the balance of payments. For structuralists, by contrast, the origins of "uncontrollable inflationary pressures" lay in the particularities of the economic, social, and political conditions of developing countries.[19]

Structuralists identified two main sources of inflationary pressure in industrializing countries. The first, associated with the work of Celso Furtado, director of the ECLA Development Division, was the presence of structural rigidities in the economy. The basic approach of the Fund presumed that prices were flexible and that people responded rationally to the signals given by changing prices—Furtado and others rejected the premises of the Fund model. In the structuralist view, as people in developing countries move from the countryside to the higher-paying jobs in the cities (or are forced out of agricultural work due to mechanization and the protectionist policies of the historically rich countries), the demand for food and basic commodities increases—a positive demand shock to which the domestic agricultural sector cannot respond with more output due to the structure of land rights in these societies (huge tracts are owned by relatively unproductive but politically powerful rural oligarchs). At the same time, the increasing cost of imports and the falling prices of agricultural exports puts pressure on the balance of payments; devaluing the currency as a way to restore the external balance simply magnifies the inflationary pressure by driving up the home currency price of imported goods.

In the ECLA framework, "mechanisms of propagation" explained why inflation spiraled out of control in some countries.[20] The underlying structural features kick the process into motion; people's reactions to rising prices sustain the inflationary drive. Structuralists described different kinds of propagating mechanisms in inflationary environments: producers keep raising prices to try to hold on to their profit margins; workers seek, individually or through organized labor unions, to make sure that their real wages keep pace with the rising prices; and so on. For Noyola Vasquez, the increase in the money supply was, contrary to the IMF monetary model, "the most passive of the propagation mechanisms; its role has been to provide the economy with enough liquidity in real terms to follow the rate of prices."[21] In Furtado's words, "the anti-inflationary policies prescribed

---

19. Furtado 1976, 99.

20. The propagation idea was introduced into structuralist thought by Juan Noyola Vasquez, a Mexican economist hired by ECLA in 1951 (Toye and Toye 2004, 157–58).

21. Quoted in Gallardo and Mansilla 2007, 82.

by the International Monetary Fund . . . provoked recessions in economic activity without achieving relative stability in the level of prices."[22]

Like Prebisch's argument about the inherent inequity in center-periphery trade relations, the structuralist approach to inflation and macroeconomic stabilization was built on a foundation that clashed with a core belief held by neoliberals. The framework did not assume that individuals' beliefs were rational. "The inflationary process," Celso Furtado claims, "always starts with the action of some agent whose operations frustrate what may be called 'conventional expectations.'"[23] Elite U.S. economists criticized the "element of irrationality of the behavior of the agents" in structuralist models; the propagation mechanisms, they argued, depended on an assumption that "human beings behave according to custom rather than to maximize profit."[24]

For many observers in the developing world, however, the assumption of rational beliefs was at odds with their own experiences. People in the countries of the periphery experienced more economic uncertainty and volatility than people in the historically rich countries; as a consequence, their beliefs were more likely to be rooted in tacit social conventions than in expected utility calculations. "The idea that peasants didn't respond to price incentives was ingrained" in the structuralist analytical framework—and this idea provided yet another justification for state intervention to direct economic activity in poor and middle-income countries.[25]

From the mid-1950s to the 1976 coup, the two dominant forces in Argentine politics—the military and the Peronists—rejected neoliberal economic ideas in favor of structuralist-inflected economic policies. Whereas the Chicago Boys were able to gain a foothold in the Chilean economic policymaking bureaucracy by the mid-1970s, Argentina was relatively inhospitable territory for U.S.-trained economists.[26] Klaus Veigel, historian, observes, "lacking attractive opportunities in Argentina, many Chicago graduates, such as Pedro Pou, Roque Fernández, Mario Blejer, Claudio Loser, and Carlos Rodriguez, remained in the United States working for international organizations or as university professors."[27] There was

---

22. Furtado 1976, 129.

23. Ibid., 125.

24. Basu 2003, 79–80. In Jonathan Schlefer's lucid discussion of different bodies of economic ideas, structuralist models differ from neoclassical theories "in that they allow different economies to have essentially different structures, shaped by social conventions outside of markets. They do not envision any single economy from which actual economies are mere imperfect deviations" (2012, 220).

25. Edwards 2014, 101.

26. Biglaiser 2002, 277.

27. Veigel 2005, 96. Rodriguez taught economics at Columbia University; Blejer and Loser had distinguished careers with the IMF; and Pou, Fernández, and Rodriguez figure into the story in chapter 5 as important neoliberal policymakers under Peronist President Carlos Menem.

no shortage of U.S.-trained Argentines; by the late 1950s, top U.S. economics departments such as Harvard, Chicago, MIT, Yale, and Columbia welcomed Argentines to their graduate programs.[28]

The Videla administration provided an opportunity for neoliberals to carve out a permanent space in Argentine society from which to influence policymaking in the future. The creation of two separate research institutions following the coup proved to be particularly important. In June 1977, a group of Argentine industrialists founded Fundación Mediterránea, an economic research institute that became a sanctuary for a number of U.S.-trained economists.[29] The next year, a newly minted Harvard economics PhD named Domingo Cavallo was invited to run a new project (El Instituto de Estudios Economicos sobre la Realidad Argentina y Latinoamericano, IREEAL) under the auspices of Fundación Mediterránea. It was through Fundación Mediterránea–IREEAL that Cavallo and a handful of other neoliberal economists developed a diagnosis of the illness of Argentina: "capitalism without the market and socialism without a plan."[30] The year 1978 also marked the founding of Centro de Estudios Macroeconomicos de Argentina (CEMA), which served as the incubator for a second set of neoliberal-oriented Argentine economists.[31]

The Martínez de Hoz Plan and Improved Relations with the IMF

The new economic policy team wasted little time in reversing the policies of the Peronist era. Martínez de Hoz outlined the economic agenda of the new government in a televised speech to the nation on April 2, 1976. Immediately, the military government would pursue a radical program aimed at liberalizing the economic system to control inflation, which had wreaked havoc at the end of the Peronist interregnum: the agricultural marketing board was abolished; restrictions on foreign investment were relaxed; real public-sector wages were slashed and new taxes implemented; the currency was devalued; and exchange restric-

---

28. Dagnino Pastore and Fernández Lopez 1988.

29. Heredia 2004, 313–77; Ramirez 2000; Corrales 1997, 56. By the late 1980s Fundación Mediterránea had expanded to include offices in every major Argentine city

30. Cavallo 1984, 26. Fundación Mediterránea was home to a number of U.S.-trained economists in the late 1970s, including Humberto Petrei and Aldo Dadone (University of Chicago), Aldo Arnaudo (Yale University), and Carlos Givogri (Vanderbilt University). Cavallo would bring many of his Fundación Mediterránea associates into the government when he became finance minister in January 1991 (Heredia 2004, 328; Ramirez 2000, 69).

31. Economists associated with CEMA included Pedro Pou, Roque Fernández, and Carlos Rodriguez (all University of Chicago economics PhDs) (Heredia 2004, 328; Veigel 2005, 96).

tions were eliminated. The program was consistent with an effort to minimize government intervention and restore the discipline of the market to Argentina.

The Central Bank governor, Adolfo Diz, initiated contact with the IMF about a lending program after the March 24 coup. On April 5, he placed a phone call to Jorge del Canto of the Fund Western Hemisphere Department to discuss the possibility of a standby arrangement. The Fund was amenable to sending a mission as soon as possible, but Diz wanted to wait until the beginning of June to allow time to implement the first round of reforms.[32]

The neoliberal economic beliefs of the key Argentine policymakers put the new team much closer to the Fund viewpoint. IMF officials, in turn, were highly confident that this government was serious about macroeconomic stabilization and pro-market reform. Vito Tanzi, a senior economist in the Fiscal Affairs Department and a participant in the 1976 missions, remarked that the ideas held by the Argentine officials were "much closer to those of the Fund: trust in the market, not too many controls, balance of payments. . . . We spoke the same language."[33]

IMF officials were, on the whole, optimistic about the Diz–Martínez de Hoz team plans. But the Argentine policymakers' room to maneuver was limited. From the outset, it was made clear to Martínez de Hoz that any package of reforms must not increase unemployment; the military regime was engaged in a pitched battle against perceived enemies from the labor movement and the universities, and the armed forces were concerned that job losses would generate sympathy for the resistance, if not add to the ranks of the left-wing insurgency.[34] The head of the mission to Argentina, Jack Guenther, flagged some concerns about the commitment of the junta for the managing director; referring to the recession that would result from an IMF-supported austerity program, he wrote, "the economic team knows this, regards it as inevitable, and seems to be willing to see it through. The military also say that they understand, but I am not sure that they comprehend fully the short-run difficulties which are ahead to lay the basis for renewed economic growth."[35]

Serious discussion about a standby arrangement with the Fund began in June 1976. Negotiations proceeded smoothly, and the two top officials from the Western Hemisphere Department, Jack Guenther and Marcello Caiola, left for

---

32. Memorandum from Jorge del Canto to the Managing Director, "Argentina," April 12, 1976.

33. Quoted in Veigel 2009, 53. See also Manzetti 1991, 95.

34. Erro 1994, 101–2; Epstein 1987, 996. One of Martínez de Hoz's opponents in the military regime, Admiral Emilio Massera, proclaimed, "For every *guerrillero* that I kill, the Minister of Economics is creating five new ones" (quoted in Veigel 2009, 61).

35. Memorandum from Jack Guenther, Argentina-IMF mission head, to the Managing Director, "Mission Review," June 15, 1976.

Buenos Aires on June 29 to iron out the final details of a $300 million (special drawing rights [SDR] 260 million) purchase under the standby arrangement. Discussions between the Fund and the Argentines proceeded alongside Martínez de Hoz's efforts to gain additional support from Western banks, efforts that proved fruitful; IMF officials reported that the Argentines had secured up to $500 million from U.S. banks during the meetings between Martínez de Hoz and a consortium of bankers in New York.[36] The financing from private sources, coupled with Argentina not having an excessively large financing gap in 1976, makes the generosity of the IMF terms all the more surprising. According to Luigi Manzetti, "the IMF was so appreciative of the 'new course' taken by Martínez de Hoz that it granted Argentina more funds than were given to any other Latin American country at the time."[37]

The IMF Executive Board approved the standby arrangement—the first high-conditionality IMF loan to Argentina since 1968—on August 6. The standby arrangement involved five binding conditions, none of which was particularly controversial or onerous. The transcript of the Board meeting shows strong support, at the director level, for the new economic team of the country. Only one ED expressed concern that "the intermingling of economic, political, and social problems in Argentina" should give IMF staff members pause before "making judgments on the speed with which measures could be taken to correct the economic position, although it was not difficult to make a broad judgment of the steps needed."[38]

Martínez de Hoz later reflected on the negotiations over the lending arrangement, "Our economic program was even more severe than the IMF demanded. *There were no disagreements or debates with the IMF.* It was easy."[39]

Performance under the 1976 Standby Arrangement

Two problems cropped up soon after the program was in place. Monthly consumer price inflation had fallen in the first four months after the coup but climbed back to 10 percent in September 1976 and hit 15 percent in December. Unable to cut wages or employment any further, Diz and Martínez de Hoz resorted to unorthodox measures to get a handle on the rising prices. In March 1977, the government imposed a six-month price freeze on the eight hundred largest Argentine firms;

36. Memorandum from Jorge del Canto to the Managing Director, "Argentina—Status of Negotiations," June 29, 1976.

37. Manzetti 1991, 112.

38. Minutes of the Executive Board Meeting, EBM/76/124, August 6, 1976.

39. Quoted in Kedar 2013, 140 (emphasis added).

the "price truce" was to be enforced officially through administrative monitoring (an ineffective approach in a government rife with corruption) and unofficially through voluntary self-restraint on the part of industrialists.[40] The authorities also lowered tariffs in an effort to impose price discipline on previously sheltered firms.[41]

More concerning from the perspective of the Fund was the failure of the government to meet the fiscal target in the August standby arrangement. The IMF set a modest target of 575 billion pesos (52 percent of total expenditures) for the cumulative deficit of the Treasury; in December, the Argentines reported a deficit of 590 billion pesos (60 percent of total expenditures). IMF economists were concerned about the fiscal situation. A November briefing by upper-level management for the mission to evaluate the status of the program noted, "the fiscal situation remains the critical aspect of the Argentine stabilization plan."[42] The final disbursement was delayed at the end of 1976 as the IMF team and Argentine officials negotiated new targets on net domestic credit of the Central Bank and the fiscal deficit for the first quarter of 1977. Despite the missed fiscal target in the last quarter of the previous year and concern that "the progress on the control of inflation has been disappointing," the staff members recommended approval of the final tranche of the standby arrangement.[43]

The Second Standby Arrangement

The Economy Minister unveiled a major policy initiative in June 1977 just before IMF officials arrived in Buenos Aires for negotiations on a second standby arrangement. Martínez de Hoz announced a far-reaching liberalization of the financial system. Private financial institutions were once again allowed to dispense credit at interest rates of their choosing, and for the first time since the end of the Peronist period, real interest rates climbed above 0. The close links of the financial sector with the government meant that the bankers were able to slip a clause into the financial reform that would have important repercussions at a later date: the government promised to fully back all private deposits held by Argentine banks.[44] As a result, when financial crisis eventually came to Argentina in 1980, the cost of the bailout for Argentine banks amounted to more than

---

40. Bonelli 2004, 33; Erro 1994, 107; Smith 1989, 237.

41. Fernández 1985, 874.

42. IMF Western Hemisphere Department, "Briefing for Mission to Argentina," November 22, 1976.

43. Staff report, "Argentina—Consultation under Standby Arrangement," EBS/77/109, April 15, 1977.

44. Epstein 1987, 996; Erro 1994, 109.

3 percent of GDP.[45] But the June reforms served the desired purpose: foreign capital returned to Argentina in droves.

Negotiations over a second standby arrangement to support the program of the economic team took place in June and July of 1977. IMF negotiators, led by Marcello Caiola, remained optimistic about the prospects of the Argentine officials' management of the stabilization effort. Although fiscal policy was still identified as the wobbly plank of the stabilization, IMF staff allowed Diz and Martínez de Hoz to offer vague promises of improvement without imposing tough conditions. The leniency of the staff was noted by an ED, William A. Beveridge, who complained in a memo to Fund management that the proposed standby arrangement contained "no reflection of efforts to intensify fiscal policies in the letter of intent," despite the suggestion in Caiola's briefing paper that "in order to strengthen the fiscal situation, the authorities should implement a substantial tax package."[46]

On September 2, 1977, Argentines submitted the Letter of Intent, drafted with the IMF staff members from the Western Hemisphere Department, which outlined policies for a new standby arrangement. The proposal was brought before the Executive Board on September 16. Several EDs immediately seized on a highly unusual aspect of the proposed loan: "the proposed standby arrangement contained the broad lines of a program for 1978 rather than any quantified targets."[47] The performance criteria included in the standby arrangement were set only for the quarter following the date of approval; one experienced ED remarked that he was not familiar with another program in which the Board was asked to approve a twelve-month program with binding conditions specified for half the length of the program. The staff and management defended the odd structure of the proposed program, arguing that delays in the preparation of the government budget had prevented the staff from formulating targets for the entire duration of the loan and that, in any case, the Argentines had indicated that they would not need to draw on the precautionary program. The last point is important: the current account balance was stable, financing was plentiful, and the June reforms of the financial system spurred large inflows of foreign investment. The need of Argentina for balance-of-payments support had eroded in the time between the mission to Buenos Aires and the Executive Board meeting.

With the caveat that the 1977 standby arrangement should not be seen as setting a precedent for future Fund lending behavior, the Board approved the SDR 159.5 million loan. In spite of concerns about the structure of the agreement and

45. Fernández 1985, 889.
46. Note from W. A. Beveridge to Sanson and Walter Robichek, "Argentina," July 7, 1977.
47. Minutes of the Meeting of the Executive Board, EBM/77/138, September 16, 1977.

lingering questions about the weakness of the program vis-à-vis inflation and fiscal policy, the record of the Board meeting indicates that, for many of the EDs, approval of the program was intended as a signal of the continued support of the Fund for the Diz–Martínez de Hoz policy team.

The End of the First Era of Neoliberal Influence in Argentina

In 1978, Argentina won the soccer World Cup in front of thousands of ecstatic *porteños* at the Buenos Aires Estadio Monumental (situated close enough to the notorious torture rooms of the Naval Mechanics School that the captives could hear the cheering). Off the soccer pitch, the news for Argentina was mostly bad. The dirty war had reached its bloody nadir, and the economic situation of the country had deteriorated. In March, the Argentine authorities notified the IMF that, in light of the strong balance-of-payments performance, they would not need to draw on the standby arrangement and would not seek to negotiate a new agreement after the current agreement expired.[48] In any case, IMF patience with the Diz–Martínez de Hoz policy team was wearing thin; inflation reached 170 percent in 1978 (the program had envisioned an increase in prices of no more than 80 percent), the fiscal deficit significantly exceeded the program targets, and the expansion of domestic monetary assets began to accelerate by the end of the year. The only good news on the economic front was the stable external balance, but this was mainly a consequence of inflows of "hot money" from abroad in the wake of the reform of the financial system.[49]

The end of the first period of neoliberal control over Argentine economic policymaking came relatively quickly. In December 1978, the economic team announced the tablita, a stabilization plan consisting of a pre-announced schedule of devaluations (literally, a small monthly table published by the government) that would push the value of the peso below the level of the monthly price increases, thereby reducing inflationary expectations and (theoretically) bringing prices back down.[50]

The tablita had some perverse consequences for economic activity in Argentina. The forward-looking crawling peg led to an appreciation of the real exchange rate; consumers, in turn, switched their spending to (comparatively) cheaper imports (the volume of which surged by 73 percent in 1979 and then

---

48. Memorandum from Marcello Caiola to the Acting Managing Director, "Mission to Argentina," March 15, 1978.

49. IMF Western Hemisphere Department, "Briefing for Mission to Argentina," March 7, 1979.

50. See Fernández 1985; Schamis 2003, 134; Sjaastad 1989, 254–75.

another 68 percent in 1980), and Argentine producers had to borrow heavily from international markets to stay afloat.

An abrupt reversal in the current account and the reserves positions of the country occurred at the end of the 1970s. The current account fell into negative territory, helped along by the real overvaluation of the peso. With the expectation of an unannounced devaluation in the near future, investors began to dump pesos in favor of U.S. dollars on a massive scale.[51]

By early 1980, many of the heavily indebted Argentine firms had failed; the banks then raised their interest rates to attract depositors to offset their losses from loans that had been made to now-shuttered companies. The tightening of credit accelerated the recession in the country. In March, the first major Argentine bank failed; following the collapse of Banco de Intercambio Regional, the government was forced to absorb the balance sheets of Banco de los Andes, Banco Oddoné, and Banco Internaciónal.[52]

By the end of 1980, time had run out for the neoliberal economic officials in the military government. Remarkably, after five years in office Diz and Martínez de Hoz had survived longer than any other Central Bank governor or finance minister in postwar Argentine history (to that point). Martínez de Hoz left office confident that, in spite of the economic trauma that Argentines had endured in the last two years of his time as economy minister, the incoming military government would remain committed to broadly neoliberal policies. "The important thing is that Argentina has accepted the principle that retaining something moderately good is better than trying to get something perfect," he remarked.[53]

Summary of the First Episode, 1976–1981

I have characterized the IMF treatment of Argentina during this period as lenient. The arrangement negotiated in 1976 was, by the standards of the organization at the time, very generous. Fund staff members were willing to overlook the missed fiscal targets to enable the government to complete the program. The second standby arrangement, approved the next year, was unusually light in terms of conditionality; rather than spelling out binding targets for entire duration of the proposed loan, the conditions included in the 1977 standby arrangement were set for only the quarter following the date of approval.

---

51. Schamis 2003, 135.

52. Epstein 1987, 998–99.

53. Quoted in Lewis Diuguid, "Argentine Finance Minister Ends Job with Confidence," *Washington Post*, October 2, 1980, p. B3.

The design and enforcement of the Fund programs with the neoliberal policy team in Videla's government was consistent with my general argument and the aggregate statistical evidence compiled in chapter 3. The confidence placed by the decision makers at the IMF in the plans formulated by the Argentines was largely a function of the proximity of the beliefs held by the two sides about how economic policies should be crafted. The course followed by the IMF staff and management provided economic (and, ultimately, political) support to a group of like-minded authorities. The institution failed to pick up on other signals that suggested a more cautious view of the trajectory of the Argentine economy would be appropriate; in particular, the internal divisiveness of the military government and its unwillingness to bear the costs of austerity should have indicated that the ability of the Fund-supported policy team to push through a sweeping reform and stabilization effort was limited.

Episode 2: Turbulence, Turnover, and the Battle with the IMF, 1981–1985

The next episode includes two political transitions—one external (a shift from the center-left idealists of the Jimmy Carter administration to the archconservative practitioners of realpolitik in the Ronald Reagan government) and one internal (the restoration of electoral democracy in Argentina)—that should have transformed the relationship of the IMF with the country. And the relationship did take a turn, albeit for the worse. The factor that best explains the breakdown in relations was the yawning gap in economic beliefs that opened up as the military ceded power to a civilian government.

This was a period in which neoliberals lost the foothold in Argentine economic policymaking that they had gained in the first years of the Proceso. The differences between the IMF treatment of the governments during this episode and the two episodes of high neoliberal influence are stark. In line with the predictions of the theoretical framework developed in chapter 2 and the cross-national evidence presented in chapter 3, the IMF applied a heavy hand during the four years in which policymakers who rejected neoliberal ideas held sway in Argentina.

Things Fall Apart: The End of the Military Regime

Between 1981 (when General Videla and his team of neoliberal policymakers left office) and 1983 (when the outgoing military government negotiated a new IMF lending arrangement), Argentina was plunged into some of the worst economic straits that the country had ever faced. The management of the economy passed through the hands of several policymakers, each of whom espoused a radically different view of how best to guide Argentina through its rolling crisis; successive policy teams of varying ideological stripes came and went while economic output invariably contracted and price inflation skyrocketed.

There were no serious negotiations with the Fund over a new loan before 1983. But the internal documents cataloging the interactions of the IMF with the different policy teams during the last years of the military regime provide some evidence about how the character of the policy team influenced the staff and management view of the situation.

The first policy team brought in after power passed from Videla and his neoliberal policy team to a different faction was composed of home-grown officials who hewed closer to the structuralist views that had influenced precoup Argentine policies.[54] The IMF viewed the developments in Argentina under the new team with growing concern. IMF staff members traveled to Buenos Aires at the end of August for an evaluation of the state of the economy; after two weeks spent analyzing the policy agenda of the new economic team, the head of the mission, Christian Brachet, presented a bleak assessment to the managing director. Of particular interest are the references in Brachet's assessment to divisions among the economic policymakers. His briefing paper expressed concerns about "the credibility of the economic program as a whole. . . . the mission could but be struck by the little confidence there remains in the economic team. Rumors of impending resignations or shake-ups in a cabinet much divided against itself and where most ministers remain first and foremost representatives of sectorial [sic] interests continue unabated."[55]

At the tail end of 1981, another member of military junta, General Leopoldo Galtieri, took control of the government. He swapped economic teams, bringing a "hard-line neoliberal group" headed by Roberto Alemann (a self-described monetarist who had previously served as the economy minister in 1961–1962) into the government.[56] Alemann was known to the policymaking elite in Washington, DC, and was well connected in international banking circles; according to Klaus Veigel, "Alemann enjoyed excellent international contacts through his work as ambassador in the United States starting in 1962 and long-standing con-

---

54. The new economy minister, Lorenzo Sigaut, held a doctoral degree in economics from Universidad de Buenos Aires; the head of the Central Bank, Julio J. Gómez, had studied commerce at Hipolito Yrigoyen in the 1940s.

55. Memorandum from Christian Brachet to the Managing Director, "Argentina—Article IV Consultation," September 23, 1981.

56. McGuire 1997, 177–78 (quotation). See also Alemann's interview in de Pablo 1977, 9–32; Kirshner 2007, 177–82.

tacts with the banking community through his advisory function for the Union Bank of Switzerland (UBS)."[57]

The new economy minister intended to undo all the policies carried out under the previous team. To that end, he made the highly unusual request that an IMF mission be brought back to Buenos Aires for the second Article IV consultation in less than six months.[58] The head of the IMF mission communicated to Jacques de Larosière (the new IMF managing director) that "the new authorities were much concerned with conveying to the Executive Board a more encouraging view of Argentina's economic policies and prospects than that presented in the staff reports prepared in the aftermath of the discussions held with the previous administration."[59] Brachet's memo is also a vivid reminder of the challenges facing Alemann's team: GDP had plunged by 11.5 percent in the final quarter of 1981; unemployment, adjusted to account for widespread underemployment, was estimated at 12–13 percent; yearly inflation was tracked in December at around 130 percent; and international reserves had dwindled to the point that they covered only four months of merchandise imports.

Alemann quickly instituted an austerity program, which seemed to set the table for an IMF loan to follow. And if the strict orthodoxy of the Alemann program was not enough to sway the IMF, Galtieri's close relations with the new Reagan administration meant that Argentina had the most powerful IMF member state back on its side.[60] But if Alemann's agenda involved going to the Fund for a lending program, his plans were spoiled by the surprise invasion by the Argentine military regime of the British-controlled Islas Malvinas (Falkland Islands) on April 2, 1982.

The Argentine defeat by British forces in the South Atlantic had profound political and economic consequences. By the time Argentina capitulated in June, the economy, already mired in a deep recession after the financial implosion in 1980–1981, entered its free-fall phase. A huge amount of money exited the country, slipping through the porous capital controls imposed by the military regime. The British government had imposed punishing financial and trade sanctions against the country. The foreign debt load of Argentina exploded—and to make matters worse, the war alienated the New York– and London-based bankers on whom the regime depended for new funds to retire old debts and (potentially)

---

57. Veigel 2009, 62.
58. Interview with Christian Brachet, Washington, DC, March 31, 2009.
59. Memorandum from Christian Brachet to the Managing Director, "1981 Article IV Consultations with Argentina—Additional Discussions," February 1, 1982.
60. On the U.S. diplomatic relationship with Galtieri on the eve of the Malvinas War, see Feldman 1985; Kirshner 2007, 183–84; Veigel 2009, 90–91.

to participate in a debt-rescheduling arrangement that would lengthen maturities, lower interest payments, and reduce the obligations of the government to its creditors.[61] Alemann and his team were removed from their posts at the end of June, paving the way for the new set of structuralist-leaning officials who were at the helm of the economy when the IMF mission members finally returned to Argentina.

Tough Negotiations over a New Standby Arrangement

Officials from the IMF Western Hemisphere Department arrived in Buenos Aires to start negotiations in September 1982.[62] The Argentine policy team was now led by Economy Minister Jorge Wehbe (a former professor of law at Universidad de Buenos Aires who twice, briefly, had served as economy minister) and Central Bank Governor Julio González del Solar (holder of a 1943 Harvard business degree and alternate ED at the IMF in 1956–1957).

The new Argentine Central Bank chief, as an (albeit short-lived) alternate ED at the Fund, knew the organization and held an advanced degree (albeit in business administration, not economics) from the most elite of U.S. universities. But González del Solar did not share the intellectual framework of the Fund; his views were much closer to those espoused by Raúl Prebisch, a structuralist and a mentor that González del Solar much admired.[63] The disagreements between the IMF mission and the Argentine team would only intensify in the next two years as structuralist-friendly officials tightened their control over the levers of macroeconomic policymaking.

A new regional (and indeed international) dynamic induced by events in Mexico City gave more urgency to the Argentine negotiations. The international financial system had been rocked earlier in the month by the announce-

---

61. On the dire financial consequences of the war in the South Atlantic, see Kirshner 2007, 182–83; Smith 1989, 246–47.

62. The IMF arrival followed an unsuccessful stabilization effort, spearheaded by two Harvard-trained economists, that was put in place in July 1982. Soon after the cessation of hostilities, the new head of the military announced plans to hold democratic elections in eighteen months and appointed José Marie Dagnino Pastore (who had earned a PhD in economics at Harvard in 1963) as the economy minister and Domingo Cavallo as the Central Bank governor, with the task of stabilizing the collapsing Argentine economy. But Dagnino Pastore and Cavallo clashed over the strategy for handling the massive war debt of the country; the plan that Cavallo settled on (called licuación) was intended to inflate away a portion of domestic debt. According to the plan, the Central Bank would, in effect, pump inflation into the system through artificially low interest rates, and the one-time inflationary shock would shrink the domestic debt burden (Veigel 2009, 89, 100–102; Smith 1989, 247). The effort was unsuccessful, and both officials resigned on August 24, 1982, after just fifty-four days in office.

63. Dosman 2008, 195.

ment by the Mexican government that it would cease making payments on its foreign debt. The capacity of Argentina to continue debt service had been questionable even before the Mexican default. The government had accumulated over $2 billion in arrears during the Malvinas conflict, and the total amount due to creditors at the end of 1982 totaled nearly $13 billion. Meanwhile, the Central Bank reserves had dropped to less than $4 billion.[64] The Mexican announcement was the shock that induced private banks to turn off the lending faucet connected to Latin America. At this point, the prospect of a chain of defaults had to be taken very seriously by the IMF. Without a quick infusion of funds from the Fund and foreign banks, it was clear that Argentina would be the next domino to fall.

Against this backdrop, the IMF mission went to Argentina in early September to start negotiations for a new loan. González del Solar, the Central Bank governor, wanted to secure a multiyear agreement with the Fund under the Extended Fund Facility (EFF) for the maximum amount allotted to the country (450 percent of the quota, or SDR 3.6 billion).[65] The EFF was the most generous loan offered at the time by the Fund and was regarded as the most serious endorsement by the Fund staff and management of the reform efforts of a country. At the time of the Argentine negotiations, Brazil was also in discussions with the IMF for an EFF worth 450 percent of its quota; in March 1983, the Fund approved the Brazilian loan for the full amount.

The IMF officials did not look favorably on the request by Argentina, however.[66] Christian Brachet, head of the IMF Argentina mission, reminded the central banker in a telephone conversation that the EFF "would be geared not only to effect a major balance of payments adjustment but also to improve resource allocation with a view to strengthening the productive base."[67] The mission report expressed concerns about the ability of the economic team to carry out a strong set of reforms: "the economic team has significantly more experience of public affairs than its predecessor but the strength of its mandate remains unclear. . . . The mission thus may find that a clearer political consensus on the need for corrective action—*as well on the nature of such action*—than exists at present

---

64. Aggarwal 1996, 410–11.

65. Memorandum from Christian Brachet to Carlos Sanson, "Telephone Conversation with Argentina's Central Bank Governor," September 23, 1982.

66. James Boughton, the former official IMF historian, reports that the director of the Western Hemisphere Department, Walter Robichek, "was receptive to the idea" of the EFF. Nonetheless, the staff members recommended against it, and Robichek in the end decided not to support the request for the EFF (see Boughton 2001, 332).

67. Memorandum from Christian Brachet to Carlos Sanson, "Telephone Conversation with Argentina's Central Bank Governor," September 23, 1982.

will have to be developed within Argentina before a workable program can be framed."[68]

The negotiations with the Argentines over a new standby arrangement were contentious. The IMF officials were encouraged by management to take a tough line with the policy team; in a handwritten note on the September mission briefing, Managing Director Jacques de Larosière advised the staff to "present the 'shock therapy' as a 1st best solution."[69] The mission was authorized by management to negotiate the terms for a fifteen-month standby arrangement worth SDR 1.5 billion (187% of the quota).[70]

The negotiations dragged on into November; at the same time, the Argentines were engaged in furious negotiations with private creditors and the Bank for International Settlements on the terms for bridge loans worth $1.1 billion and $750 million, respectively.[71] The relationship between the Fund and Argentine officials—who felt that the IMF was being excessively stringent in the face of a near complete economic collapse and amid rising political tensions in the run-up to the elections scheduled for October 1983—became strained. In a memorandum for the EDs of the G5 countries, the director of the Western Hemisphere Department reported that "negotiations on Argentina from which he and the staff had returned the previous day, had been very difficult. . . . no one on the Argentine side had tried to take an integrated view of the problem areas of the economy, nor quantify the magnitude of the problems."[72]

In November, Jacques de Larosière unveiled the new strategy that the Fund would take to deal with the Latin American crisis. The commercial banks wanted debtor countries to sign IMF agreements to lower the risk of default—but in exchange for IMF support, the managing director would force the banks to grant new money to fill the portion of the "financing gap" not covered by the IMF loan.[73] This was partly a result of practical considerations; Fund resources were simply not large enough to close the financing gaps facing most of the prospective borrowers in 1982–1983. To organize the 325 commercial banks that were involved in Argentina, the largest (and most exposed) banks formed an Advisory

---

68. IMF Western Hemisphere Department, "Argentina—Briefing for Mission (Standby Arrangement)," September 22, 1982 (emphasis added).

69. De Larosière's handwriting, although somewhat messy, is legible. Note from William B. Dale to the Managing Director, "Study: Argentina—Briefing for Mission (Standby Arrangement)," September 22, 1983.

70. Memorandum from José Braz to Walter Robichek, "Negotiations with Argentina," October 7, 1982.

71. Boughton 2001, 332–33.

72. Staff memorandum for G5 Executive Directors, "Subject: Argentina Briefing for G5 EDs," November 1, 1982.

73. See, for example, Boughton 2001, 333–34.

Committee headed by William Rhodes, legendary Citibank chairman.[74] Subsequent negotiations followed a triangular pattern: between the IMF and Argentina, Argentina and the banks, and the banks and the IMF. The outcome of the pressure from the IMF was the approval of a $1.5 billion increase in private bank exposure to accompany the standby arrangement.[75]

The remaining obstacle to the agreement was the balance-of-payments target, which the IMF limited to a deficit of no more the $500 million but which the Argentines felt was too strict.[76] Once Wehbe and González del Solar finally acceded to the balance-of-payments target, the Letter of Intent and Memorandum of Understanding containing the details of the program were signed and submitted to the Executive Board for approval.

The Board discussed the staff proposal on January 24, 1983. The fifteen-month program was much more comprehensive (in terms of conditionality) than the previous agreements signed during the Diz–Martínez de Hoz years. In addition to the inclusion of the balance-of-payments target as a binding condition, the standby arrangement included several structural performance criteria related to trade and payments.[77] Some of the EDs expressed concerns about the toughness of the program; the Belgian ED, Jacques de Groote, stated that the proposed program "could impose such a heavy burden on the government as to exclude the possibility of complete observance."[78] The Board members' uncertainty about the prospects for the program notwithstanding, the program was approved and the first SDR 300 million was disbursed in May.

Performance under the 1983 Arrangement

When the IMF mission visited Argentina in late August to determine whether the country could draw the next tranche of the standby arrangement, it was clear that the program had gone off the rails. Most concerning from the perspective of the members of the IMF mission was the fact that the country was out of

---

74. Aggarwal 1996, 411–12; ibid., 334.

75. Boughton 2001, 333.

76. The current account deficit in 1982 was $950 million. The debate between the two sides revolved around how to count the $1.5 billion bridge loan from the banks; the IMF wanted to exclude it from the ledger, whereas the Argentines wanted it to count toward achieving payments equilibrium (Memorandum from Eduardo Wiesner to the Managing Director, "Argentina—Standby Documentation," December 16, 1982).

77. The 1983 agreement included fifteen separate performance criteria ("Argentina—Staff Report for the 1982 Article IV Consultation and Request for Standby Arrangement," EBS/83/8, January 10, 1983).

78. Minutes of the Executive Board Meeting, EBM/83/17, January 24, 1983; also cited in Boughton 2001, 334.

compliance with multiple binding conditions. The Central Bank governor flew to Washington, DC, in early September to plead the Argentine case in the hopes of getting a waiver from the Fund that would allow Argentina to obtain the much-needed funding. But the managing director rejected González del Solar's appeal, and the program was suspended.[79] When González del Solar returned home empty-handed on October 3, he was promptly jailed by a Patagonian judge for violating national sovereignty by helping to renegotiate the $220 million debt of the national airline, Aerolíneas Argentinas, with several New York–based banks.[80] González's arrest and jailing (on blatantly trumped-up charges) was a manifestation of the "national rage" of Argentines against the IMF and foreign creditors (viewed by many in the country as partners in crime).[81]

Argentina teetered on the precipice in the remaining months of 1983. Pressure on the IMF from the banks to release the final tranche of the standby arrangement proved ineffectual; the only lifeline for Argentina was a series of postponements of the payments owed on the bridge loan made by the banks. The relationship between the Fund and Argentine authorities had degraded to the point that the assistant director of the Western Hemisphere Department, Christian Brachet, reported "an undisguised sense of bitterness toward the Fund."[82] In December, the IMF was given a chance to renew the relationship with a new set of policy-makers in a post–democratic transition Argentina.

The Battle with the Fund, 1983–1985

A new chapter in the relationship of the IMF and Argentina began on December 10, 1983, when Raúl Alfonsín was inaugurated as the new president of Argentina. Alfonsín was the unexpected victor of the first free elections in Argentina in a decade. He was the leader of a political party, the Union Civica Radical (Radical Party) that had not governed since the 1960s. Moreover, the Justicialista (Peronist) Party had won every previous fair, contested election since 1945.

The negotiations led by Alfonsín's new economic team illustrate the limits of domestic institutional explanations for variation in IMF lending. There was no qualitative shift in IMF treatment of the country. Instead, the rejection by the

79. Boughton 2001, 386–87.

80. Nathaniel C. Nash, "Argentine Intrigue Surrounds a Banker," *New York Times*, October 9, 1983, p. 14; *Economist*, "Why Some Argentines Want to Leave the Solar System," p. 83; Veigel 2005, 251.

81. Dosman 2008, 492.

82. Memorandum from Christian Brachet to the Managing Director, "Argentina—Meeting with Bank Working Committee," November 3, 1983.

new policy team of the neoliberal policy template made for an extraordinarily contentious set of negotiations that stretched out almost a year.

Alfonsín's new economic policymaking team consisted of Bernardo Grinspun as the economy minister and Enrique García Vásquez as the Central Bank governor. Grinspun had served as trade secretary in the brief Radical administration in the 1960s; he was described in the U.S. and British press as "a well-respected private banker who helped in Argentina's debt negotiations in 1975" as well as a figure who was "no stranger to banking circles in the United States and Europe."[83] Both Grinspun and the Central Bank governor were indigenously trained. Grinspun had become acquainted with Alfonsín while they were enrolled at Universidad de Buenos Aires. Whereas García Vásquez was slightly more sympathetic to the neoliberal orientation of the Fund, Grinspun, "imbued with nationalist and populist ideas," was staunchly in the structuralist camp.[84] He was well acquainted with Raúl Prebisch, having chaired the commodities committee at the 1964 UNCTAD meeting (a meeting at which Grinspun, much to the annoyance of the other participants, "could not stop talking").[85] Grinspun believed that the economic policies of his team should be oriented to restoring economic growth and raising real wages after several years of decline, with moderately rising prices as a perhaps necessary by-product of the effort.[86] (In current prices, per capita GDP had fallen from $7,538 in 1980 to $3,572 at the end of 1983.)[87] And he believed that protectionism and a serious dose of state intervention had important roles to play in engineering the turnaround in the economic fortunes of Argentina.

The well of structuralist-influenced policymakers ran deep in the center-left Radical Party. "Many Radical Party members close to Alfonsín," notes Edgar Dosman, had been Prebisch's "students before 1948 [the year of Prebisch's exile from Argentina] or had worked with him at ECLA, ILPES [Latin American and Caribbean Institute for Economic and Social Planning], UNCTAD or elsewhere in the UN."[88] Alfonsín had long-standing ties to the structuralist element in the Radical Party: he counted among his close advisors in his 1983 electoral campaign (in

---

83. James L. Rowe Jr., "Leaders Face Troubled Economy: The New Order in Argentina," *Washington Post*, November 27, 1983, p. H6 (first quotation); *Economist*, "Argentine Debt: Radical Rethink," November 5, 1983, p. 87 (second quotation). Grinspun had also been the Argentine representative to the Paris Club, the informal group of official creditors that meets to reschedule debt with developing countries.

84. Bonelli 2004, 58 (my translation from Spanish).

85. Dosman 2008, 401 (quotation).

86. On the economic beliefs of the new economic team, see Erro 1994, 132; Manzetti 1991, 141; Veigel 2009, 132–33.

87. Data on the per capita GDP of Argentina were drawn from the IMF World Economic Outlook database, https://www.imf.org/external/ns/cs.aspx?id=28.

88. Dosman 2008, 491.

addition to Grinspun and García Vásquez) Juan J. Alfredo Concepción, German Lopez, Aldo Ferrer, and Roque Carranza—all of whom held structuralist beliefs.[89] Raúl Prebisch himself had a role in helping to craft the Radical government economic agenda; Aldo Ferrer brought him in as a participant in a series of high-level meetings, hosted by Alfonsín and involving party heavyweights, to discuss the policy direction of the incoming government.[90]

Unsurprisingly, the IMF was not enamored with the new Argentine economic policy team. A mission had been sent to Argentina two days after the inauguration of Alfonsín as president to lay the groundwork for a new agreement.[91] The mission reported "an atmosphere of conflict" between officials in the Economy Ministry and the Central Bank.[92] Intellectual divisions in the government were also notable between Grinspun and his advisors and a group of U.S.-educated economists in the lower rungs of the Planning Ministry, which was led by Juan V. Sourrouille.[93] The IMF viewed Grinspun, in particular, with deep suspicion; one former top IMF official described him as a "walking disaster."[94] The gap in economic beliefs between Grinspun and García Vásquez, on the one hand, and the IMF, on the other, would generate the toughest, most contentious negotiations in the Fund-Argentine relationship.

In early 1984, there was an even stronger imperative on the part of the IMF to quickly hammer out the details on a loan agreement than in previous episodes. Capital flight and high inflation in the months prior to the presidential election meant that Argentina was "essentially a country without a currency."[95] The prospect of a default on the $41 billion foreign debt—nearly half of which fell due in 1984—continued to pose a threat to the international financial system. There was pressure on the Fund to extend support to the Alfonsín government for political reasons, as well. A banker observed at the time, "Grinspun will be asking the IMF

89. Bonelli 2004; Heras 2008, 190–92.

90. Dosman 2008, 490–91.

91. Manzetti incorrectly reports, "Grinspun was opposed to a standby" (1991, 141). In fact, Grinspun had secretly met with the Fund preceding the elections in September 1983 (Veigel 2009, 127). The presence of the Fund staff just two days after Alfonsín took office and the visit by García Vásquez to IMF headquarters on December 20 indicates an urgency to negotiate.

92. Memorandum from K. Burke Dillon to the Managing Director, "Mission to Argentina—December 12–16, 1983," December 19, 1983.

93. Veigel 2009, 133–34. Sourrouille's advisors included Adolfo Canitrot (Stanford University economics PhD), Mario Brodersohn (Harvard University), and José Luis Machinea (University of Minnesota). But the economy minister and (to a lesser extent) the Central Bank governor were in charge of the stabilization effort in 1984, and the U.S.-trained economists in the Planning Ministry would have to wait several years to gain influence over Argentine economic policymaking.

94. Interview with Desmond Lachman, former assistant director of the IMF Western Hemisphere Department (1984–1990), Washington, DC, April 6, 2008.

95. Boughton 2001, 388.

not to be too harsh so as not to jeopardize the experiment in democracy. He'll probably get a sympathetic ear."[96]

The Negotiations Begin

The IMF mission to negotiate a new standby arrangement began at the end of January 1984. The mission arrived just after Alfonsín announced an economic agenda that included several seemingly incompatible goals: wage increases of 6–8 percent and a 5 percent increase in output, coupled with a reduction in inflation and the fiscal deficit.[97] The first issue that confronted the IMF team, led by Stanford-trained Eduardo Wiesner, was the size of IMF support for the Grinspun–García Vásquez team. Argentina faced a large financing gap in 1984, and the mission and the Argentine authorities agreed that support should amount to 125 percent of the quota.[98] The upper-level Fund management was uncomfortable with the size of the proposed loan. William Dale, the second in command at the Fund, expressed his doubts in a handwritten note for the managing director: "I am doubtful that Argentina 'deserves' 125% of quota. . . . I think I would opt for 102% at this stage, reserving discussion of 125% for later."[99] The mission left Argentina in February without an agreement with the Argentine officials on the content of a stabilization program for 1984.

In March, the situation worsened. The Fund economists and Grinspun were at an impasse over the level of the budget deficit to be included in a standby arrangement. At the end of the month, Argentina was facing $500 million in interest payments, and the authorities began to drop hints that Argentina would not be able (or willing) to make the payment.[100] Grinspun told the Advisory Committee of the commercial banks that the country was on the cusp of negotiations with the Fund on a Letter of Intent, but in reality, Grinspun's team had just started drafting their own program without consultation with IMF economists.

Meanwhile, the rage against the IMF in Argentina had become white-hot. Grinspun's erratic and confrontational negotiating tactics left the IMF mission

---

96. "IMF Girds to Meet Bids for Aid," *New York Times*, January 2, 1984, p. 39.

97. Erro 1994, 133; Manzetti 1991, 141–42.

98. The mission reported that "Argentina has, at present, an especially large need for financing from the Fund given the high level of external payment arrears, the low level of reserves, and limited access to spontaneous sources of financing" (IMF Western Hemisphere Department, "Argentina—Mission Briefing," January 30, 1984).

99. Note from William B. Dale to the Managing Director, "Subject: Argentina Briefing," January 31, 1984.

100. Marlise Simons, "Argentine Plan Raising Doubts on Aid by Banks," *New York Times*, March 24, 1984, p. 31.

unmoved; to try to break the deadlocked negotiations, Alfonsín sent Raúl Prebisch, then in his eighties, to IMF headquarters on March 23 for eight days of talks with the staff and management to try to wrest some concessions from the Fund.[101] The IMF insisted that the budget deficit could be no higher than 6 percent; the Argentine authorities did not want to set a target below 9 percent (at the time, the fiscal deficit was around 14 percent of GDP).[102] Prebisch returned to Buenos Aires and advised Alfonsín to give way in the negotiations with the Fund. The Argentine media and academia then turned on Prebisch; Clarín, a major national newspaper, warned, "behind the structural adjustment favored by Presidential Adviser Prebisch lurks the ghost of orthodoxy." The members of the economics department at Universidad Tucúman voted to rescind Prebisch's honorary doctorate.[103]

The battle to avoid default was still being waged. On March 31, Argentina avoided a missing a debt payment only through a last-minute $300 million loan put together by Mexico, Venezuela, Brazil, and Colombia; the remaining amount came from the dwindling reserves of the country and a $100 million loan from the Advisory Committee of the commercial banks. The consequences of a missed payment would have been severe for highly exposed U.S. banks because the March 31 deadline marked the date at which the banks were to report their first-quarter earnings.[104]

The negotiations continued into the summer, with several breakdowns along the way. In a meeting with U.S. financial representatives, including Paul Volcker, chairman of the Federal Reserve, Joaquin Ferrán of the IMF expressed concern that "the economic team did not have the sufficient power necessary to take the decisions necessary to bring the situation under control." Responding to a question from Volcker about parallels between the Alfonsín administration and the experience of the Radical government in the mid-1960s, Sterie Beza, a top Fund official, expressed the belief that the IMF should hold a tough line because in the previous Radical administration, "people like Grinspun and García Vásquez gradually had come around."[105]

Unable to come to an agreement on the fiscal question, Grinspun decided to pursue a new gambit. On June 11, he and García Vásquez, the Central Bank head, submitted their own Letter of Intent to the Fund Executive Board. Grinspun's

---

101. Boughton 2001, 389.

102. Minutes of Meeting with [IMF] Management to Discuss Argentina, March 21, 1984.

103. Dosman 2008, 495.

104. Henry Giniger and Milt Freudenheim, "Latins Help End Argentine Crisis," New York Times, p. 2; Boughton 2001, 390–91; Stiles 1987, 66.

105. Minutes of the Argentine Mission Report to [IMF] Management and U.S. Representatives, March 7, 1984.

action was not necessarily a surprise to the Fund—in May, he had threatened to unilaterally submit a proposal if the IMF mission did not relent on the fiscal issue—but it was a serious breach of IMF protocols.[106] A statement from a key presidential aide at the time reflected the disagreement between the Fund and the Argentines: "There was a fundamental difference of focus. The IMF's formulas were recessionary, and we won't accept that."[107]

The timing of the Argentine move was deliberate; June 15 marked another deadline for interest payments. Grinspun and the Argentine ambassador to the United States, in a telephone call to Jacques de Larosière and other top management, emphasized the political constraints under which the government was operating, arguing that "the Managing Director had to understand the extremely charged political atmosphere in Argentina and to see the letter in its proper context."[108] In the draft Letter of Intent, the Argentines highlighted the fragility of the democratic institutions of the country:

> ...we must avert undesirable distortions both in the level of activity and employment and in relative prices and income. The Argentine government is convinced that social stability is essential for the validation and strengthening of democracy. . . . Argentine history in recent decades testifies to the repeated failure of economic policies which, for the sake of an ultimate objective of stability and progress, caused enormous distortions in the economic and social fabric.[109]

The IMF was unmoved. In Boughton's words, "to the Managing Director there was simply no question of the Fund giving a positive signal to creditors until a credible policy program was in place."[110]

An Accord Is Reached

The disagreements between Argentina and the Fund prevented an agreement from being reached through the rest of the summer and into the fall, despite several missions to Argentina and a personal visit from Grinspun to Washington, DC, to meet with the managing director in early August. Pessimism about Argentina in the Fund turned to despair. The members of the failed IMF mission in late

---

106. Memorandum from Eduardo Wiesner to the Managing Director, "Argentina," May 9, 1984.

107. Quoted in Edward Schumacher, "Argentina Bypassing IMF Staff," *New York Times*, June 11, 1984, sect. D, p. 1.

108. Memorandum for files, "Argentina," June 13, 1984.

109. Letter of Intent from Minister of Economy Bernardo Grinspun to Managing Director, June 9, 1984. Central Files Box #20 File #1, Country Files Series, Argentina Subseries.

110. Boughton 2001, 392.

June concluded that any plans for future discussions with the Grinspun–García Vásquez team about the loan may have to be scrapped: "there are serious questions whether such discussions would have a reasonable chance of success, unless the government is willing to undertake substantive policy changes that so far it has refused to entertain."[111] Argentina nearly missed another interest payment on August 15. At this point, inflation was running at nearly 20 percent per month.

Finally, in late September—nine months after the first mission to Argentina—a breakthrough occurred. The Argentines accepted a budget deficit target of 5.5 percent for 1985; in exchange, the Fund staff members decided to accept the persistence of wage indexation.[112]

The rest of the year was devoted to finding a way to close the financing gap of the country. With interest payments and arrears projected to swell to over $8 billion, the gap between Argentine resources and payments could not be filled by IMF tranches alone.[113] After furious efforts to secure financing by the managing director and his staff, the Letter of Intent and Memorandum of Understanding were presented to the Executive Board on December 28, 1984—a full year after negotiations on a lending program for Argentina had been initiated—and, despite a number of concerns expressed by individual EDs about the prospects for the program, the Board supported the proposed program for Argentina.[114] The content of the fifteen-month program was similar to the 1983 agreement (although it included several additional performance criteria), and the size was actually smaller than the previous standby arrangement in terms of the proportion of the Argentine quota (127.5 vs. 187 percent in the 1983 standby arrangement).[115]

The new program got off to a very rocky start. The Argentines had made one purchase for SDR 236.5 million following the approval by the Board at the end of December. In early February, the IMF mission arrived in Buenos Aires to check on the government performance with respect to the performance criteria for the first quarter. The news was not good; Argentina was out of compliance with multiple binding conditions. On February 18, 1985, Joaquin Ferrán notified Economy Minister Grinspun and Central Bank Governor García Vásquez that the IMF staff would not recommend a waiver to allow the program to continue.[116] Grinspun, incensed by the news that the Fund had suspended the pro-

111. Memorandum from Eduardo Wiesner and Joaquin Ferrán, "Mission to Argentina—May 6 to June 13, 1984," June 22, 1984.

112. Boughton 2001, 393.

113. Ibid., 394.

114. Boughton writes, "the Board approved the stand-by arrangement, but with somewhat less enthusiasm than was its custom" (ibid., 397).

115. "Argentina—Request for Standby Arrangement," EBS/84/251, December 3, 1984.

116. Boughton 2001, 398.

gram, reportedly confronted Ferrán in the lobby of El Palacio de Hacienda, the brutalist structure housing the Ministry of the Economy. After Ferrán advocated an across-the-board reduction in workers' wages, Grinspun unleashed a tirade that stunned onlookers: "what do you want? To bust my ass? If you insist on lowering wages, I'm going to the capitol building to publicly announce that you want to destabilize democracy in Argentina!"[117] When President Alfonsín learned about the suspension of the program, he requested the immediate resignations of both Grinspun and García Vásquez.[118] A different policy team—which included a prominent role for a new group of U.S.-trained economists—would change course, implementing a new and drastic approach to stabilizing the Argentine economy after 1985.

Summary of the Second Episode, 1981–1985

The contentiousness observed in the second episode of the case study of Argentina provides a stark contrast with cordial relations and lenient treatment by the Fund when, under Viola's repressive military regime, neoliberal-oriented officials dominated Argentine economic policymaking. Two new IMF agreements were signed during this period, the first in early 1983 and the second at the end of 1984. The pattern for both agreements was similar: protracted, difficult negotiations produced loans that were more extensive in terms of conditionality and less generous than preferred by the Argentine authorities. The Executive Board, on the recommendation of the Fund staff and management, suspended both agreements for noncompliance shortly after their approval. The quick suspension of the December 1984 program led directly to the replacement of Bernardo Grinspun, the structuralist-friendly economy minister, and his counterpart in the Central Bank, Enrique García Vásquez, with a more like-minded (from the IMF point of view) policy team. In chapter 5, I show how the transition to the new policy team altered the relationship of the country with the Fund, which continued to provide Argentina with a desperately needed economic lifeline.

Concluding Thoughts

The two episodes detailed in this chapter illustrate the important role played by the ideational composition of the policy team of the borrowing country in

---

117. The incident is recounted in Bonelli 2004, 52–53 (my translation from Spanish).

118. Grinspun rejoined the government—albeit in a much less influential position—as planning minister three weeks after his removal by Alfonsín.

shaping the Fund judgments about the country (and, subsequently, the content of the lending program and the vigilance with which it was enforced). The variation in the relationship of the Fund with Argentina during this period was stark. In 1976, a new policy team, stocked with officials who held neoliberal economic beliefs, inherited an economy in severe distress. The most materially powerful IMF member, the United States, was no friend of the military government of Argentina at the time. Yet the proximity of the beliefs held by the two sides, as predicted by the theoretical framework laid out in chapter 2, infused the relationship with confidence, and the Fund doled out (relatively) lenient programs in the first years after the 1976 coup. The teams in control of the Argentine economy at the end of military rule and at the outset of the transition to an electoral democracy faced similarly difficult economic circumstances; however, unlike the lenient treatment by the IMF of the neoliberal-oriented team, the Fund programs in 1983 and 1984 were relatively stingy (given large financing gaps of the country), loaded with binding conditions, and rigorously enforced.

The dual failures of the structuralist-dominated policy team in the first years after the democratic transition of Argentina—the failure of the Grinspun–García Vásquez team to secure uninterrupted funding from the IMF and the failure by the mildly expansionist policy agenda of the government to arrest the economic tailspin—opened the door for policymakers closer to the neoliberal orientation of the IMF to regain control over the economic policymaking institutions of Argentina, culminating in the consolidation of control by neoliberal-type economists after 1991. As I show in the next chapter, the restoration of full neoliberal control over economic policymaking also transformed the relationship of the country with the Fund.

FROM ONE CRISIS TO THE NEXT

IMF-Argentine Relations, 1985–2002

> **Since I left, Argentina has been governed by the International Monetary Fund.**
>
> —Juan Péron, 1966

The second episode in the post-1976 IMF relationship with Argentina ended with the showdown between the Fund mission head and the "wild man of Argentine politics," Bernardo Grinspun (see chapter 4).[1] The contrast between the close and collaborative relationship of the Fund with the Videla government (a period in which the top policy posts were occupied by neoliberals) and the IMF treatment of the post-democratic transition government in Argentina was stark; easy negotiations, generous terms of access, and relatively lenient enforcement gave way to disputatious negotiations, expansive conditionality, and a high degree of vigilance in the enforcement of the conditions.

The IMF won the showdown. President Alfonsín reconstituted his team with a new set of economic officials. He selected a group of individuals who were just heterodox enough in their espoused views of economic management to sidestep the political crisis that would have erupted had he picked officials in the hard-core neoliberal Diz–Martínez De Hoz mold—but he did not go back to the deep well from which the likes of Grinspun and García Vásquez sprung. Instead, Alfonsín brought in a team that included a handful of U.S.-trained economists. The new policy team, as my theoretical framework predicts, led to an improvement in the relationship of Argentina with the IMF.

I pick up the story with the appointment of the new policy team and its surprise plan to arrest the spiraling inflation problem in Argentina. From there,

---

Epigraph: Quoted in Edwards 2010, 157.
1. Dosman 2008, 497.

I discuss the successive failed stabilization plans that culminated in Alfonsín's resignation and the transformation of the Argentine economy under a group of neoliberal economic officials in the Peronist government of Carlos Menem. Last, I dissect the politics surrounding the series of IMF programs that preceded the economic collapse of 2001–2002, and I wrap up the case study by briefly discussing the aftermath of the Argentine crisis and by reviewing the evidence from the four episodes.

Episode 3: Policy Experimentation and Failed Stabilizations, 1985–1989

The Return of U.S.-Trained Economists to the Policy Team

In February 1985, there was little confidence on the part of the IMF that the Radical-led Argentine government could right the economic ship. The negotiations over the standby arrangement signed in December 1984 were torturous. Despite the demonstrable funding needs of the country and the systemic risks of failing to deliver the government from the brink of default, the deep ideational divide between the Argentines and the Fund staff and management was a major stumbling block. The IMF seemed unwilling to expend resources on a government in which it had little confidence. Once the agreement was finally reached, the Fund suspended it after just one month.

Argentina was in deep trouble, and President Alfonsín needed to take action to restore the relationship with the Fund—but he was also keenly aware that elements of his party were very unfriendly to neoliberal ideas. His new economic policy team served two audiences. The head of the Central Bank, Juan J. Alfredo Concepción, was a Radical Party stalwart and bore a resemblance in economic beliefs (if not in personality profile) to Bernardo Grinspun, the recently removed structuralist economy minister.[2] The new head of the Ministry of the Economy, Juan Vital Sourrouille, was neither a hard-core neoliberal nor an ardent structuralist in the Grinspun mold (although he was more heterodox than orthodox in his economic worldview). Sourrouille was indigenously trained (he had completed his economics degree at Universidad de Buenos Aires), but he had been exposed to U.S. economic thinking during a year he spent as a visiting scholar at Harvard University and he had formed international contacts as an official with the UN Economic Commission for Latin America. The new economy minister's

---

2. Bonelli 2004, 59; Kaufman 1990, 89.

appointment was greeted with cautious optimism at the IMF and in the broader financial community.[3]

The composition of Sourrouille's team, however, dismayed the more structuralist-oriented camp in the party.[4] After all, Sourrouille had not been among Alfonsín's core group of confidantes during the 1983 electoral campaign. And more important, Sourrouille brought with him a group of U.S.-trained economists, several of whom would later ascend to top positions in the Argentine government. This group proved to be integral to the design of a new strategy for managing the economic problems of Argentina and would help reshape the rocky relationship of the country with the Fund. Mario Brodersohn (PhD from Harvard, 1966) became the finance secretary, the economy minister's second-in-command; Adolfo Canitrot (PhD from Stanford, 1966) and José Luis Machinea (PhD from the University of Minnesota, 1983) became undersecretaries in the Ministry of the Economy.[5]

Among the officials in the Sourrouille-headed team, Machinea would go on to have the biggest impact on the Argentine economic policy agenda, serving as chief of the Central Bank at the tail end of the Alfonsín presidency and as economy minister in the late 1990s. Toting an economics PhD from the University of Minnesota, Machinea was (perhaps surprisingly, given his background) somewhat friendlier to the Radicals' left-leaning ideological agenda than the harder-core neoliberals associated with some of the conservative economic think tanks in Argentina. That being said, IMF officials regarded Machinea as a "serious and responsible" policymaker with a vision for the Argentine economy that came closer to their own.[6]

---

3. The *New York Times* reported that Sourrouille "appeared to be less abrasive than his predecessor, Bernardo Grinspun, and more committed to an economic discipline that bankers say is needed in Argentina.... many [bankers] said that the 44-year-old Mr. Sourrouille ... had pushed for export-oriented policies and an assault on inflation. These economic views generally are shared by Argentina's approximately 320 creditor banks and by the International Monetary Fund" (Nicholas Kristoff, "Bankers Warily Greet Shakeup in Argentina," *New York Times*, February 20, 1985, p. 1). See also Nancy H. Kreisler, "Two Top Argentine Officials Resign; Played Key Roles in Debt Debate," *New York Times*, February 19, 1985, p. 1.

4. The ideological conflict between Radical Party members and Sourrouille's team is described in Veigel (2009, 134, 137, 156).

5. Lydia Chavez, "Argentina's Bold Rescue Plan," *New York Times*, June 25, 1985, p. 1; Wynia 1992, 179.

6. For example, see the reflections of the former chief of the Fund Western Hemisphere Department, Claudio Loser: "nosotros negociabamos con Domingo Cavallo, Roque Fernández, José Luis Machinea, toda gente que consideramos serios y responsables" (we will negotiate with Domingo Cavallo, Roque Fernández, José Luis Machinea, all people who we consider serious and responsible) (quoted in Tenembaum 2004, 70, my translation).

The Element of Surprise: The IMF and Plan Austral

The IMF began negotiations with the new team to restart the suspended standby arrangement in March. At the same time, the Sourrouille team was devising a plan to attack inflation, which climbed to 1,800 percent in the second quarter of 1985. On April 15, Jacques de Larosière convened a meeting with Sourrouille, his advisors Brodersohn and Machinea, senior Fund management, and the head of the U.S. Federal Reserve and the assistant secretary of the U.S. Treasury, Paul Volcker and David Mulford. Over the course of the meeting the Argentine policymakers sketched a rough outline of an unorthodox shock stabilization program to be implemented in June. The managing director and the U.S. officials offered their support for the program, and the IMF staff members began an unusual set of side-by-side negotiations: one set was a public feint that focused on hammering out a typical IMF adjustment program; the other, secret set of discussions concerned the details of the June anti-inflation shock treatment for the Argentine economy.[7]

On June 11, to the relief of the creditors of the country, the Argentine authorities signed a new, more lenient Letter of Intent to restart the suspended standby arrangement.[8] Few outside of Alfonsín's and Sourrouille's inner circles (and the in-the-know officials at the IMF and in the U.S. government) were prepared for what followed three days later. On June 14, the economic authorities implemented the Plan Austral. This stabilization plan included three core components: (1) a tough set of contractionary fiscal measures to rein in the central government budget deficit (bringing it down to 2.5 percent of GDP), plus an end to the practice of financing the government deficit by running the Central Bank printing press; (2) a general wage and price freeze; and (3) a dramatic monetary reform involving the introduction of a new currency unit, the austral, to replace the by-then badly devalued peso.[9]

The June 1985 stabilization program combined elements of IMF-style orthodoxy and structuralist-inflected modes of macroeconomic thinking that

---

7. Bonelli 2004, 60–61; Boughton 2001, 399. At the time, it was widely misreported that the IMF had been blindsided by the announcement of the shock program in June (e.g., Stiles 1987, 77; Manzetti 1991, 145); the recent release of archival materials has confirmed that the IMF was aware of and involved in the planning for the heterodox approach taken by the Sourrouille team.

8. The need for secrecy about the Argentine program extended even to confidential IMF documents for fear that a leaked communiqué might spoil the plans of the government. For example, a terse memo from Joaquin Ferrán to the Fund top management about the conclusion of negotiations made no reference to the imminent shock stabilization plan (Memorandum from Joaquin Ferrán to the Managing Director, "Argentina—Revised Stand-By Program," June 10, 1985).

9. On the details of the Austral Plan, see Dornbusch and de Pablo 1990; Epstein 1987, 1000; Heymann 1991, 104–30; Kiguel 1991.

predominated in Argentina at the time. The polyglot design of the plan mirrored the mix of economic beliefs that circulated in Alfonsín's Radical Party and the Sourrouille-Concepción policy team. "Because of the team's structuralist persuasion," observes Rudiger Dornbusch and Juan Carlos de Pablo, "an incomes policy was thought to be an indispensable part of the stabilization. At the same time, *the economic team had become distinctly more orthodox since the replacement of Economics Minister Grinspun by Juan Sourrouille.*"[10]

The plan in its first months had the intended effect: the rate of monthly price inflation fell from 30 percent to 6 percent in July and dropped lower still in August and September. In the wake of the implementation of the stabilization plan, an IMF mission returned to Argentina to try to restart the standby agreement that had been approved the previous December. Privately, the top officials of the Fund expressed a high degree of uncertainty about the possible outcome of the stabilization effort.[11] But after the experience with the policy team in the first years of the Alfonsín presidency, the staff and management of the IMF showed great faith in the ability of Sourrouille's team to pull off the heterodox stabilization program. On August 9, the Executive Board endorsed the program with considerable enthusiasm; Richard Erb, the acting chairman of the Board meeting, summed up the opinion in the room:

> I recall that at the time of the initial discussion of the program in December, the Managing Director made a statement for the record reflecting the deep concerns and questions that Directors had about policy plans and the economic program of the Argentine authorities. I believe that it is fair to say, without creating a sense of unwarranted euphoria, that the spirit and the tone of the discussion today were quite different.... Directors have qualified the program as bold, courageous, and dramatic.[12]

The Argentine policymakers were able to draw on the long delayed $245 million disbursement immediately. Another IMF mission in late August gave the authorities good marks for implementing the standby arrangement, freeing up another $245 million in funds. The Argentine debt problem was eased by an additional $4.2 billion in loans approved by the consortium of private banks and by the rescheduling of maturities due from April 1982.[13]

---

10. Dornbusch and de Pablo 1990, 106 (emphasis added).

11. See, for example, comments from Veigel's (2005, 297; 2009, 151) interviews with Adolfo Canitrot and Jacques de Larosière.

12. Minutes of the Executive Board meeting, EBM/85/125, August 9, 1985. Erb is also quoted in Boughton 2001, 400–401.

13. IMF Western Hemisphere Department staff memorandum, "Argentina—Recent Economic Developments," SM/86/35, February 25, 1986.

The success of the Austral Plan was short-lived. Political and societal pressures against the Fund-supported stabilization effort mounted in late 1985 and early 1986. The powerful Argentine labor confederation, Confederación General del Trabajadores (CGT), opposed the program and, because of its historic affiliation with the Peronist party, sought to undermine Alfonsín's and the Radicals' policy agenda. The number of strikes in Argentina peaked in 1986 at 582 (with over 11 million participants in strike activities that year, about one-third of the population was at some point involved in a strike), prompting Alfonsín to seek a pact with the less intransigent factions in the overwhelmingly Peronist labor movement. Economy Minister Juan Sourrouille became "the favorite target of CGT antigovernment proclamations."[14]

Divisions in the policy team also contributed to the unraveling of the program. The Central Bank, led by Concepción, contravened Sourrouille and his U.S.-trained advisors' preferences by loosening the monetary policy through generous rediscounting to troubled banks and state-owned enterprises in politically influential provinces.[15] The fiscal situation of the government, although significantly better at the end of 1985 than in the period before the implementation of the Austral Plan, remained fragile. Much of this improvement was based on unsustainable short-term conditions; in the absence of "a major fiscal reform aimed at improving government revenues on a permanent basis," the prospects for the stabilization effort were doubtful.[16] Opponents (from both the Peronist and Radical parties) stood in the way of fiscal reform.

In late November 1985, an IMF mission returned to Argentina to assess government adherence to the conditions in the renewed standby arrangement. The mission found that the stabilization effort had veered off course, and the IMF suspended the program in December.[17]

But the IMF was not yet prepared to cut the Sourrouille team loose. In February 1986, the Argentine authorities visited IMF headquarters to convince the staff and management to waive the missed conditions and release the next tranche of the standby arrangement, and to extend the program (which was set to expire in March) through May.

---

14. McGuire 1997, 239 (strikes data), 201 (quotation).
15. Sourrouille and his advisors sought to limit the Central Bank rediscounting policies, but, as Robert Kaufman observes, "since these banks were linked closely to local political machines and smaller businesses, threats to their liquidity provoked strong protests from most segments of Radical leadership" (1990, 89). See also Bonelli 2004, 65; Boughton 2001, 401; Erro 1994, 139; Manzetti 1991, 158.
16. Kiguel 1991, 977.
17. Boughton 2001, 401, 461.

On March 10, the Executive Board considered the proposed modifications to the standby arrangement. Fernando Nebbia, the Argentine ED making the case to the Board on behalf of the government, reported that "although some of the performance criteria contained in the program were not met, my authorities are nevertheless satisfied that the overall thrust of the policy has been appropriate to achieve the objectives of the program."[18] The other EDs agreed; the modifications of the program were approved without objection, and the schedule of disbursements of the standby-arrangement funds was extended through May. During the Board debate over the proposal, one ED argued that the IMF should continue to show flexibility in its treatment of the Alfonsín government in light of "the far-reaching nature of the measures implemented and *uncertainties with respect to their actual impact on various aggregates* . . . such flexibility was amply justified by the *strong political determination shown by the authorities* throughout the past nine months and by their continued adherence to the thrust of the adjustment program."[19]

In early April, the government announced that it was weakening some aspects of the stabilization program.[20] The Fund viewed the developments with concern but continued to put its trust in the team of neoliberals around the economy minister. An internal memorandum is revealing in this regard. Vito Tanzi (of the Fund Fiscal Affairs Department), following a visit to Buenos Aires to consult with the Argentine policymakers about reform of the tax system, reported to the managing director that the stabilization effort was "showing some signs of strains." The "gloomy outlook" notwithstanding, Tanzi noted that, in the view of the Fund staff members and outside experts whom he had consulted, "*the team now in control is the best Argentina is likely to have.* They all recognized that the technical experts were making economic policy under tremendous political pressures, so that they argued that the Fund should support them in any way possible."[21]

The confidence of the Fund in the Argentines was tested again in May. Following the policy changes implemented early in the previous month, Argentina had fallen out of compliance with three performance criteria.[22] The head of the

---

18. Minutes of the Executive Board Meeting, EBM/86/43, March 10, 1986.

19. Alternate Executive Director A. A. Agah, Minutes of the Executive Board Meeting, EBM/86/43, March 10, 1986, p. 54 (emphasis added).

20. The changes included a minor devaluation of the austral and a return to the crawling-peg system of exchange-rate management, an increase in public utilities rates, and, most important, the end of the wage and price freezes (Erro 1994, 147; Heymann 1991, 104; Kiguel 1991, 979–80).

21. Memorandum from Vito Tanzi to the Managing Director, "Technical Assistance—Argentina," April 25, 1986 (emphasis added).

22. The net domestic assets of the Central Bank, the budget deficit, and the level of external arrears all exceeded the targets set in the standby arrangement (Boughton 2001, 464).

IMF mission was skeptical of the ability of the policy team to bring policies back into line, and upon his return to Washington, DC, in mid-May, he recommended against issuing a waiver that would allow the program to continue without a suspension. The Argentines were understandably concerned about the possibility that the program might be suspended. Inflation was rising again, and the country had fallen behind in clearing its arrears to creditors. The economy minister decided to send his undersecretary of the economy, José Luis Machinea, to Washington to convince the Fund top management that the missed targets should be waived. This would be no easy task; the government had missed multiple targets by significant margins, and there was seemingly little political will on the part of Alfonsin and the Radicals to tighten the policies of the country to the liking of the Fund. After a week of intense discussions with management and staff members, Machinea was able to convince the managing director, Jacques de Larosière, to support a waiver that would allow Argentina to make the final purchase under the renewed 1984 standby arrangement, and the Fund staff presented a lukewarm endorsement of the proposed waiver to the Executive Board.[23]

The Board discussion of the waiver on June 23, 1986, was more contentious than previous discussions related to the policy proposals of the Sourrouille team. Alexandre Kafka, the Brazilian ED, expressed support, arguing that "the stand-by arrangement with Argentina had far too many performance criteria. . . . The staff had rightly placed less emphasis on those criteria than on the general thrust of Argentina's remarkable achievements under the program and its policy decisions for the remainder of 1986."[24] Other Board members— particularly Western Europeans—were less positive. Bernd Goos, the alternate ED from Germany, was forceful in expressing his concerns about the threats to the credibility of the Fund itself in giving Argentina repeated waivers. In his statement, Goos emphasized that, although he did not wish to question the credibility of the Argentine economic policymakers, he worried that the "experience under the program thus far could hardly be ignored when assessing the prospects for a timely reversal of the slippages."[25] Ultimately, however, Goos and the rest of the EDs were willing to give Sourrouille and his team the benefit of the doubt, and the waiver was approved, freeing up the remaining SDR 236.5 million in the program. Once the waiver was approved and the final amount of the SBA disbursed, the obligations of Argentina to the Fund climbed to $2.9 billion (224 percent of the quota).[26]

---

23. Ibid., 465.
24. Minutes of the Executive Board Meeting, EBM/86/101, June 23, 1986, p. 42.
25. Ibid., pp. 47–48.
26. Boughton 2001, 465.

Inflation accelerated again in July, and in late August 1986, the authorities announced a renewed commitment to tight fiscal and monetary policies along with ceilings on wage and price increases. An important component of that commitment involved the replacement of the central banker, Alfredo Concepción, by Machinea, whose visit to IMF headquarters had helped unlock the last portion of the standby arrangement. The members of the top management of the Fund hailed Machinea's appointment. The outgoing managing director, Jacques de Larosière, sent an unusually candid congratulatory message to Machinea on the news of his appointment to head the Central Bank, writing that he was "particularly happy to learn" of the appointment and that the policy team could count on "the interest of the management and staff in the success of Argentina's economic program."[27]

Things Fall Apart (Again), 1987–1989

With Machinea now at the helm of the Central Bank, the Argentines immediately entered negotiations with the IMF to secure a new loan. There was a sticking point in the negotiations, however. That sticking point was the desire of Argentina for a larger drawing that would include contingency clauses linked to changes in commodities prices.[28] The worldwide decline in agricultural prices in 1986–1987 had hit Argentine farmers particularly hard. The Argentines pointed to the 1986 IMF agreement with Mexico, which included clauses linked to oil prices, as a precedent for this type of contingent loan.[29] The IMF staff and management regarded the Mexican arrangement as a highly unusual one that had not set a precedent for future loans, and they pushed instead for a standard agreement with tightened fiscal policies and a reduced current account deficit.[30]

Negotiations between the Fund and Argentine officials continued through the rest of the year. A breakthrough occurred in January 1987 when Sourrouille and Machinea accepted the lower inflation and current account deficit targets insisted on by the Fund and signed a Letter of Intent for a new $1.4 billion (SDR 1.1 billion, 100 percent of the quota), fifteen-month standby arrangement.[31]

---

27. In a second note, de Larosière wrote of his "particular pleasure . . . in view of the close working relationship" between Machinea and the Fund staff and management (Telex from the Managing Director to José Luis Machinea and Juan V. Sourrouille, September 2, 1986; Telex from the Managing Director to José Luis Machinea, September 4, 1986).

28. Aggarwal 1996, 431–32; Boughton 2001, 466.

29. Clyde Farnsworth, "Argentina Seeks IMF Loan Tied to Crop Price," *New York Times*, September 5, 1986, p. 2.

30. Boughton 2001, 466.

31. Argentina also submitted a separate request for a condition-free purchase under the Compensatory Fund Facility (CFF) to counter the effects on export earnings due to the fall in commodities prices.

Argentina faced a large financing gap in 1987; the Fund economists estimated that the country would need about $3 billion to stay current on its external payments, and the Fund could account for only around one-third of that amount.[32] The new IMF managing director, Michel Camdessus, decided to follow the "concerted lending" approach developed by his predecessor and sought guarantees from the banks that the financing gap would be filled before final approval of the IMF loan. With the understanding that the negotiations with the banks would be fruitless without at least some positive signal from the Fund, Camdessus submitted the Letter of Intent to the Executive Board to approve the Argentine request for funding "in principle." The proposal was submitted with the caveat that Argentina could not start to draw on the new standby arrangement until "satisfactory arrangements" for the financing of the balance-of-payments needs in 1987 were made.[33]

Submitting the program to the Board for approval at this early stage in negotiations with the banks was highly unusual. Typically, a program approved "in principle" would need to be fully financed in a relatively short period. A handful of EDs expressed concern about the precedent that the new managing director was setting with the proposal. In addition, the reports from Argentina indicated that the economic circumstances were deteriorating. C. Richard Rye, the ED from Australia, warned that the proposed program was a "high risk," and others agreed.[34] During the discussion, several EDs expressed concerns about the credibility of the Argentine policymakers. The goodwill that Sourrouille and the U.S.-trained officials in the policy team had engendered in the Fund over the previous two years had begun to dissipate in the face of consistently bad news from Argentina. In the end, the confidence of the staff in the Argentine policymakers helped convince the EDs, and the new standby arrangement was approved without objection. But Argentina would have to wait until the financing arrangements with the commercial banks were sorted out to draw on Fund resources.

The discussions between the commercial banks and Argentina to fill the financing gap proceeded slowly. Mario Brodersohn led the Argentine side of the negotiations with the consortium of the banks (still headed by William Rhodes of Citibank) while the IMF Managing Director Michel Camdessus and two top officials from the Western Hemisphere Department, Eduardo Wiesner and Desmond Lachman, embarked on a global "road show" to sell the program approved in

---

32. Boughton 2001, 466.
33. Minutes of the Executive Board Meeting, EBM/87/29, February 18, 1987, p. 30. See also Boughton 2001, 467.
34. Minutes of the Executive Board Meeting, EBM/87/29, February 18, 1987, p. 3. Also quoted in Boughton 2001, 467; Veigel 2005, 309.

February to the skeptical bankers.[35] Finally, in mid-June, Rhodes notified IMF top management that the banks had committed to cover 92 percent of the financing gap. On July 23, the proposal was once again brought before the Executive Board; final approval by the Board of the standby arrangement would release badly needed funds to replenish the diminishing reserves of Argentina. The program that had been approved "in principle" in February was not excessively stringent— nor was it excessively generous at 100 percent of the quota. The main difference between this standby arrangement and the previous ones was the inclusion of three separate performance criteria targeting the fiscal deficit.[36] The EDs were concerned about the "many policy slippages that had occurred since they had approved the program in principle back in February, but they felt that they once again had to give the authorities the benefit of the doubt."[37] With the supplementary financing committed through the Advisory Committee of the commercial banks, the first drawing under the new standby arrangement was approved.

In months following the July 1987 Board meeting, the inability of Argentina to gain control of economic conditions generated tensions in the IMF and between the Fund and the World Bank over the right approach to dealing with the country. Ultimately, the patience of the IMF would run out, and it would be forced to cut ties with the Alfonsín government.

Performance under the 1987 Standby Arrangement

It was clear by late August that the program was off track. The *Economist* reported that the Argentines would miss the fiscal performance criteria in the lending program "by a mile."[38] Worse, the election results were disastrous for the Radicals; the Peronist party won a majority in the national legislature, and Peronist governors took control of most of the provinces, as well. The next disbursement was scheduled for October 20, and without a significant tightening of policies, it was unlikely that Argentina would be able to access the funds. President Alfonsín's frustrations emerged in a post-election speech to the central industrial union, in which he lambasted the IMF for "trying to apply ridiculous prescriptions that have nothing to do with the people."[39]

---

35. Boughton 2001, 469–70.
36. The standby agreement included (as performance criteria) limits on the combined deficit of the nonfinancial public sector and the Central Bank, a limit on the cash deficit of the nonfinancial public sector, and a limit on Treasury outlays (Minutes of the Executive Board Meeting, EBM/87/107, July 23, 1987).
37. Boughton 2001, 471.
38. "Argentina, Anything Brazil Can Do," *Economist*, September 5, 1987, p. 76; ibid.
39. Quoted in "Argentina: Worse to Come?" *Economist*, September 26, 1987, p. 96.

But Alfonsin had little choice but to continue to delegate to the Machinea-Sourrouille policy team in the effort to secure additional financing and avert a payments crisis. After discussions with IMF staff, the Argentine policymakers announced a new set of policy measures on October 14. In addition to a new freeze on prices and wages, and a big hike in prices for public services, the policies mapped out by Sourrouille, Machinea, and the coterie of U.S.-trained economic advisors were intended to attack the fiscal deficit and inflationary tendencies through deeper structural reforms of the Argentine economy. To achieve a 2 percent fiscal deficit target for 1988, the government sent the Argentine Congress a set of tax reforms and a bill to improve revenue collection and reform revenue sharing between the central government and the provinces; developed a schedule to reduce tariffs on imports and exports of agricultural products; and set a goal for the privatization of high-profile state-owned enterprises, including monopolies in water and energy provision, the national telecommunications company (Entel), and the national airline.[40] Upon the announcement of the reforms, the U.S. Treasury approved a $500 million bridge loan for Argentina. The IMF staff and management remained broadly supportive of the Machinea-Sourrouille team, and the managing director approved the request to waive the missed conditions and modify the existing lending arrangement for submission to the Board.

The credibility of the commitment of the Argentine authorities to the program was at stake when the Executive Board met to discuss the proposal on December 2. The view among the EDs was that the prospects for the program were extremely uncertain and that the Argentine track record was poor and getting worse. The German ED "best represented the view of the Board in concluding that he was supporting the case 'with considerable reservations, and only because Argentina is an exceptional case.'"[41] Two other European EDs advocated adding more binding conditions to the agreement before future drawings could be made, but the staff representative at the meeting shot down the suggestion. In spite of the highly unpredictable economic situation in Argentina, the Board approved the program—albeit with three EDs abstaining from the vote, which is evidence of the divisions that the policy of continued support for Argentina was opening up in the institution.[42]

---

40. Statement by Mr. Feldman on Argentina, Executive Board Meeting 87/163, December 2, 1987.

41. Boughton 2001, 472.

42. The EDs from Australia, the United Kingdom, and the Netherlands abstained from voting with the Board over the proposed modification and waivers for the standby arrangement (ibid.).

U.S. Pressure on the Fund Emerges

It is at this point in the episode that evidence for the influence of the United States on the decision making of the Fund emerges. We can speculate that the leniency of the IMF staff and management toward the Argentines in late 1987 reflected pressure from the Reagan administration, given its interests in protecting U.S. banks and supporting an unstable democracy in the Southern Cone—but without direct evidence to corroborate the association this claim is too speculative. (The role of Argentina in the U.S. grand strategy, however—like that of its neighbor Chile, once dismissed as "a dagger pointed at the heart of Antarctica" by Henry Kissinger[43]—may not have been very prominent.)

A handful of news articles, however, referred to U.S. influence on IMF decision making at this point in the episode. For example, the *Christian Science Monitor* reported, "United States Treasury Secretary James Baker Jr. reportedly had to pressure the IMF to grant a waiver to release the funds."[44] And the pressure from the United States on the IMF grew in the months following the December decision.

The IMF and Argentina Reach a Breaking Point

Since the appointment of Sourrouille and his advisors in early 1985, Alfonsín had resisted strong pressure from Radical stalwarts, Peronists, and the Peronist-affiliated labor unions to remove them. A stark reminder of the precarious position of the policy team came in November, when the economy minister and his finance secretary, Mario Brodersohn, were "booed and insulted continuously by hecklers" while attempting to give a speech on government economic policies at a Radical Party convention. The economic problems emboldened the faction in the party that advocated a "neo-Keynesian alternative economic plan" and had opposed the neoliberals since their appointment. A leading proponent of the alternative approach, Guillermo Feldberg, a former Central Bank governor, observed that Sourrouille, Machinea, and the top economic advisors were viewed as "an alien body within the party."[45] But Alfonsín could not afford to jettison

---

43. Quoted in Christopher Hitchens, "Why Has He Got Away with It?" *The Guardian*, online ed., February 24, 2001, http://www.theguardian.com/world/2001/feb/24/pinochet.bookextracts.

44. Tyler Bridges, "Argentina, Sagging under Foreign Debt, Gropes for a Way Out," *Christian Science Monitor*, December 17, 1987, p. 12. Aggarwal (1996, 437) also makes reference to U.S. efforts to influence the IMF between October and December 1987.

45. Quotations from Tim Coone, "Economy Minister Faces Shaky Future in Argentina," *Globe and Mail*, December 26, 1987. See also Shirley Christian, "Argentina's Economy Seen as Out of Control," *New York Times*, April 18, 1988, p. 14.

the Sourrouille-Machinea team while the country faced an impending payments crisis and was engaged in continuous negotiations with the Fund.

The contentious approval by the Executive Board of the waivers and modifications to allow Argentina to make a drawing on the standby arrangement revealed that some officials in the institution were beginning to lose faith in the Argentine policymakers. The skepticism that greeted the December proposal was warranted. A January 1988 mission led by Desmond Lachman, a high-ranking Fund official, found that Argentina had already slipped out of compliance with the fiscal targets. The projections indicated that Argentina would breach the 2 percent ceiling for the fiscal target by 2.5 percentage points. Worse, Argentina briefly fell into arrears to the Fund after the government missed a payment due at the end of January.[46] Once again, the IMF suspended the program, and the Argentine and IMF staff were forced to seek Board approval for a waiver.

While the U.S. and other creditor governments put together a $550 million bridge loan to help Argentina clear its arrears to the Fund and stay current on its payments to the banks, the Argentines went to IMF headquarters to work out the details of a new Letter of Intent to restore the standby arrangement. The IMF and the Argentines reached a compromise of a 2.7 percent of GDP fiscal deficit target for 1988. With a new Letter of Intent in hand, the staff and management brought the proposal to the Executive Board for approval.

As described by James Boughton, at the March 18 Board meeting several EDs "made a rare show of strength and insisted that the terms of the standby arrangement be strengthened before they would approve it."[47] The thrust of the EDs' objections to the proposal focused on two issues: (1) the persistent policy slippages, particularly in the fiscal area, (2) the lack of committed financing from private and official sources to cover the huge financing gap that Argentina faced in 1988. The EDs aired their concerns about the credibility of the fiscal conditions in the program, but the Board pushback on the proposed program came on the issue of financing. Some EDs suggested that the program should be suspended until sufficient commitments to cover the financing gap of the country were in place; the ED representing Argentina, however, argued that Argentine officials would not accept a decision by the Board to suspend further drawings until a private financing target was met. The managing director proposed instead that the proposed decision be modified to simply ask that "sufficient progress" on a funding package be met by the time of the next scheduled drawing in May. Interestingly, the U.S. representative to the Board, Charles Dallara, argued that

---

46. Boughton 2001, 473.
47. Ibid., 474.

there was no precedent for Camdessus's proposal and sided with the other EDs advocating a suspension of the program until real progress was made on filling the financing gap. At the meeting, Camdessus pushed back against Dallara's objection, claiming that the situation confronting the Board was "without precedence owing to the magnitude of the possible gap that could emerge over the next few months."[48] The staff's and managing director's views won out, and the Board—in spite of the vociferous criticism of the program expressed by some EDs during the meeting—ultimately voted unanimously to approve the decision to issue waivers and apply minor revisions to the program. The Argentines were once again able to draw on the standby arrangement.

The Patience of the Fund Wears Out

The patience of the IMF staff and management was stretched to the breaking point when it became clear in May that the fiscal targets had been exceeded. Negotiations over financing from private and official sources were at a standstill. Alfonsín's government antagonized the banks by missing several deadlines for interest payments. The president further infuriated creditors by suggesting that interest rates should be lowered to the "historical" rate of 4 percent, causing one banker to ask, "is this man living on the moon?"[49] In June, the IMF staff and management agreed that the probability of the success of the program was close to zero, and the Fund officially suspended the standby arrangement.

The Argentine authorities visited Washington in late July in an attempt to restart the program. After three years of starts and stops with this policy team, the Fund officials were unconvinced that even a drastic policy shift could deliver a successful stabilization effort. Negotiations between the Argentines and the Fund continued into the fall. In early August, the economy minister announced a new shock treatment (Plan Primavera) to try to convince the IMF of the seriousness of the government. Sourrouille and Machinea publicly proclaimed that IMF support was forthcoming; in reality, the Fund had turned off the spigot.[50]

The United States had grown more concerned about the consequences of the suspension of IMF funding. Desmond Lachman recalls that the United States leaned quite heavily on the IMF top brass—and on new managing director, Michel Camdessus, in particular—to approve a waiver that would enable Argentina to

---

48. Quoted ibid.

49. Quoted in "Argentina: De Facto Default?" *Latin American Markets*, June 17, 1988.

50. Jeremy Morgan, "Fears for an Argentine Crash Package," *Guardian*, August 5, 1988; "Argentina: New Agreement to Be Signed with the IMF after 'Positive' Negotiations," *BBC Summary of World Broadcasts*, August 2, 1988.

begin drawing on Fund resources again. But in Lachman's view, "the IMF did not want to further tarnish its credibility by supporting something that was going to blow up."[51] On the horizon loomed the May 1989 presidential election; the Peronist candidate, Carlos Menem, was campaigning on a nationalist-populist platform, including a call for a five-year debt moratorium.[52] When the IMF refused to move, the Argentines, with the backing of U.S. officials, took their case to the World Bank. Here U.S. pressure was apparently more effective: on September 25, the Bank announced that it was extending a $1.2 billion loan with very weak conditionality to Argentina. The *Washington Post* and several other major news organizations reported that Barber Conable, the Bank president, "had been urged by the American government to get some help to the hard-pressed nation, lest the government of Raul Alfonsín become unstable."[53] By breaking the established tradition that the World Bank did not lend until an IMF program was in place, the actions of the Bank opened a deep rift between the two international institutions.[54]

The gamble by the World Bank was a poor one because the new stabilization plan did little to solve the inflation problem. Inflation climbed to 17 percent in March and then to 34 percent in April. Sourrouille and Machinea continued to seek IMF support, but talks in January and February ended in failure, and in early March, the World Bank suspended its program.[55] With the relationship of Argentina with the international financial institutions effectively severed, Alfonsín acceded to the calls from the rank and file of the Radical Party and replaced Economy Minister Sourrouille and the remaining U.S.-trained economists with "an old party hack" and "veteran Radical war horse" named Juan Carlos Pugliese.[56] In addition, the indefatigable Enrique García Vásquez replaced José Luis Machinea as head of the Central Bank. By the time that the Radical Party candidate, Eduardo Angeloz, was soundly defeated by the Peronist candidate, Carlos

---

51. Interview with Desmond Lachman, Washington, DC, April 6, 2009. For more evidence of pressure from the United States, see "Argentina: Not Much Luck," *Latin American Markets*, July 29, 1988.

52. Menem abandoned the moratorium later in the campaign (Shirley Christian, "Argentina Prepares Plan to Try to Rescue Economy," *New York Times*, August 2, 1988, p. 1; Stephen Fidler, "May Vote Complicates Argentina's Debt Crisis," *Financial Post*, September 26, 1988, p. 11).

53. Hobart Rowen and Robert J. McCartney, "World Bank Agrees to $1.25 Billion in Loans to Argentina; Country to Make Major Economic Reforms," *Washington Post*, September 26, 1988, p. A12; "World Bank Takes a Risk," *Independent*, September 27, 1988, p. 23; "IMF Fights for Territory," *Independent*, April 5, 1989, p. 23; "Latin America's Debt; Argentina Finds a Friend," *Economist*, October 1, 1988, p. 91; "Twins That Won't Tango," *Economist*, March 11, 1989, p. 17.

54. Interview with Christian Brachet, Washington, DC, March 31, 2009; Clyde Farnsworth, "Accord Seems Near on Roles of I.M.F. and World Bank," *New York Times*, March 30, 1989, p. 1.

55. "Argentina: Double Talk," *Latin American Markets*, February 10, 1989.

56. Erro 1994, 154 (first quotation); Smith 1990, 26 (second quotation). See also "Argentina: Down Tools," *Economist*, April 8, 1989, p. 46.

Menem, in the May presidential election, the Argentine economy was on the cusp of hyperinflation. Monthly inflation shot up from 78 percent to just below 200 percent in July. Argentine firms led a massive flight from the austral, forcing the Central Bank to sell large amounts of its dollar reserves to keep the currency afloat. When Machinea, prior to his exit as head of the monetary institution, announced that the Central Bank would no longer exchange australes for dollars, the flight to the dollar "caused the virtual collapse of the price system in domestic currency."[57] Rioting and looting spread throughout the country in late May. With the Argentine economy in shambles, Alfonsín turned the presidency over to his Peronist successor five months before the official date of succession. Within a year and a half, neoliberal economists would have a vice grip on policymaking in a manner not seen in Argentina since the military government of 1976–1981.

Summary of the Third Episode, 1985–1989

The third episode provides further evidence of the importance of shared ideas on the decision-making processes of the Fund. The rise of a small coterie of U.S.-trained advisors in the Economy Ministry of Argentina generated a very different pattern of relations than had prevailed in the second episode. The IMF enthusiastically embraced a heterodox stabilization program (the Plan Austral) and was willing to extend waivers for noncompliance at several points during the period. The ability of José Luis Machinea, the Minnesota-trained official, to personally convince the managing director to support a waiver is strong circumstantial evidence in favor of my explanation. These episodes provide some of the most compelling evidence supporting my ideational explanation for Fund decision making. It is impossible to understand how the Fund shifted from the tough line it took in February 1985 to the enthusiastic support of the Austral Plan four months later without taking the appointment of Sourrouille's team into account. The political environment was as difficult under Sourrouille and his advisors as it was for the first policy team appointed by President Alfonsín (and the economic situation of the country was just as precarious, if not more so). Faced once again with a pattern of noncompliance, the IMF had a clear political choice: it could suspend the standby agreement and risk dislodging like-minded economic policymakers that the staff trusted, or it could take a softer line, sacrificing some enforcement credibility while supporting a team that, in the staff's view at the time, was "the best Argentina is likely to have."[58] For the first three years of this episode, the IMF was

---

57. Schamis 2003, 137.
58. Memorandum from Vito Tanzi to the Managing Director, "Technical Assistance—Argentina," April 25, 1986.

inclined to overlook the missed targets to serve a broader political purpose. Only in the face of mounting evidence that the policy team was incapable of following the program strictures did the patience of the Fund give out.

Episode 4: Takeover by the Neoliberals, 1991–2001

In the first episode in the case study of Argentina (chapter 4), the military government put the Diz–Martínez de Hoz team of neoliberals at the helm of an economy that had been severely mismanaged by the deposed Peronist government. The circumstances when neoliberals again took full control of the economic policymaking institutions of Argentina were similarly dire: the economists recruited in 1991 confronted an economy that had suffered two hyperinflation episodes. The first, in 1989, forced President Raúl Alfonsín to leave office early. His replacement, Carlos Menem, also faced severe inflationary pressures after taking power.

In both episode 1 and episode 4, the neoliberal policy teams were able to engineer a few years of strong growth before a crisis erupted. One key difference between the episodes was the extent of Fund involvement during the crises that followed the recovery. Whereas the military government was not under an active program when crisis conditions emerged in the late 1970s, the Fund was deeply involved in Argentina when the problems deepened after 1998.

My theory predicts that the IMF treatment should be have been especially lenient during the 1991–2001 period. Indeed, I find a consistently generous pattern of treatment, the most remarkable aspects of which are the lack of structural conditionality in the series of loans negotiated after 1991 and the willingness of the Fund to repeatedly grant waivers for missed performance criteria. As the description of this episode makes clear, it is again hard to explain the behavior of the Fund without reference to the presence of trusted neoliberals in the government.

Menem's U-Turn

At the beginning of the 1990s, Argentina seemed an unlikely candidate for a neoliberal takeover. The head of government, Carlos Menem, was a Peronist, who, at the time of his election to the presidency in 1989, was called "an erratic populist and economic know-nothing" in the pages of the *Economist*.[59]

---

59. "Argentina; Don't Cry for Me, Weimar," *Economist*, April 29, 1989, p. 71.

Menem confronted a historic inflation crisis when he entered office. In his first year, the president recruited two top economic officials from the management of the largest Argentine agribusiness multinational, Bunge y Born, to implement yet another stabilization program (Plan BB). Forging an alliance with the management class of the country angered the labor movement, which had expected that Menem, as the leader of the Peronist party, would craft a policy agenda that mirrored the interests of labor. But Menem went even further in the liberalizing direction, appointing Domingo Cavallo, a Harvard-trained economist, as the foreign minister and installing Álvaro Alsogaray, one of the most ardent advocates of market liberalization in the country, as Cavallo's special advisor.[60] Cavallo, "a market-oriented economist and president of one of Argentina's most market-oriented think tanks," was a surprising choice for a Peronist cabinet; as Javier Corrales notes, Cavallo "was the antithesis of Peronism in terms of background and ideas. He was neither a party affiliate nor a populist."[61]

On January 30, 1991, President Menem signaled a clean break with the past by firing his Peronist allies in the Economy Ministry and the Central Bank. The officials were replaced by Cavallo, who moved over to head the Economy Ministry, and by Roque Fernández, a University of Chicago–trained economist, who became the new head of the Central Bank.

Markets were euphoric over the news; the Argentine stock market soared by 30 percent.[62] Cavallo and Fernández promised to restore the credibility of Argentina with the IMF and international investors by destroying inflationary tendencies and making the initial moves by the Menem government toward market liberalization permanent and irreversible. An important component of this strategy involved a purge of the old-school Peronists in the economic bureaucracy. In the first three months after his appointment, nearly three hundred "Cavallo Boys," recruited from the neoliberal Fundación Mediterránea think tank (established in 1977, during the first period of high neoliberal influence), from graduate economics departments in prestigious U.S. universities, and from the World Bank and the IMF, were appointed to positions in the

---

60. Throughout his nearly forty-year career in politics, Alsogaray "was driven by the goal of controlling economic policy and charting Argentina on a course toward a free-market economy" (Gibson 1996, 110).

61. Corrales 2002, 240.

62. Nathaniel C. Nash, "Turmoil, Then Hope in Argentina," New York Times, January 31, 1991, p. D1.

Economy Ministry, which had been merged with the Ministry of Public Works.[63] In February and March, Cavallo's economic team worked tirelessly to prepare a radical new stabilization program, intended to wring inflation out of the Argentine economy for good.

Convertibility Is Unveiled

In late March, Cavallo unveiled the Convertibility Plan, which quickly passed into law. Convertibility consisted of three main elements: (1) the Argentine currency was pegged to the U.S. dollar at a rate of 10,000 units of the national currency (the austral)[64] to $1; (2) the domestic currency would be freely exchanged by the Central Bank for dollars and other foreign currency; and (3) the Argentine Central Bank would be required to maintain foreign reserves to fully back the domestic monetary base.[65] The previous two decades had witnessed a series of failed attempts to control inflation. Convertibility represented a new attempt to induce price stability in Argentina, this time by essentially giving up the ability to have an independent monetary policy. From this point forward, the monetary authorities of the country could not deviate from the monetary policies followed by the global financial centers (namely, the United States).

Convertibility also reflected a return to pre-Keynesian monetary orthodoxy in Argentina. Keynes himself had strongly opposed currency board–like arrangements. (His criticism, formulated during his time working on Indian monetary system reforms, is worth quoting: "the notion that a country can only expand its domestic purchasing power when it is in a position to cover the increase 100 per cent with foreign reserves belongs, I am convinced, to an era of thought that can never return.")[66] Yet here the Argentines were, nearly eighty years after Keynes's writings, putting in place a system that essentially took the ability of the monetary authorities of the country to stimulate (or restrain) aggregate domestic demand off the table.

Cavallo's plan was bold but risky. The success of the arrangement hinged on the ability of the government to control spending. Because the Central Bank

---

63. Cavallo's close advisor, Joaquin Cottani, held a PhD in economics from Yale and had been recruited from the World Bank. Fernández recruited Pablo Guidotti (PhD from Chicago) from the IMF to serve as his top advisor (Corrales 1997, 65–65; Nathaniel C. Nash, "Argentina's Mr. Fix-It," *New York Times*, November 17, 1991, p. F12; Blustein 2005, 21.

64. In 1985, the peso was replaced with a new currency, the austral. At the end of 1991, the austral was replaced by the peso (10,000 australes = 1 peso = 1 U.S. dollar).

65. For a detailed overview of convertibility, see Starr 1997.

66. Keynes, quoted in Helleiner 2014a, 225–26.

could no longer finance the government deficit, Argentina would have to consistently run surpluses—an unlikely outcome, given its dismal fiscal performance throughout the postwar period—or tap into an uninterrupted flow of capital from abroad (also a risky bet, given its poor reputation in the international financial community). Another major risk to the program involved an overvaluation of the currency. By pegging the currency to the U.S. dollar at an (arguably) overvalued rate, the competitiveness of the export-oriented Argentine producers was threatened. Ultimately, the sustainability of the Convertibility plan depended on the perception of the credibility of the commitment by the Argentine economic authorities to the currency regime. Any hints of a wavering commitment to the system would trigger severe speculative pressures as peso-holders dumped their holdings of the currency in advance of devaluation.[67]

The IMF economists had a number of reasons to regard Cavallo's Convertibility Plan with skepticism. (Cavallo and Cottani later noted persistent "differences of opinion" between the Argentines and the IMF on the merits of the exchange rate–based stabilization.)[68] Sterie Beza, former head of the Western Hemisphere Department, recalled that, in the view of the Fund, the kind of monetary anchor that Argentina had implemented required "a very good fiscal policy. And for Argentina that would have represented a marked improvement from past experience."[69] The IMF staff report that accompanied a proposal for a new standby arrangement in July 1991 warned that the Convertibility scheme "requires that the fiscal objectives of the program be fully met."[70]

The Argentines waited until the Convertibility law was passed to begin serious negotiations with the IMF staff members. Discussions proceeded quickly, and by the end of June, the authorities had come to agreement on the details of an eleven-month, SDR 780 million ($1 billion, 70 percent of the quota) standby arrangement. The proposed program was not particularly generous, but the financing needs of Argentina had diminished; the government was expecting large receipts from a large-scale privatization effort, the trade balance had turned positive, and the reserves of the country had swelled to six times the level of holdings when Menem had taken office.

---

67. Ricardo Lopez Murphy, who later served as economy minister, presciently noted these possibilities in April 1991 (Nathaniel C. Nash, "Plan by New Argentine Economy Chief Raises Cautious Hope for Recovery," *New York Times*, April 28, 1991, p. A1; Smith 1991, 63).

68. Cavallo and Cottani 1997, 19.

69. Quoted in Blustein 2005, 15.

70. Staff report, quoted in Independent Evaluation Office of the IMF 2004, 17. Other sources that note the reticence with which the Fund viewed convertibility include Mussa 2002, 5; Veigel 2009, 179.

The 1991 Standby Arrangement

The Executive Board approved a new standby arrangement on July 29, allowing the Argentine authorities to immediately gain access to $260 million in Fund resources. The program included a fairly standard list of performance criteria related to fiscal and monetary targets. It did not contain any binding structural conditions. The centerpiece of the 1991 standby arrangement was a budget surplus target for the remainder of the year and for the first two quarters in 1992.

The Convertibility Plan spurred an impressive economic recovery after a disastrous decade marred by sky-high inflation and shrinking output. (Table 5.1 displays decadal averages for four economic indicators.) In line with similar exchange rate–based stabilizations in Latin America, the economy entered an expansionary phase after the plan was put into action; GDP growth topped 10 percent in 1991.[71] Remarkably, the expansion of output was coupled with lasting price stability, with the rate of inflation dropping to the low double digits by the fourth quarter of 1991.

But the economic indicators that greeted the IMF mission when it arrived in Buenos Aires in November to assess the performance under the new standby arrangement were disappointing: Argentina had failed to meet three performance criteria, including two separate fiscal targets. To draw the remaining amount under the lending arrangements, Argentina would have to receive a waiver from the Board, which the IMF staff and management were quick to propose.

On December 20, the Executive Board gathered to consider the proposal from the management and staff to waive the missed performance criteria and allow Argentina to continue to draw on Fund resources. There was very little resistance from the EDs, despite the fact that multiple targets had been exceeded in the October review. In fact, the tone of the discussion was overwhelmingly positive. One ED reflected, "in contrast with other occasions on which Argentina had been unable to meet its performance criteria, today many tangible results

TABLE 5.1   Economic performance of Argentina, 1980s–2000s

	GDP GROWTH RATE (%)	INFLATION RATE (%)	UNEMPLOYMENT RATE (%)	CURRENT ACCOUNT BALANCE (%GDP)
1980s	−0.9	750.4	5.6	−2.5
1990s	4.3	146.3	13.2	−7.2
2000s	4.1	9.5	13.1	3.6

Source: Data from the IMF *World Economic Outlook* database, https://www.imf.org/external/ns/cs.aspx?id=28.

---

71. Schamis and Way 2003.

of the stabilization effort can be observed." Another ED expressed his "wish that all members were prepared to show such active commitment to implementing needed economic reforms."[72] The Board members treated the deviations as minor concerns—despite the fact that the fiscal targets had been missed by wide margins—choosing instead to focus on the credibility of the Cavallo-Fernández policy team and the market-oriented structural reforms that the government had pursued.[73]

Argentina Signs Its First Multiyear Agreement

Further evidence of the increasing confidence of the Fund in Argentina came in the form of the negotiations, starting in late January, for a three-year, $3.6 billion (193 percent of the quota) EFF program. The Argentines had first pursued an EFF in 1983, but uncertainty about the prospects for such a generous program had prevented the IMF from seriously considering a multiyear package until the Cavallo-Fernández policy team arrived.[74]

The negotiations with the IMF over the first Argentine multiyear program went very quickly, with few obstacles. By late February, the two sides had come to an agreement on an outline of the program, and on March 31, Michel Camdessus, the managing director of the Fund, brought the proposal before the Executive Board for approval. The EFF, in line with the greater access to Fund resources that it offered, included more conditions than in the previous two agreements. The program set fairly stringent targets for fiscal policies, including a budget surplus through 1992 (not including proceeds from the sale of state-owned firms). But the program was relatively light in terms of structural conditionality. The two structural performance criteria (implementation of a tax reform bill and a reform of the social security system) were the only binding structural conditions in any of the programs Argentina received over the next decade, and the government had difficulty meeting them.

The Executive Board enthusiastically supported the staff and management proposal. The discussion in the Minutes of the Board provides additional

---

72. Minutes of the Executive Board Meeting, EBM/91/172, December 20, 1991, pp. 37, 43.

73. In late October, the policy team announced the implementation of Executive Decree 2284, which provided a sweeping liberalization program for the Argentine economy. The law contained 122 provisions related to the deregulation of the trade system, reform of the tax system, reform of the domestic financial market, liberalization of the international capital market, reforms of the social security system, and relaxation of labor market regulations, among other areas (Office Memorandum, "Argentina—Economic Liberalization Measures," EBD/91/296, November 12, 1991).

74. The EFF was an important seal of approval from the Fund; it would help unlock debt relief under the terms proposed by Nicholas Brady, the U.S. treasury secretary (Aggarwal 1996, 453).

evidence to support my claim that the presence of neoliberals in the borrowing government helped reassure the Fund that the borrower could be trusted. One ED praised the "radical—and, we hope—permanent *change in the authorities' policy attitude that lies at the heart of their success*" that was "rapidly translating into a growing policy credibility for the authorities."[75] The Cavallo-Fernández policy team signaled to the Fund that the like-minded Argentine officials could be counted on to "do the right things." A comment from the Belgian ED is revealing in this respect. Jacques de Groote reminded his fellow Board members: "we can all recall how skeptically we viewed Argentina's request [in June 1991] for a standby arrangement; with the benefit of hindsight, it was clearly a good decision to approve that request and to be rather generous in financing it."[76] The willingness of the Fund to give the neoliberals the benefit of the doubt seemed to have paid off.

The news from Argentina was positive through most of 1992. Program reviews in both June and August showed that all of the quantitative performance criteria were met within comfortable margins.[77] Inflation remained low, the Central Bank holdings of foreign reserves reached the $10 billion mark, and a flood of foreign investment began surging into the country. Significantly, the external debt load, under which successive policy teams had struggled since the buildup under the neoliberal Diz–Martínez de Hoz team in the late 1970s, lightened considerably. In April, shortly after the approval of the IMF program, Argentina and the private banks reached an agreement on a voluntary debt reduction, and in August, the authorities secured a more manageable repayment schedule from the official creditors of the country. The events prompted the *Financial Times* to (cautiously) observe, "Argentina may be on the road to a fundamental economic recovery," thanks in large part to the influence of Domingo Cavallo, the "Harvard-trained economist who provides the intellectual firepower for reform."[78]

But problems emerged again in the review of the progress in the fourth quarter of 1992. Specifically, the government failed to carry out the reform of the social security system, as specified in the agreement. The staff and management proceeded to bring a waiver before the Board to allow the program to continue without interruption. The Board gave its approval on December 30.[79]

---

75. Minutes of the Executive Board Meeting, EBM/92/41, March 31, 1992, p. 23 (emphasis added).

76. Minutes of the Executive Board Meeting, EBM/92/41, March 31, 1992, p. 50.

77. Staff memorandum, "Argentina—Review under Extended Arrangement," EBS/92/144, September 1, 1992.

78. Stephen Fidler, "Don't Cry for Argentina," *Financial Times*, May 18, 1992.

79. Minutes of the Executive Board Meeting, EBM/92/158, December 30, 1992.

Even at this stage, there were mounting problems in Argentina—which Fund officials consistently overlooked. The first was the inability of the government to pass the reform of the social security system. In July 1993, the Board accepted another modification of the program to allow the authorities to push back the date for legislative approval of the social security reform bill. The other problem that the Fund noted was the real appreciation of the peso. Between March 1991 and the end of 1993, the currency appreciated by 50 percent.[80] Yet the IMF did not apply any serious pressure on the Argentines to tighten fiscal policy as the current account balance turned negative.

Dangerous Debt Buildup and the Durability of Convertibility

The Argentine economic policy team had also discovered the support of international investors. In December 1993, foreign investors purchased—in a single day—over $1 billion in ten-year notes issued by the Menem government. The debt burden of the country, which had become more manageable after the debt-rescheduling negotiations were completed in 1992, began to climb once again. The voracious appetite for Argentine dollar-denominated bonds fed a doubling of the external debt over the 1990s (from $62 billion in 1992 to $142 billion in 1998), an increase that had serious repercussions when economic performance weakened later in the decade.[81] Only Turkey bested Argentina in the race to feed the appetite of the market for government bonds. From the perspective of the Menem government, the renewed appetite of international investors for Argentine debt was an external seal of approval for the neoliberal-helmed policy agenda that, although still relatively popular with average Argentine citizens, had begun to reveal its costs—namely, a spike in the unemployment rate (which doubled between 1991 and 1994) and a deterioration in the current account balance (the counterpart of which was the large inflows of capital from abroad).

There was, however, a hidden vulnerability in the government borrowing binge. Almost all the debt instruments issued by the central government, provinces, and municipalities in the 1990s were denominated in foreign currencies (mostly U.S. dollars). The inability of Argentina to sell debt to foreign investors in pesos fed a problem that has come to be known in the economics literature as currency mismatch.[82] The different currency denominations of assets and liabili-

---

80. Minutes of the Executive Board Meeting, EBM/93/99, July 14, 1993; Independent Evaluation Office of the IMF 2004, 17.

81. Jonathan Fuerbringer, "Argentine Notes Draw Investors," *New York Times*, December 10, 1993, p. D16; Mussa 2002, 16.

82. On currency mismatch in Argentina, see Dominguez and Tesar 2007, 314.

ties on balance sheets can create a wave of bankruptcies, from the individual borrower to the central government, when the price of the currency on the liability side shoots up relative to the currency on the asset side. Such adverse exchange rate moves multiply the real value of external debt. When the Argentine peso strengthened (as it did by almost 25 percent between 1991 and 1993), the risks of the debt structure could be elided; but if the market price of the home currency weakened vis-à-vis the price of the currency in which the debt was denominated, the exploding debt dynamics could trigger a severe financial crisis. The new love affair of Argentina with the international financial community was fraught with dangers.

The Convertibility system faced its first serious test at the end of 1994. Earlier in the year, the IMF mission had noted that fiscal progress had slowed and that the Argentines had failed to meet the fiscal targets for the first quarter of the year. Nonetheless, the country passed its July review without facing a suspension or tightening of the fiscal performance criteria, thanks to another set of waivers. Noting that her authorities were "happy to accept the waivers recommended in the proposed decision," the U.S. ED, Karin Lissakers, remarked, "with an election approaching, some relaxation of spending discipline might be expected, *even in a team as determined as the Argentine authorities*."[83] In late September, Cavallo felt confident enough to announce that Argentina would not need the final two drawings under the EFF. Outside observers worried that the cancellation of the final tranches of the EFF indicated that the authorities had lost control of the fiscal situation in the run-up to the May 1995 presidential elections, in which Menem sought reelection.[84]

In late December 1994, the Mexican currency crisis exploded. The international shock triggered a confidence crisis among investors in Argentina, which ignited a massive capital outflow. Between January and April 1995, $8 billion—accounting for 18 percent of all bank deposits—were drained from the country. The stock market lost 30 percent of its value in the first two months of the year. Cavallo compared the events of early 1995 to the financial panic of 1929.[85] The Argentines hoped that a series of auctions of short-term treasury bills would staunch the bleeding, but the severity of the crisis forced the Cavallo-Fernández team to turn back to the Fund in late February

83. Minutes of the Executive Board meeting, EBM/94/64, July 18, 1994, p. 15 (emphasis added).

84. "The Foundations Have Been Laid," *Economist*, November 26, 1994, p. 5; Martin Krause, "Argentina's IMF Battle Doesn't Excuse Wasteful Spending," *Wall Street Journal*, December 30, 1994, p. A7.

85. Pastor and Wise 1999, 484; Calvin Sims, "Argentina, a Victim of Mexico's Fall, Tries to Recover," *New York Times*, March 12, 1995, p. C12; Starr 1997, 98.

to negotiate terms to restart the EFF.[86] Although investors continued to bet on an Argentine devaluation and the end of the Convertibility system, in March the Fund announced that it would allow Argentina to draw on the remaining $400 million and would begin negotiations to supplement the existing arrangement with an additional $2 billion. The stakes were high: the system under which Argentina had conquered inflation was at serious risk in the wake of the Mexican devaluation.

In retrospect, the months following the Mexican crisis might have been an ideal time to leave the Convertibility system. The regional crisis presented a dramatic, unanticipated contingency that would explain such a choice by the policy team without undermining government credibility. But the Argentine elites were strongly committed to the arrangement. Cavallo announced a new set of austerity measures while the crisis in the financial system continued, and the country teetered on—but managed to avoid—a total economic collapse. At this point, the position of the Fund on the hard peg shifted from acceptance of the commitment of Argentina to the system to outright support for the currency board.[87] In September, the Executive Board approved the $2 billion augmentation of the EFF along with waivers for missed performance criteria in the previous months. For the first time since 1977, Argentina was able to draw the full amount of the resources promised it under an IMF lending program.

The Slow Unraveling of the Argentine Miracle

In February 1996, a mission led by Tomas Reichmann of the IMF Western Hemisphere Department began negotiations with Cavallo and the Central Bank governor on a new agreement. Despite the fact that Argentina had exceeded the Fund targets for the fiscal deficit in 1995 by 144 million pesos, the IMF issued a waiver to allow the government to obtain the final drawing under the EFF and was receptive to the interest of the policy team in signing a new agreement. Negotiations were quick and easy, and in April, the Executive Board approved the proposal for a twenty-one-month, SDR 720 million ($1.04 billion, 46.8 percent of the quota) standby arrangement. The proposed program was relatively small in size, but it was also very light in terms of conditionality. No binding structural conditions were included in the agreement. The approval of the program raised the outstanding obligations of Argentina to the Fund to $4.5 billion (290 percent of the total quota).

---

86. "Peso Crisis May Force Argentina Back to IMF," *Financial Times*, February 22, 1995, p. 10.

87. Independent Evaluation Office of the IMF 2004, 18–19; Mussa 2002, 21.

At the outset of the twenty-one-month standby arrangement, the IMF staff members flagged fiscal performance as crucial for the success of the program.[88] But the IMF was anything but vigilant in enforcing the fiscal targets. The leniency of the Fund has been well documented. The comprehensive report issued by the Independent Evaluation Office (IEO) summarizes the weak enforcement efforts of the IMF: "the IMF repeatedly accommodated Argentina's slippages in meeting fiscal performance criteria from mid-1996 onwards, either to give the authorities credibility or in view of their good faith efforts in the face of political constraints."[89] Michael Mussa, who served as the Fund chief economist, noted that between 1995 and 1998 "the deficit of the Argentine government was within quarterly limits prescribed at the beginning of each year under the IMF-supported program less than half of the time."[90]

Rampant noncompliance emerged early in the life of the standby agreement. During the review of the end-of-June targets, the staff found that Argentina had missed all six performance criteria in the agreement. Nonetheless, the staff and management pushed the program forward, proposing, first, waivers for the missed conditions and, second, raising the fiscal deficit target from $2.5 to $6 billion when the Executive Board convened in October to discuss the program. The Board approved the staff proposals. Charles O'Loghlin, the Irish ED, although emphasizing that he was "deeply concerned about the repeated failure of the authorities to adhere to the performance criteria . . . in every arrangement that they have had with the IMF over the past five years," told his fellow Board members that he was "willing to give the Argentine authorities the benefit of the doubt one more time and agree to the present request for waiver and modification of the performance criteria. The decision is based on the fact that there is a new economic team, which appears more committed to reform." O'Loghlin warned, however, "completion of the next SBA review would be very difficult if the authorities did not *fully* adhere to the revised performance criteria."[91]

It is hard to understand the willingness of the Fund to tolerate repeated deviations from the program without looking to the composition of the Argentine policymaking team. The IEO review suggests that, in spite of the pattern of non-

---

88. The Executive Summary that accompanied the Letter of Intent of the Argentine authorities reported that "there is general agreement on the need to maintain convertibility. . . . The staff believes that it is crucial to monitor fiscal developments closely" ("Argentina—Request for Standby Arrangement," EBS/96/45, March 15, 1996).

89. Independent Evaluation Office of the IMF 2004, 37.

90. Mussa writes further that "it is difficult to understand why the Fund did not make active use of its conditionality to press the Argentine government to maintain a more responsible fiscal policy" (2002, 18–19).

91. "Statement by Mr. O'Loghlin on Argentina (Preliminary)," GRAY/96/197, October 29, 1996.

compliance, within the Fund "there was *almost universal confidence expressed in the authorities' ability and willingness to implement the appropriate policies*."[92] The confidence of the Fund in the Argentine authorities remained high even after the departure of the architect of the Convertibility Plan, Domingo Cavallo.

On the afternoon of July 26, 1996, Cavallo was sacked after a heated argument with the president. (Cavallo's public denunciation of the lack of transparency of Menem's administration proved to be the final straw.) After five and a half year in office, Cavallo left as the longest-serving finance minister in modern Argentine history.[93] Cavallo's enemies inside and outside the government rejoiced, but his ouster did not signal the shift away from the neoliberal policymakers that had run Argentine economic policy since 1991.

Menem immediately moved Roque Fernández, the "ultraliberal" Chicago-trained Central Bank governor, to head the Economy Ministry; another economist touting an economics PhD from the University of Chicago, Pedro Pou, became the new Central Bank governor.[94] The international financial community viewed the cabinet shakeup with relief. The *Economist* called Fernández "a respected economic technocrat" and "another pillar of orthodoxy."[95]

During a visit to Buenos Aires, the managing director noted that the relationship in the previous decade had been strained over "important doctrinal differences." With the neoliberal consolidation of economic policymaking in Argentina (evinced by the smooth transition from Cavallo to Fernández), "today there is no longer any doctrinal divide."[96] Camdessus expressed confidence that neoliberal policies would not be reversed "not just *because I trust in the men who manage it*, but because the process is irreversible."[97]

---

92. Independent Evaluation Office of the IMF 2004, 37 (emphasis added).

93. Cavallo's remarkable durability in the 1990s was probably due to three main factors: the confidence of the IMF and international creditors, the apparent victory over inflation, and his personal efforts to curry favor with the members of the Peronist Party, who regarded him with great skepticism and distrust. Although "Cavallo was the antithesis of Peronism in terms of background and ideas," Javier Corrales notes that, in his time as economy minister during the Menem administration, Cavallo made some overtures to the party rank and file, including creating an office within the ministry charged with "conducting negotiations with the PJ [Peronist Party]." Corrales continues, "although few party leaders ever believed that Cavallo was truly committed to safeguarding the party's interests and dogma, they nonetheless came to appreciate his overtures" (2002, 240, 173–74).

94. Kedar 2013, 172 (quotation).

95. "Argentina: Dropping the Pilot," *Economist*, August 3, 1996, p. 37 (first quotation); "Argentina after Cavallo," *Economist*, August 3, 1996, p. 17 (second quotation). Upon his removal, the *Economist* assayed Cavallo's importance: "Brusque at home, Mr Cavallo was a brilliant salesman to the world. Rightly or wrongly, it is the world that counts; and here too it wants to be reassured, promptly, that there will be continuity." "Argentina after Cavallo," *Economist*, August 3, 1996, p. 17 (quotation).

96. Quoted in Blustein 2005, 29.

97. Quoted in "Argentina: Dropping the Pilot," *Economist*, August 3, 1996, p. 37 (emphasis added).

The IMF chose to focus on the ideational continuity among the policy elites rather than the signs that the broader political consensus that had supported the neoliberal agenda since 1991 had started to unravel. The head of the center-left opposition complained that removing Cavallo was not enough: "we must change the dog, not its collar."[98] The labor movement, which had been relatively quiescent under the early years of the Menem government, began to mobilize against high unemployment and budget cuts. On August 8, the central labor confederation announced a general strike against the IMF-led program; in late September, a second general strike ended with 100,000 angry protesters camped in front of the presidential palace.

IMF officials also downplayed serious structural problems in the Argentine economy. Two issues loomed large from the day that the Convertibility system was implemented in April 1991. First, the Argentine labor market was excessively rigid. Sebastian Edwards, the former World Bank chief economist, enumerated the problems: "payroll taxes are close to 40%; collective bargaining procedures favor monopolistic behavior by unions and severely limit negotiations at the firm level; labor taxes earmarked for social services provided by unions are a source of corruption; and a surrealistic system of severance payments burdens small and medium enterprises."[99] The inflexible labor market practices were incompatible with the hard peg; because exchange rate manipulation was off the table, adjustment to the negative terms of trade shocks had to come from a fall in real wages. The staff and management of the Fund were aware of this weakness and, from the mid-1990s, encouraged the Argentine authorities to pass comprehensive labor market deregulation. In fact, the IMF tried to include the submission of labor market legislation to Congress as a prior condition in several agreements. But even the watered-down labor market reform bills that the government produced were rejected by the legislature; it was not until 2000 that a bill made it through Congress.[100] It is remarkable that none of the programs after 1996 included even a single binding structural condition related to some aspect of the labor market regulatory system in Argentina.

The distorted revenue collection and distribution systems of Argentina were another structural problem identified by the Fund officials. In figure 5.1, I plot the track record of the Argentine central government as a revenue collector (captured by total tax revenues as a proportion of GDP), as well as revenue data from comparable South American countries and the average for the region as a whole.

98. Quoted ibid.

99. Sebastian Edwards, "The Americas: More IMF Austerity Won't Cure What Ails Argentina," *Wall Street Journal*, August 30, 1996, p. A9.

100. Independent Evaluation Office of the IMF 2004, 31–32.

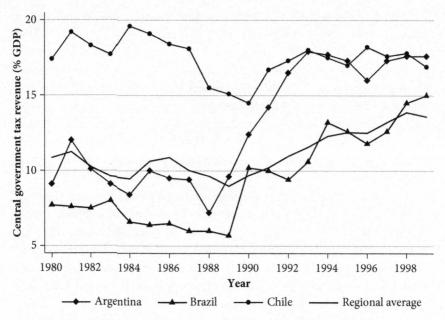

FIGURE 5.1 Total tax revenues (as a percentage of GDP) of South American governments, 1980–1999. The regional average includes revenue-collection data from Bolivia, Brazil, Chile, Colombia, Paraguay, Peru, Uruguay, and Venezuela (*Source:* Tanzi 2003).

The Argentine tax-collection effort before Menem became president was weak but did not fall far below the regional average. The improvement in revenue collection engineered by the Menem government reforms is clear. But the long-term success of the Convertibility system required very strict fiscal discipline, and the upward trend in revenue collection notwithstanding, tax evasion in Argentina remained a pervasive problem. Estimates of the shortfall in value-added tax (VAT) receipts due to evasion ranged as high as 40 percent in the 1990s; survey evidence from 1999 indicates that up to 55 percent of potential taxpayers did not file that year.[101]

The other side of the taxation issue involves the fiscal relationship of the central government with the provincial governments. Briefly, Argentina suffered from a high degree of vertical fiscal imbalance; the twenty-three provinces delegated most of the revenue-raising in the country to the central government in

---

101. Fenochietto 2003, 394–95.

Buenos Aires while retaining significant discretion in social spending.[102] In 1997, the provinces accounted for 47 percent of total spending but were responsible for only 24 percent of the revenues collected in the country.[103] The peculiar Argentine system of fiscal federalism was enshrined in a series of tax-sharing agreements (*coparticipación*), which established the rules by which the central government shared with the provinces the taxes collected by the central government.

IMF officials understood that *coparticipación* posed a threat to the fiscal sustainability of the Convertibility system. In the first Executive Board meeting after the hard peg was implemented, one ED expressed concerns about the long-term implications for Convertibility: "There are, of course, uncertainties. Perhaps the major one is the fiscal behavior of the provinces. Past experience shows that this is a particularly difficult area."[104]

IMF pressure on Argentina to reform the fiscal imbalance between the provinces and the federal government was mainly rhetorical. Although the Fund may not have been able to exert much influence on center-province relations due to the complex political dynamics at play, it also did not even try to enforce changes in this area. Only in the March 2000 standby arrangement was reform of the provincial revenue-sharing system included as a (nonbinding) structural "benchmark." Indeed, one of the most striking aspects of the IMF-Argentina relationship from 1991 onward was "the paucity of formal structural conditionality, particularly in the form of performance criteria." Further, "what little conditionality the programs contained was not vigorously enforced."[105]

El Divorcio: The Argentine Crisis, 1998–2002

The IEO report on the Fund-Argentina relationship in the 1990s concludes that, by 1998, "the information available at the time—the authorities' poor compliance record with earlier programs, the unraveling of the political consensus that had backed the reform program of the early 1990s, the absence of a clear balance of payments need—would have been sufficient reason to end the program relationship."[106] Nonetheless, in February 1998 the IMF plowed ahead with another three-year EFF worth SDR 2.08 billion ($2.8 billion, 135 percent of the quota).

---

102. The peculiar Argentine form of fiscal federalism has spawned its own literature, which I do not review here. Some important work includes Eaton 2005; Gibson and Calvo 2000; Remmer and Wibbels 2000; Spiller and Tommasi 2007.

103. Pessino 2003, 423–24.

104. Minutes of the Executive Board Meeting, EBM/91/102, July 29, 1991, p. 44.

105. Independent Evaluation Office of the IMF 2004, 36.

106. Ibid., 37–38.

The 1998, EFF was intended as a precautionary program. Argentina hardly needed the funds. In the previous year, the government had floated a record amount of debt on the international financial markets. But, at the time of the agreement, global financial markets were roiled by crises. Turbulence had spread across East Asia in late 1997, and financial contagion from Asia to other emerging-market economies was not unthinkable.

The precautionary EFF was also an extremely lenient program. It included the fewest number of binding conditions in any IMF agreement since 1977. The generosity and leniency of the proposed program prompted some concern among the staff members outside the Western Hemisphere Department. A memo from Teresa Ter-Minassian, the new deputy director of the Western Hemisphere Department, to the Fund management highlighted serious concerns from the Research, Policy Development and Review, and Fiscal Affairs departments "about the adequacy of the proposed reform agenda for an extended arrangement." A separate memo from the Research Department at the time of Board approval warned, "the program is not ambitious enough to warrant Fund support in the form of a high access extended arrangement."[107] Ultimately the concerns fell on deaf ears. On February 4, the Executive Board approved the precautionary multiyear arrangement.

Over the next two years, the situation confronting the Argentine economic policy team steadily worsened. Some of the problems were created by the government itself; several of the problems were not. A detailed examination of the conditions that led to the crisis and default of late 2001 is beyond the scope of this chapter, but several factors that set Argentina on a path toward financial ruin can be identified: the strong appreciation of the U.S. dollar; the 20 percent fall in international agricultural prices, which harmed Argentine farmers; a drawback of international investment in the wake of the East Asian Financial Crisis and the Russian default; the devaluation of the Brazilian real in January 1999; and excessive deficit spending by the Argentine government in the period prior to the 1999 presidential election (which the Peronists lost to the Alianza[108] candidate, Fernando de la Rúa).[109]

107. Staff memoranda quoted in Blustein 2005, 51. Dissent among the staff is also reported in Independent Evaluation Office of the IMF 2004.

108. The disintegration of the Radical Party in the mid-1990s led to the creation of a new center-left party, the Front for a Country in Solidarity (FREPASO), which captured much of the Radical Party middle-class support base. In 1997, FREPASO and the remaining Radicals combined to form Alianza por Trabajo as a viable electoral alternative to Carlos Menem's Peronist political machine. Menem attempted to run for a third term, in contravention to the Argentine Constitution; when he was barred from running, the Peronists selected Eduardo Duhalde as their candidate.

109. On the conditions that led to the crisis, see Independent Evaluation Office of the IMF 2004, 20; Powell 2003, 1–44.

In April 1998, Teresa Ter-Minassian let slip in an interview with a journalist that "the Argentine economy contains a sort of Molotov cocktail."[110] The sustainability of the debt burden of the country became more and more uncertain as its economic performance slackened. In 1999, the economic output of Argentina contracted by 3 percent. As tax revenues plunged in the midst of the deepening recession, investors became nervous and the cost to the government of external borrowing increased. Rather than using its leverage to enforce better fiscal discipline or to entertain a possible exit strategy from Convertibility, the Fund continued to place its trust in the hands of the Argentine policymakers.

The performance of Argentina under the 1998 program was poor. It missed fiscal targets by wide margins, and its legislators dragged their feet on the passage of a new bill mandating changes to the labor laws.[111] By mid-1998, the current account deficit had widened again. With international financial markets still roiling from the crises in East Asia, Russia, and Brazil, serious concerns about the trajectory of Argentina began to emerge in the private discussions of the Fund with Argentine authorities. Publicly, the IMF feted Argentina; Carlos Menem, as the leader of a "star" emerging-market reformer, was invited to deliver the keynote speech at the fall 1998 IMF meeting. But in a closed-door meeting with Economy Minister Roque Fernández, the managing director of the Fund pressed the minister on the worsening external imbalance of his country, pointing out that Malaysia had recently followed a similar path before it was plunged into a crisis. According to the account of the meeting by Marcelo Bonelli, Teresa Ter-Minassian reassured Camdessus and the other participants that the staff mission remained fully confident in the Argentines' commitment to the program: "if they have to cut spending, they'll do it, and if they have to raise taxes, they'll do it."[112]

At several points in the life of the program, the IMF overlooked noncompliance with performance criteria. In July, September, and December 1998, the Board approved waivers for missed conditions, and in March 1999, the Board approved the staff request to revise the fiscal targets upward by $150 million (with one long-standing ED, Abbas Mirakhor, heaping praise on the country during the meeting: "the Argentine economic policy managers have demonstrated, once again, their agility and prudence").[113] Ultimately, private sources of financing proved to be sufficient, and the Argentines did not need to draw on the precautionary loan.

---

110. *Clarín*, April 3, 1998; Blustein 2005, 54 (quotation).
111. *Ambito Financiero*, April 2, 1998; *Ambito Financiero*, July 21, 1998; Blustein 2005, 56.
112. Quoted in Bonelli 2004, 80 (my translation from Spanish).
113. Minutes of the Executive Board Meeting, EBM/99/56, 26 May 1999, p. 11 (quotation).

A House Divided: Fernando de la Rúa's Government

Neoliberals retained control of Argentine economic policymaking institutions after the election of Fernando de la Rúa to the presidency in October 1999. José Luis Machinea, the Minnesota-trained economist who had played a central role in the interactions of Alfonsín's government with the Fund in the mid- to late-1980s, became the new economy minister. Chicago-educated Pedro Pou was the holdover from the Menem team, staying on as the head of the Central Bank.

Factionalism divided the loyalties of the policymakers in de la Rúa's administration. Under the Alianza banner, there were distinct camps with very different visions for steering Argentina through its deep recession. On one side stood the Alfonsístas—a group with long-standing ties to the Radical Party and former President Raúl Alfonsín—with Carlos Winograd (who had received his economics training in Brazil and France) and Daniel Marx, the lead debt negotiator, as the key allies of the group in the new administration. The Alfonsístas were open to more heterodox policy alternatives to the recession than those that the IMF was willing to countenance. Allied with the Alfonsísta group was the structuralist-oriented Roberto Frenkel, who made the case in secretive strategy meetings (organized in September 1999 by the incoming president) that the best option for Argentina was to unshackle itself from a "suicidal" IMF-approved austerity program by exiting the Convertibility Plan and undoing the "Menemist" agenda.[114]

On the other side stood the Marketinera group of advisors to President de la Rúa, united in their defense of the hard peg of the peso to the U.S. dollar, their advocacy of even more extensive market-oriented reforms, and their support for neoliberal economic ideas. Among the key figures in the Marketinera group were Mario Vicens, soon to be the secretary of state; Miguel Bein, economic advisor; Ricardo López Murphy, Chicago-trained professional economist; and Fernando de Santibañes, the incoming secretary of intelligence and a former student of Arnold Harberger at the University of Chicago.[115] Machinea was suggested for the position of economy minister by the vice president in the incoming de la Rúa administration, Carlos "Chacho" Alvarez; Machinea was not anathema to the Alfonsístas (unlike the individuals associated with the "more [economically] orthodox Radical faction headed by Ricardo López Murphy"[116]), and he seemed to be an acceptable choice to the Marketinera faction in the Alianza government.

---

114. Bonelli 2004, 127–30.
115. Ibid., 135.
116. Quoted ibid., 131.

A New Standby Agreement

By the time an IMF mission arrived in Buenos Aires in January 2000 to negotiate a new program to replace the expiring precautionary EFF, the external imbalance of Argentina had become even more precarious. Yet the Fund remained optimistic about the fortunes of the country for the next year, forecasting economic growth at greater than 3 percent. The IMF mission, jointly led by Teresa Ter-Minassian and Thomas Reichmann, focused on the key issues that had plagued previous agreements: the fiscal balance of the central government, excessive social spending by provincial governors and the government willingness to cover provincial debts (totaling nearly $4 billion in 1999), and the stalled labor market reform.[117] In late February, the lower house of Congress finally approved the long-delayed "flexibilization" of the labor laws, paving the way for the staff to submit a new Letter of Intent to the Executive Board.

The new standby arrangement was approved on March 10. The program was for three years and was very generous at SDR 5.4 billion ($7.2 billion, 255 percent of the quota). The Argentine debt burden had spiked in the previous two years, but the country retained some access to external financing (albeit with rising costs), so the policy team indicated that its intention was to use the program as simply a precaution.[118] Conditionality was light; the Argentine policymakers saw no great difficulties in achieving the modest fiscal targets, and once again, the program did not include structural performance criteria. All of the structural content in the agreement was treated as benchmarks, which would be assessed at the time of reviews but, if violated, would not trigger an automatic suspension without a waiver.

The EDs seized on two aspects of the proposed agreement in the discussion of the staff report and accompanying documents: the large amount of access granted to the borrower and the limited number of performance criteria. Two EDs (from Italy and Albania) wondered why the structural benchmarks were not, in light of the poor track record of the country in implementing benchmarks in the 1998 EFF arrangement, set as either prior actions or performance criteria.[119] Noting the meaninglessness of claiming that the program was "precautionary" (on approval, the Argentine "authorities will have immediate access to a substantial amount of money, around $1.3 billion"), Stephen Pickford, the British

---

117. *Buenos Aires Economico*, January 14, 2000.

118. In the week before the Board approval of the standby arrangement, the Argentine government sold $1 billion in ten-year, dollar-denominated bonds (Tamar Han, "New Issues: Argentina Sells Some More," *Emerging Markets Debt Report*, March 13, 2000).

119. Minutes of the Meeting of the IMF Executive Board, EBM/00/24, March 10, 2000, pp. 120–23.

Board representative, expressed the view that debt management "is central to the success of the program and . . . should have been reflected in a performance criterion."[120] The French ED pushed the staff representative to justify the large (and front-loaded) program, fearing "it might be hard to explain to other borrowers that we agreed to unlock 1.3 billion dollars without any prior actions and regardless of the fact that most of the targets of the December 1999 program review were missed."[121]

The response to the EDs' concerns came from the Policy Development and Review staff representative, who argued, in part:

> Regarding how the staff and management had determined the amount of Fund support and what kind of vehicle was considered most appropriate, the country had had enormous difficulties for a decade ending in 1989–1991, but had had a rather exceptional track record since then, the staff representative recalled. . . . The question was how to provide support to a new set of authorities, who were determined to move quickly, and to live up to the strategy that had been developed over the past ten years.[122]

Toward the end of the discussion, Willy Kiekens, the long-serving Belgian ED, weighed in. Noting that debt management needed to be a priority for the de la Rúa government but that he "would not go as far as Mr. Pickford by requiring performance criteria," his confidence in the "overall good track record" of the country meant that the Fund "can be somewhat less demanding" than usual.[123] In the end, the Board members unanimously approved the proposed program.

Over the next six months, economic circumstances in Argentina worsened. By May, the policy team led by Machinea and Pou was forced to implement emergency belt-tightening measures to achieve the budgetary targets laid out in the agreement. The deep budget cuts generated massive protests organized by CGT (the central labor organization). President de la Rúa blamed the social discontent on the IMF, claiming that the 80,000 anti-austerity protesters on the Plaza de Mayo were "a wake-up call to international financial agencies, for them to pay proper attention to social solidarity as well."[124] The events caused consternation among investors, and the already shaky access of Argentina to sources of external financing became even more questionable. Consequently, Machinea flew to

---

120. Ibid., p. 124.
121. Ibid., p. 138.
122. Ibid., p. 147 (emphasis added).
123. Ibid., pp. 160, 162.
124. *El Cronista*, June 1, 2000, p. 5.

Washington in August to try to gain access to the undrawn portion of the standby arrangement. He succeeded in getting the Fund to waive the nonobservance of the fiscal target for August (Argentina had missed the binding target by over $500 million) and to raise the fiscal deficit ceiling from $4.7 to $5.3 billion.[125]

Then a major political crisis in October forced the Fund and Argentina to take drastic actions to stave off an impending economic collapse. Vice President Chacho Alvarez resigned, ostensibly in protest of the public revelation of bribes offered to legislators during the fight over the labor market bill. (Bonelli argues that Alvarez, concerned about the influence exercised by the hard-core Marketinera, Fernando de Santibañes, on de la Rúa's agenda, left before he would have to govern in a regime dominated by the hard-core neoliberal faction.)[126] In the wake of Alvarez's resignation, the spreads on Argentine debt (the difference between the price the U.S. government pays to borrow and the price paid by the Argentine government to lure in investors) began to rise. Servicing the $120 billion Argentine external debt became much more difficult. Depositors became increasingly nervous about the possibility of a devaluation of the peso. Nearly $800 million exited the banks of Argentina in October alone.

Argentina Gets Its "Shield"

The Fund, responding to the increasingly desperate situation in Argentina, acted quickly to put together a new package to help preserve the Convertibility system and avoid a complete financial collapse. The staff and management focused on two issues: dramatically increasing access by Argentina to external financing resources and forcing the Argentine authorities to commit to an ever tighter set of fiscal targets. Between October 2000 and January 2001, Argentine and Fund officials worked to put together an augmented bailout package that could stave off the coming crisis. Machinea, Mario Vicens, and Julio Dreizzen (a subsecretary in the Department of Finance who had served as an assistant to the Argentine ED in 1984–1986 and as an alternative ED in 1986–1987) traveled to Washington to work with the mission staff and top management in the Western Hemisphere Department on the technical details of the plan. Daniel Marx, meanwhile, worked with the U.S. foreign economic policy corps to drum up support for the package.[127] In January, the $40 billion augmentation (known informally as the *blindaje*, or "shield") to the initial agreement was announced. With the new infusion of resources, the drawing by Argentina climbed to SDR 10.6 billion ($14 bil-

---

125. *Buenos Aires Economico*, August 15, 2000; *El Cronista*, September 8, 2000.
126. Bonelli 2004, 149.
127. Ibid., 151–52.

lion, 500 percent of the quota). The remaining amount in the bailout package came from the other international financial institutions and from creditor governments such as the United States and Spain.

The toughness of the fiscal requirements in the agreement was a source of tension in the institution. Some IMF economists—particularly those in the Policy Development and Review Department (which evaluates the content of all programs)—pushed for a tightening of the fiscal and structural targets. But Machinea had a high-ranking ally in the Fund management. Deputy Managing Director Stanley Fischer accepted the Argentines' claims that the most they could plausibly do in terms of the fiscal deficit in 2001 was $6 billion (the target in the 2000 agreement was for a deficit of no more than $4.7 billion). The new Letter of Intent included fiscal performance criteria to limit the fiscal deficit to $6.5 billion. With the U.S. Treasury firmly in support of the freeing of additional resources for the Argentines, the Executive Board unanimously approved the modifications on January 12.[128]

"If Machinea Does Not Announce the Shield, Then No Shield"

The *blindaje* episode supplies another corroborating piece of evidence for my argument linking the IMF treatment of its borrowers to the composition of the policy team of the borrowing country. By the time the augmentation was announced, the pressure on President de la Rúa to bring in a new economy minister, coming from both the Marketinera and Alfonsísta camps, had become intense. In Marcelo Bonelli's recounting of events, the top officials of the Fund were increasingly concerned about the possibility that Machinea might be sacked before the new bailout program was rolled out. The episode culminated in a phone call that Stanley Fischer, the IMF second-in-command, placed to the president. Fischer warned de la Rúa that the confidence of the IMF in the program was bound up in their relationship with Machinea: "we negotiate with Machinea. For us Machinea is the guarantor of the agreement. If Machinea does not announce the *blindaje*, then no *blindaje*."[129]

The January 2001 augmentation of the standby arrangement did not, however, succeed in restoring the faith of the market in Argentina. (In the Board discussion, one ED cited a client survey run by an investment bank on the likeliest candidates for sovereign default. Argentina tied for the top position in the poll with Nigeria.)[130] The data on fiscal performance from the first two months of the year indicated that Argentina had fallen out of compliance.

---

128. Blustein 2005, 96–97, 106.
129. Quoted in Bonelli 2004, 155–56.
130. Minutes of the Meeting of the IMF Executive Board, EBM/01/5, January 12, 2001, p. 74.

On March 2, Economy Minister José Luis Machinea resigned in the face of the growing economic and political crisis. Machinea's replacement, Ricardo López Murphy, Chicago-trained economist, took immediate action to get control of the fiscal situation, proposing a draconian package of spending cuts and tax hikes. The IMF regarded the new economy minister as "a strong choice." In the estimation of Claudio Loser, López Murphy was "a man with solid ideas."[131] The Alfonsístas in the government, on the other hand, were not so pleased with de la Rúa's choice, and their simmering anger over the unwillingness of the administration to consider alternatives to IMF-enforced austerity spilled over into outright opposition to the economy minister and his agenda. López Murphy's tenure as economy minister lasted less than three weeks.

The Fading *Magia* of Domingo Cavallo

Desperate to regain the confidence of international investors, President de la Rúa brought back Domingo Cavallo to head the Economy Ministry. The vying factions in the government hoped that Cavallo's *magia* had not worn off in the years since he left the Menem government.[132] But Cavallo's headstrong tendencies emerged early in his second term as economy minister. In April, he controversially engineered the replacement of the Pedro Pou, the Central Bank governor, with a more agreeable official; later that month, Cavallo proposed modifying the Convertibility system to tie the peso to a combination of the euro and the dollar. The announcement was regarded in financial circles as a warning sign that devaluation was just over the horizon, heightening the flight from the banking system.[133]

With Cavallo once again at the helm of Argentine economic policy, the IMF reviewed the progress of the standby arrangement in May. The news was bad. As expected, the government had missed its fiscal targets. Further, an increase in the effective rate of protection on the import of consumer goods, engineered by Cavallo as a way to staunch the currency outflow, violated a basic performance criterion (an injunction against the intensification of trade controls) that appears in essentially all IMF conditional lending agreements.

Nonetheless, the Fund approved four waivers for missed conditions, thereby allowing the country to access another $1.2 billion tranche of the lending arrangement. The Dutch ED, J. Onno de Beaufort Wijnholds, summed up the

---

131. "A Surgeon without a Scalpel," *Business Week*, March 19, 2001, p. 30 (first quotation); Tenembaum 2004, 181 (second quotation).

132. Bonelli 2004, 145.

133. Di Tella and Vogel 2004, 3; Blustein 2005, 120.

spirit of the Board meeting: "Thanks to Mr. Cavallo and his quick response unit, sufficient action has been taken for us to proceed with the next disbursement as scheduled."[134] The actions of the IMF did not do much to assuage nervous financial markets. The spread on Argentine debt remained around 1,000 basis points. A sovereign default was by each passing week becoming the likeliest end point.

Over the next three months, Cavallo charted an increasingly erratic course in his effort to stave off the collapse of the Argentine economy. Cavallo's policy changes were announced with little advance warning and with almost no input from the IMF mission members. For the head of the Western Hemisphere Department, the Argentine policymaker had become "almost a nightmare."[135] Briefing the IMF Executive Board on his return from a trip to Buenos Aires in June, Stanley Fischer noted that he had spoken with Cavallo "about the Board's concern with the lack of consultation on the recently introduced measures. [Cavallo's] answer was that he hardly had time to consult with anyone, including members of his own staff."[136]

In June, the Argentine policy team announced a massive voluntary debt swap (the *megacanje*) that lengthened the maturities and changed the yields on around $30 billion of foreign debt.[137] This gave the debt managers of the country a small amount of breathing room by deferring a large amount of the interest payments until 2006. In an effort to stimulate exports to grow Argentina out of the crisis, Cavallo proposed a dual exchange rate for exports (1.08 pesos to the dollar). The policy was a de facto 8 percent devaluation and another signal to financial actors that the commitment of the authorities to Convertibility was wavering.[138] Finally, in a last-ditch attempt to convince markets of the sustainability of the hard peg, Cavallo announced the "zero deficit" policy: going forward, Argentina would commit to eradicating fiscal deficits at both the federal and provincial levels. Financial market players treated the announcement as a sign of desperation rather than fortitude, and the spreads on Argentine debt shot to 1,600 basis points.

The September 2001 Augmentation

On September 7, the Executive Board approved the addition of an extra $8 billion to the standby arrangement. The approval enabled the Argentines to immedi-

---

134. Minutes of the Meeting of the IMF Executive Board, EBM/01/53, May 21, 2001, p. 61.
135. Claudio Loser, quoted in Tenembaum 2004, 180.
136. Minutes of the Meeting of the IMF Executive Board, EBM/01/65, June 27, 2001, p. 7.
137. Blustein 2005, 129.
138. Di Tella and Vogel 2004, 4; Blustein 2005, 131; Independent Evaluation Office of the IMF 2004, 51; Clifford Krauss, "Argentine with a Headache: The Economy," *New York Times*, July 18, 2001, p. A12.

ately draw on $6.3 billion in IMF resources—the second-largest single disbursement in IMF history. The total resources in the Argentine program amounted to 800 percent of the quota.

Here the strongest evidence of intervention by the United States and other powerful member states in the decision-making process of the Fund emerges. The dissension in the ranks of the staff over the successive augmentations to the Argentine program was *not* communicated in the reports that were circulated to the EDs before the Board meetings. The staff reports, which contained relatively optimistic projections for the program, were, in Randall Stone's view, sanitized under pressure from the United States.[139] Important meetings in which the management position on the Argentine program cohered were not open to all Board members—an issue seized on in the Board discussion by the Estonian ED, Oli-Pekka Lehmussaari, who complained, "The Board never managed to have an open discussion on the options that were put forward to us by the Managing Director. Instead, Management came up with a recommendation based on an agreement that had been sealed by a handful of major shareholders."[140]

Although evidence abounds that "informal governance" procedures had kicked in during the last months of the IMF involvement in Argentina, the direction of the influence of powerful states on IMF decisions is not entirely clear. The United States did not present a unified front on the Argentine issue. Stone argues that the U.S. Treasury had a strong interest in maintaining the flow of IMF resources to Argentina to avoid triggering a crisis that could spill across borders. But Treasury Secretary Paul O'Neill's unsympathetic comments about Argentina in late July 2001 indicate that he had effectively written the country off. (Argentina, in his view, had "been off and on in trouble for 70 years or more. They don't have any export industry to speak of at all. And they like it that way. Nobody forced them to be what they are.")[141] The transcripts of the meetings of the U.S. Federal Open Market Committee (FOMC) contain a scant few references to Argentina in 2001, suggesting that fears of contagion in South America were not high on the FOMC members' agenda. Karen Johnson, the director of the Federal Reserve (the Fed) Division of International Finance, even publicly stated that the Fed had "no confidence" in Argentina.[142] The U.S. security establishment may have worried about the political risks of an economic meltdown in Argentina, but there is no evidence to suggest that State Department officials leaned on decision makers at the IMF to push through the augmented programs.

---

139. Stone 2011, 201–2.
140. Minutes of the Meeting of the IMF Executive Board, EBM/01/91, September 7, 2001, p. 57.
141. Quoted in Taylor 2007, 78.
142. Bonelli 2004, 189.

The Board held an unusually contentious meeting in which the September 2001 augmentation was the main item on the agenda. In a stunning display of dissatisfaction, two EDs (Wijnholds from the Netherlands and Roberto Cippa from Switzerland) abstained from the vote. Tomas Reichman, the head of the staff mission to Argentina, took to the floor after the abstentions to, once again, defend the confidence of the staff that the policy team would avert a total economic meltdown: "Even if the program does not succeed—meaning the Fund will be faced with the possibility of waivers, and that the process takes longer—the program will eventually show results."[143] The remaining EDs who cast their vote in favor of the program "appeared impressed by the strength of what they saw as the authorities' resolve, and some wished to give them the benefit of the doubt on their ability to implement the measures they had announced."[144] The September augmentation of the standby arrangement briefly helped improve market sentiments, but soon the spreads climbed back to 1,400 basis points. Over the next three months, the Fund would "essentially adopt a passive stance" while Argentina hurtled toward a default.[145]

Full Collapse

The crisis finally arrived in December. At the end of November, the run on banks accelerated to the point that the banking system was losing $1 billion each day. On December 1, the government decided to place limitations on bank withdrawals and other personal financial transactions (the *corralito*). Four days later, the IMF pulled the plug on Argentina, announcing that it would not disburse the next $1.24 billion tranche of the standby arrangement. Officially, the violation of the fiscal deficit target by over $2 billion was the reason for the suspension of the program.

After the remaining staff members left Buenos Aires and Cavallo returned home from a last-ditch attempt to win support from the IMF managing director, the capitol exploded in violence. A group of leading industrialists, labor leaders, and top figures in the Peronist party (Núcleo Nacional) convened to formulate a plan for a post-Convertibility, post-default Argentina; after Cavallo angrily walked out of a meeting with the group, his fate was sealed.[146] Cavallo resigned

---

143. Minutes of the Meeting of the IMF Executive Board, EBM/01/91, September 7, 2001, p. 51.
144. Independent Evaluation Office of the IMF 2004, 54. Michael Mussa, formerly the chief economist of the Fund, argues that an important reason for the September augmentation was that "Argentina was generally seen as a country deserving sympathy and support" (2002, 47).
145. Blustein 2005, 157.
146. Bonelli 2004, 207–8.

shortly thereafter, followed by President de la Rúa, who exited the Casa Rosada by helicopter to escape the protesters. In the three subsequent weeks, four different presidents were sworn in. On January 3, 2002, Eduard Duhalde, the interim president, announced in front of a room full of wildly cheering legislators that Argentina would no longer make payments on its debt. Three days later, Argentina officially ended the Convertibility Plan and let the peso float. And after thirty years of nearly continuous engagement, the IMF relationship with Argentina had effectively ended.

The Aftermath

After the withdrawal of IMF support, the shuttering of banks and imposition of capital controls, and the announcement by the government that the country was insolvent and could no longer pay its debts, Argentines were subjected to yet another horror: pesofication. While the banks were closed, dollar deposits were converted overnight into pesos at the rate of 1.4 pesos per dollar. Pesofication on top of a massive wave of bankruptcies, combined with the government default on its debt (a good deal of which was held in the country by ordinary Argentines), brought economic activity in the country to a near standstill. The Argentine economy contracted by over 10 percent in 2002.

The crisis ushered in a new era of economic management in Argentina. With the abrupt handover of power from the Alianza government to the Peronist party, a new set of non-neoliberal economic policymakers entered office. Contravening Michel Camdessus's triumphalist claim that the economic liberalization in Argentina was "irreversible," successive sets of Argentine policy teams reshaped the policy agenda along structuralist-populist lines. Jorge Remes Lenicov, a leader in the new wave of Peronist policymakers in the months following the crisis, explained that desperate economic times created the imperative for heterodox policy experimentation.[147] With the ascendance of Néstor Kirchner and Cristina Fernández de Kirchner from the left wing of the Justicialista party to the Casa Rosada, the relationship of Argentina with the IMF went from strained to outright antagonistic. In 2003, the Argentines signed a small, short-term standby arrangement and a larger emergency program with the Fund, but the arrangements were unusual: the standby arrangement was set up mainly to supply funds to enable Argentina to pay off the obligations to the IMF that the country had built up in the run-up to the crisis of 2001–2002, and like the IMF

---

147. Bonelli 2004, 231.

programs for countries hit by natural disasters, the emergency loan contained no performance criteria. The Kirchner government subsequently delayed several payments to the Fund. In 2006, with a fast-growing economy and coffers swelled by foreign-exchange reserves thanks to a worldwide surge in commodity prices (and with the added help of a generous loan from Hugo Chávez's government in Venezuela), Argentina paid in full its remaining $9.8 billion in obligations to the organization. Kirchner observed, "I received an Argentina devastated by an economic program supported by the IMF, [but] there is life after the IMF, and it's a very good life."[148] Argentina would never return after the crisis to the kinds of neoliberal economic policies it followed in the 1990s, warned Roberto Lavagna, Kirchner's influential economy minister (a man widely credited, according to the *Financial Times*, as "the architect of Argentina's economic revival").[149] "Nor," Lavagna added, "can the Fund be back."[150]

Summary of the Fourth Episode, 1991–2001

The evidence presented in the fourth and final episode of IMF-Argentina relations shows that the staff members were well aware of the risks engendered by the Convertibility arrangement; the issues of fiscal indiscipline, stunted structural reforms in the areas of the labor market and relations with the provinces, and the rapid buildup of (foreign currency–denominated) debt were all on the radar of the Fund. Yet the IMF chose not to enforce those policies. There is good reason, then, for the former chief economist of the Fund, Michael Mussa, to call the behavior of the institution in Argentina in the 1990s a "failure of intellectual courage."[151]

The Fund programs in an Argentina dominated by neoliberals in the decade after 1991 were, in general, very lenient. The first program in the episode, negotiated in June 1991, was completed with the help of waivers for noncompliance with multiple binding conditions. The structural conditions in the 1992 multiyear arrangement were not enforced; later agreements did not include any binding structural conditions. Another set of waivers allowed the Argentines to restart the EFF after the Mexican crisis in late 1994 and later to augment the arrangement. The programs negotiated in 1996, 1998, and 2000 were each completed only after multiple waivers for noncompliance with the fiscal targets—in some

---

148. Quoted in Kedar 2013, 180.
149. Benedict Mander, "Greek Woe Brings Powerful Sense of Déjà Vu for Argentina," *Financial Times*, online ed., July 9, 2015, http://www.ft.com/cms/s/0/5d8c9462-25c2-11e5-bd83-71cb60e8f08c.html.
150. Quoted in Bonelli 2004, 262.
151. Mussa 2002, 47–48.

cases, waivers were issued when the limit on the fiscal deficit had been exceeded by wide margins. In 2000 and 2001, augmentations of the standby arrangement brought the size of the Fund disbursements to 800 percent of the Argentine quota. Reflecting after the crisis of 2001, the former head of the Fund Western Hemisphere Department accepted that that the organization had been too permissive: "the Argentine political class thought that the IMF was always giving them a new chance, no matter what they did. So they kicked the problem down the line. The behavior of the Fund confirmed this perception."[152]

Concluding Thoughts

The two chapters of the case study were organized around four episodes spanning a quarter century in which Argentina and the Fund were tightly connected. In two of the episodes (1976–1981 and 1991–2001), neoliberal economic ideas were ascendant. Another period was marked by oscillation between teams that varied in their embrace of neoliberal ideas (1981–1985). In the opening section of this chapter I considered relationship of Argentina with the Fund in a mixed case (1985–1989). The purpose of the within-unit episodic comparisons was twofold: (1) I wanted to see whether the degree of neoliberal influence tracked the IMF treatment of Argentina in each period (was the treatment by the Fund more lenient during the high-neoliberal episodes?), and (2) I used material from the IMF archives to find out whether evidence shows that the degree of shared beliefs between the institution and the policy team was important in the decision-making process of the Fund. On both counts, the case-level evidence was supportive: the variation in the relationship of the Fund with the Argentines across episodes matched the predictions from my theoretical framework; in addition, I found more direct evidence of the causal mechanisms linking the IMF treatment of Argentina to its support for policy teams composed of like-minded authorities in the internal memoranda and records of Executive Board meetings.

The four episodes of Fund-Argentine relations, each featuring a complex mix of actors (executives, economic policymakers, IMF officials, and powerful states) and intentions, are not perfectly explained by any of the existing explanations. But combined with the quantitative evidence in chapter 3, the findings suggest that the ideational approach to IMF lending behavior I develop here has powerful empirical implications (see table 5.2 for a compact summary of the findings from the case study).

---

152. Quoted in Tenembaum 2004, 195 (my translation).

TABLE 5.2 Overview of the case study of Argentina

PERIOD	TREATMENT BY THE IMF	DEGREE OF NEOLIBERAL INFLUENCE
1976–1981	*Lenient*: Two programs signed during the period (1976 and 1977). Conditionality is weak and weakly enforced. Government does not draw on second loan.	*High*: Central Bank Governor Adolfo Diz was a University of Chicago economics PhD; Economy Minister Martínez de Hoz did not possess neoliberal credentials but was friendly to the IMF; other U.S.-trained officials occupied advisory positions.
1981–1985	*Tough*: Two standby arrangements signed following difficult negotiations. Both programs (January 1983 and December 1984) include numerous conditions and are suspended without waivers.	*Low (during periods of IMF program participation)*: Rapid turnover of officials and policy switching marked the final years of the military regime (1981–1983); officials in the new democratically elected government were non-neoliberals, skeptical of IMF advice
1985–1989	*Mixed*: Lending arrangement restarted in June 1985 and completed thanks to waivers issued in March and June 1986. New agreement signed in July 1987; waivers issued in December and March 1988. Program canceled due to noncompliance in May 1988 in face of apparent pressure from U.S. officials on Fund to extend program.	*Medium-low*: The appointment of Juan Sourrouille as economy minister brought a group of U.S.-trained economists into government, albeit in advisory positions until Machinea's appointment as Central Bank head in September 1986.
1991–2001	*Lenient*: Five separate programs signed during the period (July 1991, March 1992, April 1996, February 1998, and March 2000). Multiple waivers issued for missed performance criteria; programs contain limited conditions (only the March 1992 EFF contains binding structural conditions).	*High*: U.S.-trained economists (Cavallo, Fernández, Pou, and Machinea) controlled both the Economy Ministry and Central Bank throughout the period.

Domingo Cavallo well understood that his neoliberal credentials helped the relationship of his country with the Fund. When asked to reflect on the importance of his background in his relations with IMF officials, Cavallo replied that his Harvard economics training was "enormously helpful in establishing a relationship of confidence."[153] IMF judgments are shrouded in the fog of uncertainty (thicker in some contexts than in others, but always present), and the presence of like-minded authorities helps reassure the staff and management that the authorities will try to "do the right things." In Argentina, the IMF was "willing to give Domingo Cavallo more slack than Bernardo Grinspun. The Fund is more likely to take someone who shares our worldview at their word."[154]

---

153. "Ayuda muchísimo el establecimiento de una relación de confianza" (quoted in Heredia 2004, 329).

154. Interview with Desmond Lachman, Washington, DC, April 6, 2009.

STAYING ALIVE

IMF Lending Programs and the Political Survival
of Economic Policymakers

The theory and evidence adduced to this point in the book connects to a question that has long preoccupied students of world politics: How do the agencies of global economic governance, empowered by an ever-more-extensive web of cross-border, market-based transactions in goods and services, production, money and financial products, actually govern?

I argue that decision making by the IMF has been systematically affected by the makeup of the policy team charged with managing the economy of the borrowing country. The aggregate quantitative evidence (chapter 3) and the more fine-grained historical evidence from Argentina (chapters 4 and 5) points in this same direction: when the IMF decision makers and key members of the policy team of the borrowing country shared similar beliefs, the conditions in the program were often less numerous, the access granted to the country was usually more generous, and the enforcement of the conditions was typically less stringent.

But there are other potentially interesting and important consequences of shared economic beliefs in the context of IMF lending that merit further investigation. The analytics and empirics in the book have to this been point been focused on how the interaction between policy teams and the IMF affected the products of the IMF decisions. I pivot in this chapter to a different question: How did the IMF interactions with its borrowers affect the politics shaping the survival of top economic officials? I test an argument that links participation in IMF programs to the prospects for top economic officials' tenures in their appointed positions. That argument has its origins in scattered observations from the literature on economic policy reform in the developing world, which, taken together, suggest the Fund may have served as an important player in promoting not just the diffusion of market-oriented policy changes but also the installation and retention of neoliberal-type economic policymakers in borrowing countries.

Anecdotal Evidence for IMF Impact on the Appointment and Retention of Economic Officials

That the policymakers at the center of negotiations with IOs (on which the government depended for financing) were often empowered in their battles with rivals in and outside the government by dint of their seats at the negotiating table is a *leitmotif* in the literature on market-oriented policy reform. References to this pattern can be found in general analyses of policy reform as well as in region- and country-specific case studies. Miles Kahler, for example, argues that the IMF and World Bank seek to identify and empower "allies within the government whose interests are aligned more closely with the policy preferences of the IFIs [international financial institutions]."[1] The IMF, in particular, attempted to "create such interlocutors and allies . . . ensuring that this critical transnational link is sustained over time."[2] Harold James, a historian, observed, "one of the main functions of the IMF has been concerned with the transmission of ideas . . . by bolstering the position of reformers in the bureaucratic structures, usually the finance ministry and the central bank."[3] Peter Kenen, an MIT economist, argues, "as ministers of finance and governors of central banks represent their governments in dealings with the Fund, their own 'seal of approval' on a policy package is essential for access to financing from the Fund, and they might carry more weight in their own countries' councils than they would if they could not invoke the Fund's authority and promise of Fund credit."[4] And in the view of Malcolm Fairbrother, a sociologist, loan programs "can shift the balance of power in domestic politics, providing an advantage to those who agree with the external

---

1. Kahler 1992, 126. Kahler recognizes that, despite the efforts of the IMF and World Bank to strengthen their neoliberal allies in borrowing countries, "in many cases, the technocratic allies of external actors are in vulnerable political positions, despite their importance for a government's reputation and its access to external finance" (130).

2. Kahler 1993, 377.

3. James 1996, 133.

4. Kenen 1986, 52.

actors' policy priorities and allowing for market-oriented policy revolutions to be implemented as an 'inside job.' . . . technocrats may gain power vis-à-vis more statist and nationalist domestic competitors because of support and resources from the IFIs."[5]

Similar arguments abound in comparative studies of policy reform. James Fearon posits that, in mid-1980s sub-Saharan Africa, the IMF "used its power to ration balance of payments credits to influence appointments in key ministries, and missions have occasionally refused to negotiate unless a more 'suitable' finance or economics minister was installed, typically a younger man with a western Ph.D. in economics. In this manner, external pressures for reforms have helped create factions of African 'technocrats' who derive their political strength and legitimacy not only from presidential grace but also from their alliance with the IMF and other international agencies."[6] Catherine Conaghan and James Malloy's careful study of policy change in the Andean countries yields a similar insight: "the neoliberal clique inside the executive found a powerful set of external allies in the IMF and World Bank."[7] In her study of the tug-of-war over Mexican economic policy in the early 1980s, Sylvia Maxfield argues that the finance minister (and holder of a master's degree in economics from Yale University), Jesús Silva Herzog, had a "key role in the [creditor] negotiations" and left President Lopez Portillo "no choice but to keep him in the cabinet." In the pitched battles over the regulation of the Mexican banking sector, Silva Herzog's "leverage in the domestic debate stemmed from his links to international creditors and his key role in solving Mexico's extreme foreign exchange crisis."[8] Reflecting on the rise of neoliberals in the Augusto Pinochet regime in Chile, Rolf Lüders, a University of Chicago economics PhD and the Chilean finance minister in the early 1980s, stated, "the support of the International Monetary Fund and World Bank was crucial to us. They were very enthusiastic because *our team thought the way they did*; we were following their prescriptions more closely than any other country."[9]

Scholars have thus proffered several variants, backed by intriguing but anecdotal evidence, of the same basic argument: the neoliberal-type policymakers in governments involved in IMF programs parlayed their cozier relationships with the decision makers based in Washington into political capital at home.

---

5. Fairbrother 2014, 1332.
6. Fearon 1988, 127.
7. Conaghan and Malloy 1994, 155.
8. Maxfield 1990, 146, 149. See also Babb 2001, 176–79.
9. Quoted in Hira 1998, 99 (emphasis added).

The evidence behind the arguments, however, has been to this point fragmentary and incomplete; it consists, effectively, of a set of similar impressions reported by scholars of economic policymaking in developing and emerging countries.

In this chapter, I provide systematic tests of the link between the economic beliefs held by policymakers, participation in IMF programs, and the politics of selection and retention of top economic policymakers. I show that IMF loans extended the tenures of neoliberal-type officials. The statistical relationship between policymaker type and political durability is strong and significant—but only for the subset of country-year units in which there was an IMF program in place. The quantitative evidence amassed here suggests that neoliberal officials were not more durable in general; rather, their tenures were lengthier only when the government in which they served was under an IMF lending arrangement. I also show, using cross-sectional data from eighty-two developing countries, that there is a correlation between the fraction of time a country spent under the watchful eye of the IMF in the previous decades and the ideational composition of the policy team (measured as the average level of the proportion neoliberal indicator) during the 1990s—a decade marked by, first, extensive and sustained involvement of the IMF in the economic affairs of developing and emerging countries and, second, by a wavelike spread of market-oriented, liberalizing economic policy changes that swept through many countries.

Promoter of Neoliberal Policies—or Neoliberal Policymakers?

The statistical evidence suggests that the power of the IMF extends beyond influencing *how* borrowing economies are governed. I argue that the institution, through its conditional lending programs, also influences *who* governs the economy.

But that relationship—between participation in IMF conditional lending programs and the political durability of different economic policymakers—has been underplayed in the large literature on the effects of the IMF, which looks almost exclusively at the impact of lending program participation on macroeconomic outcomes and structural policies, and treats the organization as an instrument of coercive policy diffusion.

Coercive policy diffusion works when a more powerful actor consciously mobilizes resources to get the weaker target to ditch the status quo policy regime (because either the rewards for bringing the policy closer to the preferred point of the coercive actor are perceived to be very high or because the punishment for sticking with the disliked policy is too costly to bear).[10] It is easy to make the case that the borrowers from the IMF were situationally dependent (due to the crisis conditions that led the governments to request access to its resources) and perhaps structurally dependent as well (being, in most cases, smaller, more vulnerable, and materially less powerful countries). As a consequence, the coercive pressure of the IMF, transmitted through the machinery of conditional lending, was (according to conventional wisdom) a key factor in the turn toward greater openness in developing countries. The problem with the conventional wisdom is not that it is wholly wrong but, rather, that the existing evidence is simply too ambiguous to let us close the book on the issue of the role of the Fund in promoting market-oriented policy change. In a different study I reviewed thirty-one studies of the covariates of market liberalization in developing countries.[11] Less than half (fourteen) of the thirty-one studies provided unambiguously positive evidence for an association between the IMF and/or the World Bank and policy liberalization. That partly fits with the counternarrative about the fecklessness of the IMF and its sister institution, the World Bank, that began to emerge in the late 1990s—that the pro-liberalization conditions attached to the conditional loans of the Fund and World Bank were largely ineffectual.[12]

Perhaps the transformative effect of the IMF on policymaking in the countries that turned to the organization for loans in the 1980s and 1990s came not only (or even primarily) through the narrowing of the "policy space" of the borrower via the instrument of binding conditionality. The impact of widespread (and for some developing country members near-continuous) participation in IMF lending arrangements may have also come through effects on the political processes that shaped the makeup of the teams in charge of managing the economies of the countries. Next I explain how IMF program participation could change the political landscape facing executives in such a way that it makes good sense, from a country leader's perspective, for her to retain a particular kind of policymaker—specifically, the kind of official in whom decision makers at the IMF have a good deal of confidence.

---

10. Simmons, Dobbin, and Garrett 2006.
11. Nelson 2016.
12. The futility of IFI efforts at generating durable reforms in borrowing countries is illustrated by episodes such as the one related by Paul Collier, a development economist: "during a 15-year period, the Government of Kenya sold the same agricultural reform to the World Bank *four times*, each time reversing it after receipt of the aid" (1997, 60).

Valorizing Neoliberal Economic Policymakers

An economic policymaker's durability in office is, as Christopher Adolph reminds us, "the outcome of a *political process*."[13] The factors shaping the prospects for officials' tenures (and hence their ability to craft economic policies) extend well beyond the macroeconomic track record of their country during their tenure. The performance of the economy clearly matters for political survival (a finance minister presiding over a tanking economy would be well advised to start looking for alternative, nongovernmental career opportunities), but other parameters also influence the durability of individual officials. Those factors range from individual-level attributes and events (officials lose or leave their positions on account of health problems, embroilment in scandals, lucrative job opportunities outside government, and personality conflicts with the head of government, among other idiosyncratic reasons) to formal institutional features at the national level (e.g., the legal terms of appointment of central bankers vary by country, and central bank chiefs are more likely to live out their full terms when there is an institutional firewall between the central bank administrators and the government) to forces emanating from the international level.

Although there are a number of studies of the determinants of the political survival of national leaders and the duration of governments, we have almost no systematic evidence on the factors shaping the politics of the survival of economic officials.[14] The theory and evidence on the IMF-borrower relationship I develop in this book can shed some light on the issue. I start to build the argument linking political survival to IMF program participation by revisiting two claims about the involvement of the organization in low- and middle-income countries.

In the 1980s and 1990s, many developing and emerging countries entered into conditional lending arrangements offered by the Fund. The lengthiness of the participation periods of some of these countries is a feature that remains underappreciated by many observers of the institutions of global economic governance.[15] The fact that many developing countries, grappling with payments crises and struggling under onerous debt overhangs, came to depend on the lifelines extended by IMF lending arrangements made the organization a much more

---

13. Adolph 2013, 290 (italics in original).

14. Adolph's (ibid.) analysis of the covariates of the survival of central bankers in twenty advanced industrial countries is an important exception.

15. Jeffrey Sachs is an exception, noting that "the Fund has been unable to wean many countries away from IMF support, in spite of being only 'temporarily available.' ... the lengthy reliance on Fund loans is a contemporary feature of the system" (1989, 272). Conway (2007) and Reinhart and Trebesch (2015) provide more recent evidence on repetitive entry of members into IMF loans.

important force in the domestic political processes of those countries (a point illustrated by the vignette from Argentina in chapter 1).

The second element of the argument builds on the key finding so far in the book. When individuals with neoliberal backgrounds occupied the top economic policymaking positions in the borrowing government, the relationship between the government and the IMF shifted. As the gap between the beliefs of the two sides narrowed, confidence in the willingness and ability of the borrower to make the right decisions increased among the decision makers at the Fund. Greater confidence in the policy team in office, in turn, yielded larger programs with fewer performance criteria. And, seeking to preserve the relationship with neoliberal policymakers that were often in politically precarious situations, Fund officials were more likely to approve waivers when the program in their country went off track. As we have seen, the statistical relationship between the presence of neoliberals in the top economic policy posts in the borrowing country and the IMF treatment of countries stands up even when variables to account for potentially confounding factors—macroeconomic conditions, the strategic importance of the borrower to powerful member states (such as the United States), the relative openness of the policy environment of the borrower, the partisan makeup of the government, and the regime type—are included in the statistical models.

With these building blocks in place, I can develop a straightforward, testable argument linking the lenient treatment by the Fund of neoliberal economic policymakers to the incentives facing government leaders when they choose to retain or jettison members of their economic policy teams. Leaders ultimately control the appointment and retention of government officials. The executives themselves are concerned with political survival, and these concerns are heightened during period of economic distress. Leaders in all types of regimes face rising pressure as economic conditions worsen. If a member of the policy team can credibly claim to be able to deliver better treatment by an IO that has served as the economic lifeline for many low- and middle-income countries over the past several decades, then the executive has an added incentive to keep that policymaker in a position of influence.

Executives incur some cost when they engineer the removal of top economic officials. In normal times, leaders may face pressure to jettison neoliberal policymakers in favor of officials who hold different economic beliefs; assuming that leaders in low- and middle-income countries appoint neoliberals with the expectation that they will pursue a set of market-conforming policies, the leaders have to weigh the costs of rolling back reform efforts against the political benefits of changing course.

The cost of removing a neoliberal finance minister or central bank governor increases when the IMF is involved. For crisis-stricken governments, ditching a neoliberal policymaker risks souring the relationship with the IMF—a turn that could mean tougher conditions and stingier loans in the future (not to mention more contentious relations with private financial actors because the IMF acts as a gatekeeper for the international financial community).[16]

Leaders of governments that were under IMF programs, then, had strong incentives to appoint and retain policymakers that deliver results while in office, but results can mean more than just higher rates of economic growth or lower price inflation; for governments that were involved in IMF agreements, results could also mean an improved relationship with the officials based in Washington. Retaining the officials in whom the IMF decision makers had vested a good deal of confidence—even if those officials' policy preferences were at odds with the views of the public or the ministers in other cabinet positions—could be a sensible strategy for executives in countries buffeted by payments and capital account crises.

The argument generates two central implications: (1) neoliberal economic policymakers in governments under IMF programs should survive in office longer than non-neoliberal policymakers in countries under IMF programs; and (2) neoliberals should be more common fixtures in government in the countries that had lengthier spells under IMF lending arrangements.

The IMF and the Political Survival of Economic Policymakers

Next I examine the covariates of the political survival of economic officials in countries under active IMF programs; the analysis is limited to the two top economic officials in borrowing countries: finance ministers and central bank governors.[17] I do not examine the survival of heads of governments; there is now an active literature on leaders, and the dynamics that govern the removal of leaders

---

16. During and after the sovereign debt crisis of the early 1980s, private banks and official creditors (organized through the Paris Club) usually made debt-rescheduling contingent on the debtor having signed an IMF agreement (see Boughton 2001).

17. It might seem surprising to argue that both types of economic policymakers are subject to similar political forces. After all, finance ministers are political appointees who are members of cabinets, whereas the central banks in many countries are, in principle, insulated from political pressures. Most countries have a legal term of appointment for central bank governors; in the historically rich Northern countries, the executive's ability to intervene in the functioning of central banks is severely proscribed. But the independence of central banks in many, if not most, developing countries is more myth than reality. For this reason, some researchers measure central bank independence in low- and middle-income countries using the turnover rate of the governors rather than the legal independence of the bank (Cukierman 1992; Dreher, Sturm, and de Haan 2008).

are very different from the processes by which economic policymakers gain and lose office.[18]

I have data for 905 finance ministers in developing and emerging countries (810 of them were recorded as "failures," meaning that they exited the data set at some point during the 1980–2000, observation window) and 471 central bank governors (396 failures). The smaller number of central bankers is a consequence of their longer average duration in office compared to their counterparts in the finance ministry, the exclusion of a number of African countries that were in monetary unions and did not have independent central banks, and difficulties identifying reasonably precise entry and exit dates for central bankers in several countries that appear in the finance ministers data set. When the entry or exit dates are very uncertain, the official (or country, if information is very unreliable) is excluded from the data set. The data are right-censored, meaning that policymakers who remained in office after December 31, 2000, contribute information on survival but are not recorded as failures.[19] The average duration for the 810 finance ministers who exited office at some point in the two decades was 711.6 days.[20] Central bank governors had, on average, lengthier tenures than their counterparts in the finance ministry. The mean duration in office for the 396 central bankers who entered and exited the data set was 1,200 days.

Figures 6.1 and 6.2 provide an initial cut at the question. In the figures, I compare the Kaplan-Meier survivor functions for neoliberal (coded 1) and non-neoliberal (coded 0) finance ministers (figure 6.1) and central bank governors (figure 6.2) in IMF program countries. Recall from chapter 3 that a policymaker is coded as holding neoliberal beliefs if she obtained graduate training in a highly ranked U.S. economics department and/or gained significant work experience in the Fund or World Bank.

Only 62 percent of non-neoliberal finance ministers in countries under active IMF programs survived past the one-year mark, whereas 73 percent of neoliberals remained in office after one year. By two years after the date of appointment, the difference between neoliberal and non-neoliberal finance ministers is more pronounced: 35 percent of the non-neoliberals made it past the 730-day mark,

---

18. Since Bienen and van de Walle's path-breaking analysis, quantitative studies of the factors that affect the tenure of executives have proliferated. A comprehensive review is far beyond the scope of this chapter; for some important research, see Bienen and van de Walle 1991; Chiozza and Goemans 2004; Goemans 2008; Londregan and Poole 1990; Marinov 2005; Bueno de Mesquita et al. 2003.

19. I also treat policymakers who exited because of death from natural causes or an incapacitating illness as censored.

20. This does not mean that 810 different finance ministers exited the data set at some point between 1980 and 2000; if a policymaker was removed but returned to office at a later date, I record the entry as if she were a new policymaker.

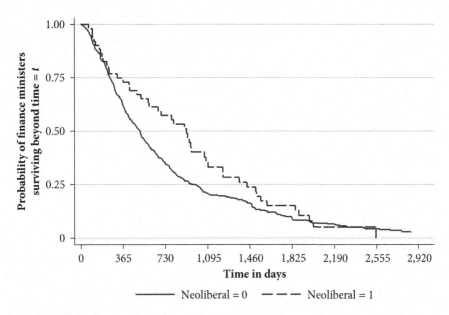

FIGURE 6.1 Kaplan-Meier survival estimates for finance ministers under IMF programs, stratified by neoliberal indicator

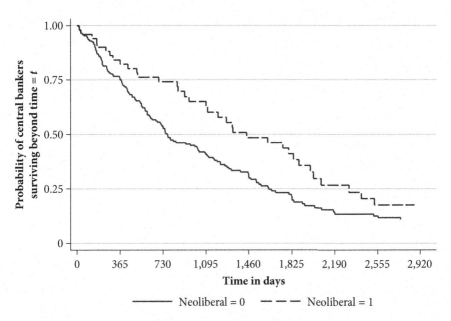

FIGURE 6.2 Kaplan-Meier survival estimates for central bankers under IMF programs, stratified by neoliberal indicator

whereas 58 percent of the neoliberals were still in office after two years. Only after five years do the survivor functions intersect: 9 percent of non-neoliberals and 10 percent of neoliberals in countries with IMF programs survived past 1,882 days.[21]

Figure 6.2 illustrates that difference in survivor functions between neoliberals and non-neoliberals is even greater for central bank governors. By the end of the first year following the appointment, there is a nearly 10-point gap between neoliberals (84 percent surviving) and non-neoliberals (75 percent). The gap increases as more time passed; after four years, 48 percent of the neoliberal central bank governors in countries under IMF programs were still in power, compared to just 30 percent of bankers without neoliberal credentials.[22]

COVARIATES IN THE STATISTICAL MODELS OF POLITICAL SURVIVAL

To see whether the differences in survival prospects persist after I control for other variables that affect the hazard for individuals in policymaking positions, I test the dichotomous neoliberal policymaker indicator alongside several other covariates. I draw the other covariates from two explanations for the durability in office of policymakers. In the first approach, the risks that individual economic policymakers faced were mainly influenced by specific attributes of the governments in which they served (e.g., whether the government was a "caretaker" between elections); the nexus of practices and political institutions that distinguished different regime types (democratic or autocratic); and political events such as elections, no-confidence votes, and coups that led to the replacement of the head of government.

One place to look for possible covariates of durability of economic policymakers is the growing body of research on the tenure of political leaders. Evidence suggests that regime type has an important effect on the prospects for political survival; because autocratic leaders tend to outlast their democratically elected counterparts, we would expect to find that economic policymakers face elevated risks in democratic regimes.[23] Consequently, I include a set of dichotomous variables as proxies for the domestic institutional explanation of varying survival times. I use the same approach as Chiozza and Goemans: dichotomous

---

21. I used log-rank tests to assess whether the differences in survivor functions were statistically significant. The test reveals that the difference between neoliberal and non-neoliberal finance ministers under IMF programs is in fact statistically significant ($\chi^2 = 4.21$; $p = 0.04$).

22. The log-rank test confirms that the difference in survivor functions between neoliberal and non-neoliberal central bankers is highly statistically significant ($\chi^2 = 6.20$; $p = 0.013$).

23. For the logic of the argument, see Bueno de Mesquita et al. 2003.

indicators for mixed regimes, parliamentary (democracies), and presidential (democracies) are created based on scores from the Polity IV data set. Democracies are countries that receive a score of 7 or higher on the 21-point Polity scale; mixed regimes have a score between −6 and +6, and autocratic governments have scores less than −6. In the pool of democratic countries, Chiozza and Goemans distinguish parliamentary from presidential systems.[24] I rely on their coding of political systems in the analysis. I expect to find that the likelihood of exit is higher in democracies than in autocracies and that, among democracies, it is higher in parliamentary systems due to the greater instability of coalition governments.

I include two other covariates to capture political factors that can influence survival. Frequently, the replacement of the leader of a country leads to a turnover of all the important officials in the previous government. To account for this dynamic, I create an indicator (change of executive) that takes a value of 1 if the chief of government was replaced at any point in the policymakers' tenure.[25] I also create a variable (caretaker government) that measures whether a finance minister was a member of an interim (caretaker or transitional) government (this variable does not apply to central bankers, who are not cabinet members).[26]

Economic performance affects the prospects for policymakers in all types of regimes. Previous work shows that the hazard rises as the state of the economy worsens. The relationship between macroeconomic conditions and political survival should be heightened for finance ministers and central bank governors. After all, their jobs involve the management of the economy. If the economic situation degrades, they bear the primary responsibility. It has long been recognized that the stewards of the economy face special risks. Richard Cooper's classic study, for example, reveals that, in a majority of the twenty-four cases he studied, the finance minister was removed after a large devaluation of the currency.[27]

I rely on three variables to assess the impact of economic conditions on political survival. High inflation is an indicator of poor economic performance. Consequently, I use a transformed measure of the annual change in consumer

---

24. Chiozza and Goemans 2004, 617.

25. This includes the policymaker's last day in office. The measure captures the replacement of an entire government after, for example, an election or a coup. The list of leaders and their dates of entry and exit from office comes from the *Archigos*, version 2.8, data set put together by political scientists Hein Goemans, Kristian Skrede Gleditsch, and Giacomo Chiozza, http://www.rochester.edu/college/faculty/hgoemans/data.htm (last accessed June 24, 2015).

26. I relied on the *Keesings Record of World Events* resource to generate the caretaker/transition variable, http://www.keesings.com/.

27. Cooper 1971.

price inflation (inflation).[28] In many studies, economic growth has been linked to the survival of leaders, and it is included in both of the models reported here.[29] Finally, I incorporate a covariate to account for the impact of dramatic events in the exchange market. The currency crisis indicator comes from Laevan and Valencia; it takes a value of 1 in the year in which a country experiences a nominal devaluation of its currency of at least 30 percent that is also at least a 10 percent hike in the rate of depreciation compared to the previous year.[30]

Before discussing the findings, it is necessary to explain the manner in which the tests are designed. Recall that I am evaluating the claim that the hazard rate for neoliberal finance ministers and central bank governors is lower under IMF programs. To observe the impact of the neoliberal policymaker variable on political survival, I control for the presence of IMF lending arrangements; in other words, conditional on being under an IMF program, neoliberals should remain in office longer than non-neoliberals, after I account for other factors.[31] Consequently I restrict the sample to countries under active IMF programs during the 1980–2000 period.[32] This strategy, along with some data being missing, reduces the number of finance ministers I observe to 539 (of whom 401 were failures) and the number of central bankers to 295 (192 failures).

STATISTICAL METHODS

I make use of the workhorse of event history modeling, the Cox proportional hazards model, in the data analysis. The Cox model has become the preferred approach to analyzing survival data because of its flexibility; although the

---

28. To reduce skewness due to a few episodes of hyperinflation, I transformed the measure of inflation using: $(\pi/100)/(1 + (\pi/100))$, where π is the annual percentage change in the consumer price index. This is the same transformation used in Dreher, Sturm, and de Haan 2008.

29. Data for inflation and GDP growth are taken from the World Bank *World Development Indicators*, http://data.worldbank.org/data-catalog/world-development-indicators.

30. Laevan and Valencia 2008.

31. The wrong test would be to compare the survival of neoliberals under IMF programs to the survival of non-neoliberals in countries *not* under IMF programs; in that case, it would be impossible to tell whether the differing hazards were due to the IMF or to neoliberal credentials. Looking only at IMF borrowers enables me to observe whether being a neoliberal under the IMF offered the anticipated payoff in terms of lower hazard. This approach also mitigates some of the concerns about selection effects. For example, if I compared the survival of neoliberals in countries that were under IMF programs to neoliberal policymakers in countries without IMF programs, we might reasonably ask whether officials whose tenure was more durable (for reasons that are potentially unobservable) disproportionately sought out IMF funding. It does not make sense to claim that more durable policymakers, once in office, obtained neoliberal credentials because the experiences that transmit neoliberal economic beliefs in my coding scheme must occur *prior* to their gaining office.

32. I use data from Vreeland (2003) and my own archival research on IMF lending arrangements to create an indicator that takes a value of 1 for each year that a country was under a program and 0 otherwise.

covariates are parameterized, the shape of the baseline hazard (rising, decreasing, or constant) is unspecified.[33] I use the Efron method to handle coterminous failure events in the data.[34]

I make two modifications to the basic Cox hazard model. The first modification deals with country-level heterogeneity in the political durability of policymakers. It is clear from a look at the data that the rate of turnover of economic policymakers is very high in some countries and relatively low in others. For some (possibly unobservable) reason, policymakers in certain countries may be more prone to failure. To handle country-specific heterogeneity, I add a parameter to the specification (a frailty term), which is akin to a random effect. For identification, the unmeasured frailty parameter (v) is sampled from a gamma distribution and is assumed to have a mean of 1 and an unknown variance equal to θ.[35]

The other modification concerns the proportionality assumption of the Cox model. The assumption of proportional hazards implies that the effect of covariates on the hazard is constant over the time that each policymaker is in office. If the proportionality assumption is violated, a correction (an interaction between the covariate and the natural logarithm of time) has to be applied to obtain unbiased estimates.[36] I first implemented global tests for nonproportionality in both data sets, which were easily rejected. I then followed the standard practice and examined the plots of scaled Schoenfeld residuals against survival times.[37] The only covariate that displayed clear patterns of nonproportionality was the transformed inflation variable. Consequently, the models include Inflation as well as an interaction between the covariate and the log of time.

I report coefficients rather than hazard rates in the presentation of the results. Negative coefficients imply a decreasing hazard (longer survival); positive coefficients indicate that the covariate increases the risk of losing office.[38] As in

---

33. The Cox model takes the form: $h(t) = h_0(t)\exp(X_{it}\beta)$, where X_{it} is the vector of covariates and $h_0(t)$ represents the unspecified baseline hazard. For a very lucid discussion of the Cox model, see Box-Steffensmeier and Jones 2004, 47–67. Box-Steffensmeier and Jones make their view about handling multivariate analysis of duration data clear: "apply the Cox model. . . . The Cox model makes no assumptions about the distributional characteristics of the baseline hazard rate, yet can provide estimates of the covariates of interest that have desirable properties allowing the usual kinds of hypothesis tests" (193).

34. Ibid., 55.

35. Ibid., 142–48; Chiozza and Goemans 2004, 607.

36. Box-Steffensmeier, Reiter, and Zorn 2003.

37. Blossfeld, Golsch, Rohwer 2007, 233–37; Box-Steffensmeier and Jones 2004, 120–21, 131–39.

38. I interpret the substantive impact of coefficients in terms of percentage change in the hazard. I use the following simple formulas to assess the impact of unit changes in a covariate on either increasing or decreasing the hazard rate for policymakers: $[(1 - e^\beta) \times 100]$ for negative coefficients and $[(e^\beta - 1) \times 100]$ for positive coefficients obtained from the Cox model. For a different formula that yields the same point estimates, see Box-Steffensmeier and Jones 2004, 60.

chapter 3, I visualize the regression results using dotplots, which display the point estimates and 95 percent confidence intervals for each of the covariates in the models.

RESULTS OF THE SURVIVAL ANALYSIS

I start the discussion with the model of the survival of finance ministers ($N = 1,253$). Based on the point estimate reported in the visualization of the results in figure 6.3, neoliberal finance ministers were approximately 30 percent less likely to be removed from office than non-neoliberals in countries that borrowed from the Fund (the 95 percent confidence interval around that point estimate, however, is wide, ranging from a minimum of 1.3 percent to a maximum of 51 percent). The most important implication from the results of the Cox hazard model of the survival of finance ministers is that neoliberal policymakers were politically advantaged when their governments entered into IMF lending programs, an effect that is observed in their lengthier tenures.

Several other interesting patterns emerge from the model of the political survival of finance ministers. Compared to their counterparts in autocratic regimes, finance ministers in democracies and mixed regimes face greater risks of removal. For finance ministers under IMF programs, presidential regimes provide the

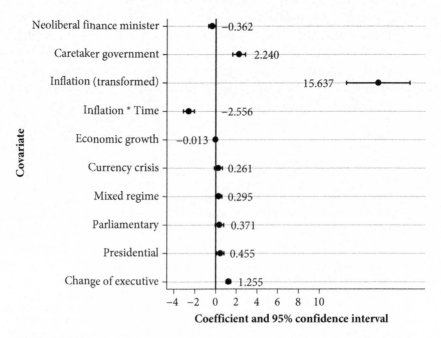

FIGURE 6.3 Covariates of the tenure of finance ministers in IMF program countries

riskiest institutional setting: the coefficient on the presidential democracy covariate indicates a 57 percent increase in the hazard of removal. According to the results reported in figure 6.3, the replacement of the leader in countries under IMF programs increases the odds that a finance minister will be removed by 250 percent. Inflation has an interesting impact on the political survival of finance ministers in the subsample. In the early stages of a policymaker's time in office, high inflation was deadly; however, the impact of inflation on political survival dissipates over time (based on the negative coefficient for the interaction between inflation and the log of time, Inflation * Time). Few finance ministers survived a bout of hyperinflation early in their time in office, but for those who did, continued price instability had diminishing effects on their prospects for survival

In figure 6.4, I present the results from a Cox model of the determinants of the survival of central bankers in countries under IMF lending arrangements ($N = 846$). The results dovetail with the findings for finance ministers in several ways. Inflation damaged their prospects for survival (although, again, the impact decayed over time). Central bankers found it difficult—although less difficult than finance ministers—to survive the removal of the chief of government (the hazard increased by, on average, 67 percent for central bank governors when the executive was replaced; it increased 250 percent for finance ministers). The main

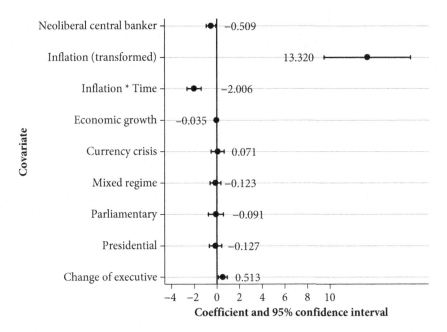

FIGURE 6.4 Covariates of the tenure of central bankers in IMF program countries

difference in the results for the two top economic officials is that the proxies for regime type have no impact on the political duration of the central bank governors. There were apparently no significant differences in the risks for central bankers in democratic, mixed, or autocratic regimes in the pool of countries that borrowed from the IMF.

A negative and significant coefficient is additional evidence in favor of the claim that neoliberal policymakers become more valuable under IMF programs, and this is indeed what I observe: holding other covariates constant, the hazard rate for neoliberal central bankers in countries that turned to the IMF was lowered by about 40 percent (with the uncertainty band around that estimate spanning 8.5 to 61 percent).

In an alternative specification, I included an indicator that measures the degree of central bank independence (CBI index) as a covariate of the survival of central bank governors. I wanted to make sure that the neoliberal indicator is not just a stand-in for the delegation of an official by the government to an independent central bank (presumably, a monetary authority freed from government control has more leeway in appointing and retaining its top officials).[39] The limitation of CBI index is its relatively limited country coverage: it does not include any African or Eastern European states; thus, the number of observations drops from 846 to 360 when the CBI index variable is included in the specification.

Nevertheless, the correlation between the neoliberal indicator and time in office held up when CBI index was included as an additional covariate. In fact, the substantive impact was of the neoliberal indicator was slightly larger: the estimated coefficient ($\beta = -0.572$) implies that the hazard of removal for neoliberal central bankers in countries involved in IMF lending programs was reduced by 43 percent (the 95 percent confidence interval range around the point estimate was 6–66 percent).

The findings from the models of the survival of finance minister and central bankers are consistent with my argument. For countries that needed to make use of IMF resources, the ability of neoliberal economic officials to deliver tangible benefits in the form of more generous, less onerous loans increased their value and, in turn, their durability in the political positions to which they were appointed. In the pool of countries that signed IMF programs, the individuals whom I identified as neoliberals kept their positions longer than their non-neoliberal counterparts.

As an additional test of the argument, I compared the average duration of neoliberals and non-neoliberal policymakers in countries that were *not* under

---

39. The index of central bank independence is taken from the data set compiled by Acemoglu et al (2008).

IMF lending arrangements using simple difference-of-means tests. If neoliberals are more politically durable in general, they should outlast, on average, non-neoliberals in countries that were not participating in IMF programs, as well. Table 6.1 provides further evidence that the politics surrounding the retention of economic officials is affected by participation in IMF lending programs. While the average tenure of neoliberal finance ministers exceeded the tenure of non-neoliberals by 200 days, the small t-statistic and p value (0.18), which fall below conventional levels of statistical significance, suggests that we should view the difference in the means of the two types in the sample with some caution. The bottom row in table 6.1 shows that there was essentially no difference in the average survival of the two types of central bankers when the subsample was limited to countries not under IMF programs ($t = 0.32$; $p = 0.75$).

The statistical analysis of the determinants of the tenures of a large sample of finance ministers and central bankers from low- and middle-income countries—the first of its kind, as far as I am aware—confirms what some scholars of the process of economic policymaking have long suspected: the presence of IMF lending programs raises the political value of the neoliberal-type officials in the economic policy team.

The argument and analysis cast the politics of the relationship of the IMF with its borrowers in a different light. Most of the existing work on the impact of the IMF on its borrowers uses the mechanism of coercive diffusion as the analytical point of departure for understanding how (and how much) the lending programs of the Fund promote changes in the domestic and foreign economic policies of countries. This is an important ongoing research agenda. Nevertheless, too much attention has been directed to the policy-change-by-IMF-coercion theme. The imbalance of scholarly attention means that, when it comes to other politically consequential effects of the extensive involvement of the IMF in the economies of countries, international relations scholars are, comparatively, in the dark. The evidence that we have is often fragmentary and untethered to any clear

TABLE 6.1 Average tenure of policymakers in countries not under IMF programs, 1980–2000 (in days)

GOVERNMENT POSITION OF POLICYMAKER	TYPE OF POLICYMAKER		T-STATISTIC FOR DIFFERENCE OF MEANS
	NEOLIBERAL	NON-NEOLIBERAL	
Finance minister	873.82	673.55	−1.37
	(N = 39)	(N = 342)	(p = 0.18)
Central banker	1,355.72	1,288.74	−0.32
	(N = 36)	(N = 164)	(p = 0.75)

theoretical propositions. This chapter is a modest step toward a better understanding of how participation in IMF programs can transform the politics of countries. My entry point for that effort came through the question of how the politics of political survival are affected by participation in IMF lending facilities. I have found evidence that, for the individuals identified as neoliberals in the data set, the hazard rate fell (hence, their expected tenures increased) when the governments in which they served entered into agreements with the Fund.

Out of the entire sample of policymakers that I collected for this study, I identified just over two hundred episodes during which an official with neoliberal socialization experiences in her background occupied a key position in the government. Those episodes were not evenly distributed among the countries in the sample; in some cases (e.g., Argentina), neoliberals had by the mid-1990s consolidated their grip on the domestic policymaking institutions, but in other countries, the types of individuals whom I would code as being most likely to view the economy through the neoliberal lens were nowhere to be found.

IMF Program Participation and the Composition of Economic Policy Teams

Next, I take one more look at the question of how the IMF, through its conditional loans, impacted policymaking in borrowing countries—this time by exploring the relationship between cross-sectional variation of countries in their proportion neoliberal scores and the frequency of their involvement in IMF lending programs over a several-decade span of time. To explore the relationship between the share of neoliberals in the top ranks of an economic policy team and the fraction of years countries spent under IMF arrangements, I calculated two country-level averages. I first calculated the average value of the proportion neoliberal variable for each of the countries in the sample during the 1990s. Recall that this indicator is constructed by combining the information about the key policy positions in each country extracted from the Letters of Intent submitted to the Fund with biographical information on the individual policymakers. The economic policy team in the analysis thus consists of the signatories to the agreement (usually, but not always, the finance minister and central bank head) plus the head of government; proportion neoliberal is constructed as the proportion of the individuals on a policy team who met the coding criteria for being recorded as a neoliberal. To capture the extensiveness of the involvement of different countries with IMF lending programs, I took the fraction of the years between 1975 and 2000 in which each country was enrolled in one of the Fund lending facilities (including information from the decade and a half preceding

the 1990s is a way to mitigate the possibility that countries with higher proportion neoliberal values were more likely to be frequent users of IMF resources,
rather than the other way around).

The bivariate relationship between the two indicators is shown in the scat-
terplot displayed in figure 6.5. The average value of proportion neoliberal for
eighty-two countries is plotted on the y axis; the indicator of the frequency of
involvement in IMF programs is tracked on the x axis. The observed values on the
two dimensions for each country appear in the plot as three-letter abbreviations
of the country name. The regression line that appears in the plot is fitted from a
robust estimator to reduce the influence of outlying observations.

There is a positive—although not particularly strong—association between
the two variables. The regression line slopes upward, suggesting that values of
the proportion neoliberal variable were higher in the countries that spent more
time under IMF programs. Further, the coefficient on the indicator measuring
the fraction of years that a country was under IMF arrangements proves to be
both positive and statistically significant in a regression analysis. The coefficient,
standard errors, and p values from the regression model are each reported in
table 6.2. I modeled the statistical relationship using a robust estimator to handle
the problem posed by outliers.

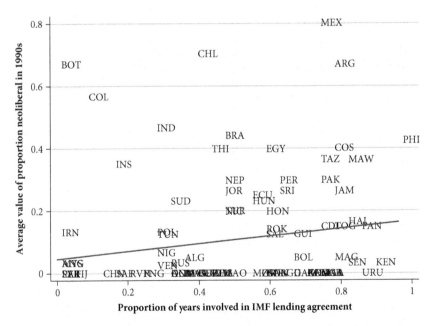

FIGURE 6.5   The bivariate correlation between the average value of proportion
neoliberal in the 1990s and fraction of years spent under IMF agreements since
1975

TABLE 6.2   Statistical relationship between proportion neoliberal and time spent under IMF lending arrangements

	COVARIATES OF AVERAGE VALUE OF PROPORTION NEOLIBERAL IN THE 1990S (*N* = 82)	
	(1) Robust regression model with %years under IMF arrangements as the only covariate	(2) Robust regression model with additional covariates: log of per capita GDP, per capita oil production, Polity2 score, and left-wing government
%YEARS UNDER IMF ARRANGEMENTS	$0.139^{0.031}$ (0.063)	$0.147^{0.025}$ (0.067)

Notes: Standard errors appear in parentheses. The *p* values appear as superscripts on the coefficients.

The positive correlation between the extensiveness of the involvement of countries in IMF lending programs and the commonness of neoliberals in policy teams holds when I include several other covariates that might also have impacted the country-specific value of proportion neoliberal in the 1990s. In the second model specification reported in table 6.2, I add indicators for the level of development (the log of per capita GDP), a measure of per capita oil wealth,[40] a measure of the share of years in which the executive was from a left-wing party and/or a left-wing party was the dominant political force in government, and an indicator of the level of democracy (the Polity2 score).[41] None of the other covariates were significant in the regression; hence, I do not report the full set of results in the table. The conclusion that I draw from the analysis is that there is a small but positive and robust association between the degree to which the IMF was involved, through the instrument of conditional loans, in the economic and political affairs of countries and the proportion of neoliberals in the composition of the economic policy team.

The findings are consistent with the expectations laid out in the first sections of the chapter. The pattern of favoritism evinced in the differences in the size, conditions, and enforcement of loans signed by governments with and without

---

40. The measure is taken from Humphreys 2005. Sachs and Warner (2001) suggest that natural resource wealth diverts attention from more productive economic activities; Ross (2001) argues that oil income retards social changes that might otherwise lead to better governance. It is no great leap to expect that the supply of and demand for neoliberal economists is weaker in countries where oil is the main driver of economic activity.

41. The other indicators were calculated as the average between 1980 and 2000 for each country in the cross section.

neoliberal officials spilled over into the politics determining the composition of governmental economic policy teams. Confidence among the decision makers at the home base of the Fund in Washington translated into greater power and more durable influence for the neoliberals on the policy team at home.

Conclusion

One of the emerging themes in the literature on market globalization is that, contrary to the "flattened world" imagery propagated by journalist Thomas Friedman,[42] the effects of globalization are in fact highly spatially uneven. The disciplining effect of globalized financial markets, for example, appears to be considerably more powerful in the developing world than in the historically rich Northern countries.[43] The narrowing of the range for macroeconomic policy experimentation in developing countries is a central concern in Ilene Grabel's work on the politics of macroeconomic "policy credibility"; in her view, the delegation of policymaking authority in many countries to unelected monetary bodies reflects the influence of powerful transnational economic interests more than the apolitical logic of economic efficiency.[44]

A broader normative implication emerges from this line of work: to the extent that greater openness to the forces of market globalization and market-friendly institutional change in the realm of policymaking has meant the abrogation of some sets of policy alternatives, there has been a concomitant diminution in the democratic quality of economic governance. The gap between what the masses want from their governments and what the policymakers at the helm of the economy will actually deliver widens. And in trying to "depoliticize" economic policymaking by putting the instruments in the hands of largely unaccountable experts, some fear that "it may prove difficult to sustain a minimal social consensus around this latest project of modernity . . . [exposing the project] to potentially destabilizing resistance and even backlash."[45]

The evidence in this chapter shows that the IMF, through its lending facilities, has become a player in the politics surrounding the composition of the economic policy teams of countries. When countries entered into IMF arrangements, neoliberal-type officials benefited from their links to the decision makers in Washington, DC. Greater confidence abroad yielded bigger loans with fewer

---

42. Friedman 2005.
43. Mosley 2006; Wibbels 2006.
44. Grabel 2000.
45. Santiso and Whitehead 2012, 447–48.

(and more lightly enforced) conditions; at home, the ability of neoliberals to deliver more favorable treatment by the Fund extended their tenures in office. For the developing countries that spent large parts of the 1980s and 1990s under IMF-led adjustment programs, politics were still mostly local but also increasingly global, shaped as they were by a powerful institution of global economic governance.

My key finding in this chapter—that IMF program participation affected domestic-level decisions to appoint and retain a certain type of policymaker (distinguished by the socializing experiences in her background prior to entering office)—connects to the issues of accountability and representation raised by the work on the political consequences of market globalization. IMF decisions are not subject to evaluation and, if found wanting, not subject to correction by the masses in the borrowing countries—yet its decisions are highly consequential for domestic political processes (including the selection of the governors of the borrowing economies) that many believe *should* be consistent with practices of democratic accountability. The implications of this study for the reform of the organization are among the issues that I take up next.

IMPLICATIONS, EXTENSIONS, AND SPECULATIONS

The IMF and Its Borrowers, in and out of Hard Times

> **The IMF has behaved with the same level of misunderstanding, recommending the same old adjustment plans that just don't work. They have learnt absolutely nothing at all.**
>
> Roberto Lavagna, former Argentine economy minister, July 2015

"Differences in beliefs regarding the range of legitimate macroeconomic policies," Jonathan Kirshner observes, "clearly exist across nations, within nations across time, and in distinct global eras as well—and these differences matter."[1] Few scholars of international relations (save, perhaps, for the most ardent materialists) would object to this observation. Yet international relations scholars have not always been able to explain precisely *how* differences in economic beliefs matter—nor have they always shown *how much* they matter compared to alternative explanations. In this book, I advance a framework with pathways connecting neoliberal economic beliefs held by IMF decision makers and by policymakers in borrowing countries to variation in the relations between the two sides. In the empirical sections of the book, I have shown that shared beliefs are indeed a powerful explanatory factor.

I am far from the first to highlight the embeddedness of neoliberal economic ideas in the organizational culture of the Fund.[2] But in this book I push an ideational framework in new directions, first, by developing several testable mechanisms that link the degree to which IMF officials and top policymakers in borrowing countries share (and do not share) common beliefs to the decisions made by the organization about access to credit by the borrowers, the comprehensiveness

---

Epigraph: Quoted in Benedict Mander, "Greek Woe Brings Powerful Sense of Déjà Vu for Argentina," *Financial Times*, online ed., July 9, 2015, http://www.ft.com/cms/s/0/5d8c9462–25c2–11e5-bd83–71cb60e8f08c.html.

1. Kirshner 2007, 217.

2. Babb 2007; Barnett and Finnemore 2004; Chwieroth 2010; Stiglitz 2003; Woods 2006.

of conditionality in IMF programs, and the laxity of enforcement of those conditions and, second, by testing the strength of argument with new quantitative data on IMF treatment and the composition of the policy teams of the borrowing countries, as well as by closely examining the relationship of the organization with Argentina over a twenty-five year period (1976–2002).

Here, I first briefly review my ideational argument and compare it to the alternative political explanations for the puzzle that motivates the analysis: the sources of systematic variation in IMF-borrower relations. I then pivot to a discussion of the main implications of my arguments and findings for the reform of the IMF. Finally, I extend the argument about how shared beliefs shape IMF-borrower relations to the environment after the onset of the Global Financial Crisis of 2008, providing some preliminary statistical evidence suggesting that the IMF is, in fact, still "playing favorites" in its lending decisions.

Political Explanations for the Variation in Treatment

Why does the Fund systematically treat some borrowing members differently than others? As I point out in chapter 1, the answers proffered by international relations scholars writing on the Fund in recent years have usually focused on factors such as the strategic and economic interests of powerful member states and private economic actors (and the outsized influence that these actors may wield over the organization), the domestic political institutions and interest groups that structure bargains struck between the two sides, and the incentives and constraints facing the self-interested individual bureaucrats who have a hand in designing the programs of the organization.

Shared economic beliefs fade into the background in these kinds of explanations for variation in IMF-borrower relations.[3] Many seem to doubt the sincerity of the rhetorical volleys launched by hostile policymakers at the Fund and its neoliberal-oriented approach to adjustment and economic development; lurking behind the (ostensibly) heated ideological debates, they argue, is the cold, simple truth that governments do not want to take the blame for making hard decisions that might make citizens' lives more difficult and that the IMF serves as

---

3. Barnett and Finnemore's (2004) approach, built on the concept of organizational culture, is an important exception—but (as I note in chapter 1) their argument is limited in its empirical scope. It is better suited to explaining the expansion of conditionality over time than to explaining variation from borrower to borrower, and it sheds little light on the other elements of conditional lending (the relative generosity of access to IMF resources and the enforcement of conditionality).

a convenient scapegoat onto which political elites can shunt some of the blame. Scapegoating is not an uncommon feature of the interactions of the IMF with its borrowers—but in dismissing the possibilities that, first, there are sincere (and enduring) differences in decision makers' economic beliefs and, second, that the distance between the actors' beliefs exerts a powerful effect on IMF-borrower relations, we risk limiting our understanding of how this linchpin of global economic governance works.

The ideational approach that I develop in this book is built on several empirically- and theoretically informed claims about the IMF and its borrowers, starting with the argument that IMF thinking has (since the early 1980s, at least) been rooted in a set of neoliberal economic principles and policy implications. To explain why the dominance of neoliberal economic beliefs in the Fund can be a powerful source of variation (rather than consistency) in the treatment by the organization of its borrowers, I have described how, at each step in the lending process, the IMF staff and management must engage in making subjective judgments about the prospects of the borrowers. And IMF officials' subjective judgments are, in my argument, made under conditions of strong (or Knightian) uncertainty.

Uncertainty plays two important roles in my argument. First, it helps us understand why the staff and management of the organization have managed to attain such a high degree of autonomy from outside forces that might otherwise seek to use the Fund to advance their own narrow interests. And second, the uncertainty facing both the Fund decision makers and the policy elites at the helm of borrowing economies is a key reason why sizable differences of opinion can persist—even when both sides share the same information.

The more closely the beliefs of the officials occupying the top posts in government match the beliefs held by the Fund decision makers, the greater is the confidence of the Fund that the borrower will "do the right things." More confidence in the team that manages the borrowing economy, in turn, leads to programs that are more generously funded (because IMF officials are more likely to believe that a program managed by neoliberal-oriented policymakers will succeed), less comprehensive in terms of conditionality (because trusted policy teams need less oversight), and more laxly enforced (because leniency can be a way for the Fund to supply political support for like-minded policymakers struggling to stay in office).

The novel elements of the ideational approach—and the explanatory power of my arguments—are made clearer when situated alongside the other prominent explanations for systematic variation in how the IMF treats its borrowers. In table 7.1, I group together four explanations under the material-rationalist label. What all these explanations share is a basic assumption that the decision-making

TABLE 7.1 Explanations for variation in the treatment of borrowers by the IMF

	MATERIAL-RATIONALIST				SOCIOLOGICAL-CONSTRUCTIVIST	
	GREAT POWER POLITICS	PRIVATE ECONOMIC POWER	BUREAUCRATIC PUBLIC CHOICE	STRATEGIC DESIGN AND ENFORCEMENT	PATHOLOGIES OF ORGANIZATIONAL CULTURES	SHARED ECONOMIC BELIEFS
Key analytical assumptions (level of discretion/ decision-making environment)	Low discretion/ (mainly) risk	Low discretion/ (mainly) risk	High discretion/ (mainly) risk	High discretion/(mainly) risk	High discretion/ (mainly) uncertainty	High discretion/(mainly) uncertainty
Implications for IMF-borrower relations	Materially powerful members influence staff and management (through formal and informal means) to give easier terms of IMF programs to strategically important borrowers	Powerful private economic actors (e.g., financial sector) exert influence (formally and informally) to bring terms of IMF programs closer to their preferences	Self-interested staff members strategically use instruments of lending to maximize their power, prestige, and income (and ensure IO survival)	Strategic bargains struck by IMF and borrower shaped by economic (e.g., market size) and domestic political features (e.g., regime type, government partisanship, societal interests)	Bureaucratic culture generates predictable "pathologies," including a tendency toward "mission creep" (conditionality driven by IMF expansionary drive)	Degree to which IMF officials and key policymakers in borrowing country share set of neoliberal economic beliefs drives decisions about loan size, conditionality, and enforcement
Strength of fit between explanation and evidence	Weak (no clear link between indicators of strategic importance and IMF treatment variables in chapter 3)	Mixed/weak (indicators weakly correlated with loan size, conditionality, and enforcement)	Mixed/weak (inconsistently associated with IMF treatment variables in chapter 3)	Mixed (GDP–loan size correlation is strong; domestic variables sometimes correlated with treatment indicators)	Mixed (link between number conditions and passage of time confirmed in chapter 3, but explanation has very limited explanatory scope)	Strong (very strong links between proportion neoliberal and IMF treatment in chapter 3; qualitative evidence in Argentina case study)

setting facing IMF officials is primarily one of calculable risk (rather than of strong uncertainty). The material-rationalist approaches part ways, however, on another basic issue: the degree to which the organization can act autonomously. Two of the explanations (labeled in table 7.1 as "Great Power politics" and "Private economic power") assume that any discretion accorded to the Fund staff and management on matters of program design and enforcement is usurped when materially powerful actors (states motivated primarily to advance their strategic interests or private (typically financial) interests exerting their influence indirectly by getting state officials to serve as their agents or by lobbying the organization more directly) intervene in the IMF decision-making processes. The other two explanations ("Bureaucratic public choice" and "Strategic design and enforcement") assume a greater degree of autonomy for the Fund from the controllers identified by the Great Power and Private economic power varieties.

The two explanations grouped together in table 7.1 as sociological-constructivist assume, by contrast, that uncertainty is a fundamental condition of the choice settings of the IMF (and the borrowers). The analytical attention in these approaches shifts away from the influence of the materially advantaged actors in world politics, the incentives facing self-aggrandizing staff members, and the formal institutions and organized domestic-level interests that structure strategic IMF-borrower bargaining and toward, instead, how the content of the organizational culture of the Fund affects outcomes. In Barnett and Finnemore's trail-blazing work, the drive by the Fund to bring more and more elements of the economies of its members under the purview of conditional lending is an outgrowth of its bureaucratic culture. Expansionism at the Fund is, in their argument, primarily staff- and management-led, and best understood as a bureaucratic response to the challenges posed by uncertainty and complexity. The argument is a powerful one but limited in its empirical application—it predicts only an incremental increase in conditionality over time. My argument builds on Barnett and Finnemore's effort to endogenize IO interests, but I focus more closely on the mechanisms connecting the neoliberal intellectual culture of the Fund to variation in each of the different elements of conditional lending.

Strengths and weaknesses of different explanations in the field of international political economy can, of course, be revealed by close investigation and comparison of their theoretical foundations; ultimately, however, as Rawi Abdelal argues, "their relative usefulness for understanding world politics is an empirical question, not a matter of whether one or another grand perspective on IPE [international political economy] is more right."[4] The bottom row of table 7.1

---

4. Abdelal 2001, 35.

compares the fit between the measures I use to capture the implications of different approaches to Fund-borrower relations and the evidence amassed in the book. The data on which I tested my argument and the most plausible alternatives are another major contribution of the book.

For the initial tests of the argument, I constructed several new data sets. I directly measured the indicators of the treatment by the IMF of its borrowers by first collecting from the Fund archives the documents spelling out the terms of nearly five hundred programs between 1980 and 2000. I then recorded the relative size and number of performance criteria in each program. I also gathered a record of all the Executive Board decisions to approve waivers in the 1980s and 1990s. I developed a measure of the ideational composition of the economic policy teams in a large number of low- and middle-income countries; to create the indicator (which I call proportion neoliberal), I identified the most important economic officials of the borrowing countries by looking at the signatories to the IMF agreements (plus each leader of the country); then I used an indirect method to pick out the policymakers that were likely to hold neoliberal economic beliefs: I looked for two socializing experiences in policymakers' backgrounds (graduate economics training in highly ranked U.S. economics departments and work experience in the ranks of the IMF and/ or the World Bank) that were likely to bring policymakers' beliefs closer to the views held by IMF officials.

The results of the statistical analyses, conducted using the large sample of IMF programs and a new measure of the makeup of the policy teams of the borrowers, fit well with the implications drawn from the theory: on average, policy teams filled with neoliberal-type officials received bigger loans (relative to the quota), received loans with fewer performance criteria, and received more waivers. I find that the statistical relationships between the proportion neoliberal covariate and the measures of IMF treatment are both strong and significant—and the findings are, in addition, relatively insensitive to changes in the way the models were specified.

In the statistical tests described in chapter 3, I find that, among the various explanations, the currency of confidence argument (connecting shared beliefs to favoritism in the treatment by the IMF of its borrowers) produced a measure that was both more powerful (in terms of accounting for variations in the loan size, number of conditions, and issuance of waivers) and more consistently significant than the variables suggested by the other prominent explanations.

The case study of the relationship of Argentina with the IMF supplied another way to examine the fit between the argument and the evidence. I selected Argentina for the in-depth case study because the turnover in its economic policy teams—not just in terms of the replacement of the individuals but in the (more relevant for my argument) changes in the ideational center of gravity of each team—during a twenty-five-year period in which the country was a frequent participant in IMF lending programs provided another opportunity to observe the link between shared beliefs and IMF-borrower relations. The fact that several of the Argentine programs were watershed moments in IMF history also motivated my choice to closely examine the case. The evidence in the case study (chapters 4 and 5), compiled from a rich secondary literature, news reports, interviews, and a treasure trove of documents recovered from the IMF archives, conforms well to the currency of confidence argument. IMF officials' greater confidence in the country when its top policymakers shared their basic beliefs (and, on the flipside, its lower confidence when policymakers in the country hewed more closely to the non-neoliberal, structuralist body of economic beliefs) sheds a good deal of light on some of the more puzzling episodes in the relationship: Why, for instance, did the Fund dole out relatively generous programs to the team working in an extraordinarily repressive (and diplomatically isolated) military regime? Why was the first team in the Alfonsín government treated so roughly, when the fledgling democracy of the country was under threat and the precariousness of its debt load threatened to spill over into other major countries in the region facing similarly difficult-to-manage debt burdens? Why were the Argentine programs of the 1990s essentially free of structural performance criteria and so laxly enforced? We cannot fully understand the outcomes of those episodes without looking to the shared economic beliefs that bring together or drive apart the IMF and its borrowers.

In chapter 6, I turn my attention to how participating in IMF programs impacts the politics shaping the tenures of top economic policymakers. I tested a claim that has emerged from the vast literature on the varied paths of developing countries to market-oriented policy reform: the Fund may have served (via its conditional lending programs) not just as a promoter of the diffusion of market-oriented policy changes but also as a key outside force in the reshaping of the national politics surrounding decisions to install and retain neoliberal-type economic officials. The analysis of the covariates of the tenures of a large sample of finance ministers and central bankers reveals that survival prospects were improved for neoliberals when their government was involved in an IMF lending program. I also find evidence of a positive statistical association between the influence of neoliberals in the national policy teams in the 1990s (measured as the average values of the proportion neoliberal indicator in a cross section of eighty-two countries) and the fraction of years that the countries spent under IMF arrangements.

Implications and Extensions

Exporting the Argument to other International Organizations

Can the theory and the findings in the book be applied to other IOs? The purpose of the book is to deepen our understanding of the interactions between the IMF and its borrowers, but my findings suggest more generally that the organizational cultures of IOs are at least as important for understanding their decisions as the formal organizational rules and the marching orders given by powerful member states. There are, however, some clear scope conditions for the theory. The IMF is unique in several ways, and the particular aspects of the institution suggest that the theoretical framework needs adjustment before it can be exported.

There are three aspects of the Fund that make an ideational explanation particularly useful in this setting. First, the complexity of the task at hand—managing global financial stability—means that states have been willing to delegate a particularly large degree of authority to the institution.[5] Related to the complexity of the external environment is the peculiar relationship between the Fund staff and management, on the one hand, and the putative representatives of state interests in the institution, the EDs, on the other. The capacity for interested member governments to influence the content of IMF programs through official channels is limited because the staff members have significant informational advantages. By the time the proposal is brought before the Executive Board, the content of the agreement is, for all intents and purposes, decided. Some suggest that government officials use informal means to lean on staff and management, but aside from a handful of high-profile cases of meddling by Treasury officials, I find scant evidence that the IMF consistently favored countries that scored highly on the measures of U.S. strategic interest.

The third unique characteristic of the Fund is the degree of ideational coherence in the institution. The IMF is composed of around 2,600 staff members, the majority of whom are U.S.-trained macroeconomists; in Ngaire Woods's description, "the institution prides itself on being cohesive, consistent, and tightly disciplined."[6] At the upper reaches of the institution, the profile of the decision makers is remarkably similar. The fact that the Fund is a cohesive, tight-knit organization dealing with complex and unpredictable crisis situations enables it to act independently of sovereign states in the international system that might seek to use the institution for their own ends.[7] The contrasts between the Fund and

---

5. Barnett and Finnemore 2004.

6. Woods 2006, 7.

7. A claim by Koremenos, Lipson, and Snidal comports with the notion that the degree of IMF independence is unusual: "states rarely allow international institutions to become significant autonomous actors" (2001, 762).

less formal organizations, such as the World Trade Organization and the Bank for International Settlements, are stark. The other international institutions are more frequently viewed as empty vessels used by self-interested states rather than as autonomous actors in their own right.

Policy Implications: Reforming the Fund

An IO that asks its members to undertake painful policy changes will never win a popularity contest, but the problems of the IMF may run deeper. In the years before the global financial meltdown in 2008, many observers diagnosed the IMF as suffering from a legitimacy crisis.[8] *Crisis* implies that the perception of the efficacy of the institution or the perception of the rightfulness of its rules, principles, rights, and obligations "declines to the point where the actor or institution must either adapt . . . or face disempowerment."[9] Because the IMF is (arguably) a *more* indispensable element of the system of global economic governance after 2008 than it was before the onset of the Global Financial Crisis, even though its organizational adaptations before the financial market meltdown were modest (at best), calling the problem of the IMF a "legitimacy crisis" suggests a misdiagnosis. The IMF has been, and remains, a key player when national, regional, and global financial markets enter states of turmoil, as they have regularly over the past thirty years.

Perhaps the IMF did not suffer a full-blown legitimacy crisis; the emerging challenges threatening the authoritative position of the organization near the apex of global economic governance, however, are serious. There are two perennial candidates for organizational reform and renewal, each intended to address the governance problems of the Fund.

The first reform issue, on which there has been significant movement, is the gulf between the lendable resources of the Fund and the financing needs of its borrowers. As the global pool of "stateless" money grows, the cost of borrowing falls. Cheap money enabled millions of Americans to purchase mortgages that, once home prices tumbled, they could not repay—and it has allowed governments to accumulate massive debt loads. A case in point: by 2009, Greece—a country of 11 million people with an economy about the size of Massachusetts—had racked up a debt that exceeded the foreign debts of Argentina, Brazil, and Mexico, combined.[10]

---

8. Seabrooke 2007.
9. Reus-Smit 2007, 158.
10. Chinn and Frieden 2011, 187.

When Lehman Brothers collapsed in September 2008 the IMF war chest was less than $250 billion. Recognizing that the Fund was severely underpowered as the crisis deepened, the G20 agreed in April 2009 to expand the IMF coffers to the tune of $750 billion. In January 2012, the Fund, expecting additional demands as the Eurozone Debt Crisis threatened to spread from Ireland, Greece, and Portugal to the much larger economies of Spain and Italy, sought further commitments to raise its pool of resources to $1 trillion. The trebling of IMF resources, important as the reform may be, is unlikely to help the Fund become a more effective overseer of larger, faster, more fragile, and (increasingly) seamlessly integrated financial markets. Before the three recent (and devastating) financial market meltdowns (the East Asian Financial Crisis of 1997–1998, the implosion of the U.S. financial system in 2008, and the eruption of the eurozone sovereign debt crisis in 2010), the Fund displayed a curious lack of concern about developments in the financial markets while they were perched on the cusp—a forecasting track record so poor that it could not help but reduce the authority of the organization over its members.[11] The IMF can try to move from its back foot to its front foot and take a proactive rather than the reactive approach to managing the risks of overlending by the financial community. But to do so, its officials will have to answer a criticism posed by the Australian ED Michael Callaghan in his discussion of the staff report on a previous crisis: "What is not sufficiently covered in the paper are the circumstances which resulted in the private financial community being willing to finance a growing borrowing requirement by Argentina to the point that its debt level was unsustainable."[12] Heterodox views of the inherent instability of deregulated financial markets, such as those espoused by Hyman Minsky, the late Washington University economist, historically had little to no resonance with IMF staff members.[13] There is little reason to believe that the 2008 crisis was a "Minsky moment" for the more orthodox IMF economists.

Another focal point for organizational rejuvenation deals with the contentious issue of voting rights. The institutional avenue for the assertion of national interests is the Executive Board. The twenty-four EDs who constitute it are appointed by their home governments and are apportioned voting rights. Many argue that the distribution of votes fails to match the balance of material power among the member states. The growing economic might of the emerging markets is not

---

11. In the run-up to the 2008 crisis, the IMF endorsed the views of people such as Alan Greenspan, approvingly quoting from one of his speeches in its *Global Financial Stability Report*: "increasingly complex financial instruments have contributed to the development of a far more flexible, efficient and hence resilient financial system than the one that existed just a quarter of a century ago" (IMF 2006, 1).

12. Minutes of the Executive Board Meeting EBM/03/106, 17 November 2003, p. 32.

13. Boughton 2012, liv–lv.

captured by a formula that awards more votes to Belgium than India. After years of deadlock (mainly due to northern European intransigence), voting rights are up for a mild reapportionment. The scheduled shift in votes (which finally passed through the gauntlet of U.S. legislative politics in December 2015) is far from sweeping: 6 percent of votes are set to be transferred to low- and middle-income member states, and as a result, Brazil, Russia, India, and China will then join the list of the top ten largest IMF shareholders.[14]

How important is the vote casting of the Executive Board to the activities of the IMF in general? Less than we might expect. It is true that some decisions—such as revising the Articles of Agreement—require an 85 percent supermajority to pass, which gives the United States (possessing just under 17 percent of the votes) a veto. The voting on proposals for lending programs delivered to the Board by the staff and management, however, is informal and recorded on an up-or-down basis, and the Board almost always unanimously approves staff proposals. For this reason, meddling by powerful governments to influence the terms of IMF agreements works mainly through back channels.[15] The limit of Board influence on staff decision making was evident in the approval in July 2009 of a loan for Sri Lanka, despite official abstentions by the U.S. and British representatives from the vote of the Board on the staff proposal. Abdelal's study of the push for the amendment to make capital account liberalization a membership obligation illuminates the social sources of power in the institution: the most advantaged state in terms of material resources (the United States) was outmaneuvered by representatives from a savvier and more determined member state (France).[16] The fact that power has both material and social sources means that formal institutional changes such as the redistribution of voting rights are less consequential for institutional behavior than casual observers might imagine.

My findings suggest that an issue that has ranked low on the organizational reform agenda should be pushed up higher on the list. Although it is easy to find critics (mostly in the developing world) who bemoan the dominance of neoliberal economic ideas at the IMF, efforts to change the recruitment patterns of the organization have made little headway.[17] My evidence indicates that the economic beliefs of the staff and management have important consequences for how the organization relates to its developing-country members. The homogeneity of

---

14. Grabel 2011, 809.
15. Stone 2008, 2011.
16. Abdelal 2007.
17. Take, for example, comments by Trevor Manuel, the long-serving South African finance minister: "[There is] a sense of sameness about the people. They are all very smart. They go to the same Ivy League universities and get their PhDs. It is not innovative" (*Financial Times*, 17 March 2009, p. 2).

IMF economists—not in terms of their national origins but in their training—is the key factor driving the finding that the Fund has played favorites in the design and enforcement of its lending programs.[18] And intellectual homogeneity has been and remains a sore spot for many members of the organization. Consider the view of Raghuram Rajan, economic counselor and head of the IMF Research Department from 2003 to 2006: "Many of these multilateral organisations are dominated by U.S. trained economists, and certainly when I was at the Fund I heard again and again countries like France saying there's a French view of things, why does it have to only be the U.S. view from economists, no doubt from all over the world, but trained in the U.S.?"[19]

Intellectual homogeneity is a submerged source of the governance problems of the organization. But this book is not about the poor forecasting track record of the IMF but rather about the neoliberal-dominated culture of the organization, which I have tied to the decisions about the elements of conditional lending and which has been linked elsewhere to the blind spots that prevented the Fund from acting in advance of (rather than reacting to) the eruption of financial market conflagrations. The official watchdog of the IMF, the Independent Evaluation Office (IEO), identifies "a high degree of groupthink" and "intellectual capture" in a report on the performance of the IMF before the crisis of 2008.[20] Another survey conducted by the IEO finds that "many [national policymakers and outside experts] . . . thought IMF research was biased and that 'the IMF was fixated on certain messages and did not consider alternative views.'"[21] These critiques, coupled with the argument and evidence presented here, strengthen the case for opening the ranks of the Fund to include more individuals who approach the most pressing economic problems of the member countries—and especially of the developing-country members—from different vantage points.[22]

---

18. Gender imbalance is another serious problem in Fund staffing decisions. In the data set of 983 appointees to upper-level positions between 1980 and 2000, less than 10 percent (8.8 percent, to be precise) of the appointees were women.

19. *Quoted in Financial Times*, online ed., November 1, 2010, http://www.ft.com/intl/cms/s/0/9671f282-e5bb-11df-b023–00144feabdc0.html (accessed November 16, 2012).

20. Independent Evaluation Office of the IMF 2011, 17.

21. Alan Beattie, "Carstens Urges IMF to End Wealthy Bias," *Financial Times*, online ed., June 11, 2011, http://www.ft.com/intl/cms/s/0/a7a675fc-9be9-11e0-bef9-00144feabdc0.html.

22. Historically, UN economic agencies supplied the rejoinder to the neoliberal policy recommendations of the Fund. Jolly, Emmerij, and Weiss drive the point home: "on development matters—economic problems and policy issues from the perspective of developing countries—mainstream economics has mostly stuck to the tools and frames of neoliberal analysis. Outside this mainstream, there has been a significant and vocal professional minority, especially in developing countries and somewhat in Europe, sometimes economists working within structuralist frames of analysis, sometimes social scientists working within other disciplines or multidisciplinary frames. The Bretton Woods institutions have mostly worked within the mainstream. . . . the UN has mostly approached

And although phenomena such as groupthink and excessive organizational insulation are observed to some degree in *all* bureaucracies, the "specific empirical conditions of the organization" can intensify or weaken these behavioral predispositions. Recruiting the bulk of the staff members of an organization to ensure that they share one kind of professional background tends to exacerbate rather than mitigate the pathologies that impede the ability of the IMF to carry out its mission; not just recruiting from a single discipline (economics) but fixating on a relatively narrow (in the context of an organization with global scope) set of graduate programs in that discipline risks further amplifying the pathological tendencies.[23]

The IMF and Its Borrowers in the New Hard Times

The IMF lending activities peaked in the early 2000s—and then, after a decade marred by financial crises around the world, the international economy entered a period of relative quietude. The great moderation in the world economy, ensuring a few years of relative international financial stability, raised questions about the future role of the IMF in the international economy. Some (e.g., John Taylor and Alan Meltzer, well-known macroeconomists) asked publicly whether the world even needed the institution. In 2005, Barry Eichengreen compared the IMF to a "rudderless ship adrift on a sea of liquidity."[24] By 2007, interest payments on outstanding loans—the institutional lifeblood—had all but dried up. The IMF Executive Board announced plans to trim the staff by 15 percent and to sell a portion of its gold holdings just to stay solvent. In the wake of the IMF mismanagement of the East Asian Financial Crisis in 1997–1998 and the collapse of Argentina in 2001, some middle-income countries self-insured by accumulating huge quantities of foreign reserves.

The forecasting models of the Fund itself, calibrated using historical data, offered some sobering predictions about the drop-off in the members' use of

---

development issues from outside mainstream economics" (2009, 46–47). The UN agencies, although playing important roles as incubators for alternative views, were nonetheless often sidelined in the discussions surrounding the "official" response to international economic problems. For example, in the wake of the Global Financial Crisis, UNCTAD efforts to shape the post-crisis landscape and ensure that the voices of the developing countries were heard were delegitimized. A U.S. official was transparent on the subsidiary role that the UN organizations should play: "We don't want UNCTAD providing intellectual competition with the IMF and World Bank" (Wade 2013, 15).

23. Barnett and Finnemore 1999, 719 (quotation), 722–23.

24. Eichengreen 2005, 495.

institutional credit. The outstanding stock of IMF credit, economists in the Research Department reported, would fall to SDR 10 billion in 2010; between 2006 and 2010, the models predicted just twenty-six new arrangements—only three of which would necessitate exceptional access (more than the 300 percent of the quota threshold).[25] The institution appeared to be moving at an advanced rate down a path to irrelevance.

But by the end of 2008, with the Global Financial Crisis in full swing, it was clear that predictions of the demise of the IMF were premature. The next several years were marked by a burst in the lending activities of the Fund (and this time around, not just in developing countries). Between 2008 and 2010, the IMF established seventy-four new lending programs; in the next three years, another thirty-seven new arrangements followed. The sizes of some of the new programs were unprecedented: although the average size of the programs signed between 2008 and 2010 was SDR 3 billion, the 2010 loan to Greece enabled the country to borrow, over a three-year period, up to SDR 26 billion. Between two separate programs in Greece (a second arrangement in 2012 followed the expiration of the 2010 standby agreement) and massive loans for Ireland and Portugal, the outstanding use of credit by the Fund came to just under SDR 100 billion—and that figure does not include the disbursements set out in the nearly one hundred other IMF programs that came into effect between the start of 2008 and the end of 2012.

The uptick in IMF lending during the credit crunch that followed on the heels of the chaotic bankruptcy of Lehman Brothers was demand-driven. Financial globalization meant that the balance sheets of banks around the world were exposed to the collapse of the U.S. housing market; by 2007, at least $3.8 trillion of assets derived from securitized mortgages had spread around the world.[26] Governments scrambled to recapitalize vulnerable banks and to stay current on payments as capital inflows dried up and exports plummeted (the global value of exports fell by 28 percent, or $761 billion, between quarter 1 [Q1] 2008 and Q1 2009). At the time, the IMF was one of the few actors in the international economy that could mobilize, with relative speed, a sizable pool of resources for countries plunged into difficulty.[27] And with the Eurozone Sovereign Debt Crisis spreading from its patient zero, Greece (which fell into difficulty in December

---

25. Ghosh et al. 2008.

26. Fligstein and Goldstein 2011.

27. The United States—and more specifically, the U.S. Federal Reserve—also played a key role in the international response to the crisis in its first months (the foreign exchange swap lines of the Fed, used by other countries to inject much-needed dollars into seized-up national banking systems, peaked at $750 billion in 2009). On the U.S. efforts to stabilize financial markets around the world in the wake of the 2008 crisis, see Drezner 2014; Helleiner 2014b; Kirshner 2014.

2009), north to Ireland and then west to Portugal (with mounting fears that Spain or even Italy could become infected), the demand for the IMF resources spiked to record levels.[28]

Everything Old Is New (Again)

The increase in the size of the post–Global Financial Crisis programs is striking. The average size of IMF loans between 1984 and 2000 was 78 percent of country quota. The average size of 104 loans signed between 2008 and 2013, by contrast, was 412 percent.

Although the post-2008 programs were larger in terms of access, changes in the design of the Fund lending arrangements have been subtle (some might say nearly imperceptible). The high degree of continuity is perhaps surprising, considering that the perceived intrusiveness and inefficacy of conditionality was a major target for critics both in and outside the Fund in the years between the financial crises of the late 1990s and the crisis of 2008.[29]

In 2001, the IMF initiated a review of its conditionality policy. Representatives from low- and middle-income countries on the Executive Board pushed for a reduction in the number of conditions per program. In the wake of the review, the IMF devised new guidelines to drastically streamline conditionality, focusing in particular on the structural conditions that were often the target of the ire of borrowers. The gap between the intentions of the initiative and the observed outcome was wide. A report issued in 2007 by the IEO "concluded that the streamlining initiative had not reduced the number of conditions."[30]

Prior to the eruption of the Global Financial Crisis, the IMF had streamlined its lending programs but not dramatically. The data in the most recent IMF review of conditionality (covering programs signed between 2002 and September 2011) reveal that the average number of conditions per program has fallen after peaking in 2004—but only back to the 2002 level.[31] The evidence suggests that the crisis of 2008 was not a breaking point in either the scope or content of conditionality. Although the IMF management publicly advocated the use of countercyclical macroeconomic policies (lowering interest rates and increased government spending) to boost economic output during the depths of the credit crunch in 2008 and 2009, the bulk of the programs designed by the staff looked anything but countercyclical; stringent fiscal measures, including limits on

---

28. Reinhart and Trebesch 2015.
29. Grabel 2011, 823.
30. Best 2012, 12.
31. IMF 2012.

(or big cuts in) fiscal outlays and tax increases, were enforced in loans drawn by Iceland, Latvia, Hungary, Romania, Greece, Portugal, Pakistan, Ukraine, and El Salvador.[32] The IMF, in a September 2009 review of fifteen post-crisis programs, contended that the enforcement of fiscal targets was more flexible than it had been in the past, with frequent revisions to loosen the conditions. But the report also admits that this was due at least in part to more dramatic declines in output than the staff anticipated when they negotiated the terms of the programs.

The Fund did, however, create several new lending facilities after 2008, intended to rapidly disburse funds to member states. The Flexible Credit Line (FCL), established in April 2009, is intended to "shift IMF loan policy from ex post conditionality to ex ante conditionality for . . . states that have a good track record of policy implementation under IMF reform programs and strong economic fundamentals."[33] Members that prequalify for access to the FCL do not face conditions. A second new facility, the Precautionary Credit Line (PCL), sets a lower bar for prequalification but includes light conditionality. But, like in previous experiments with programs for members suffering exogenous and temporary troubles, few members have made use of the new lending facilities (Mexico, Poland, and Colombia accessed resources through the FCL; Macedonia is the only member to access the PCL).[34]

The crux of my argument about the IMF in the post–Global Financial Crisis era, then, is that the changes in the way the organization interacts with its members, mediated by the instruments of conditional lending, have been incremental rather than fundamental. Comparing IMF lending programs before and after 2008 is a study in continuity rather than revolution. For some readers, this contention might be controversial. What about the surprising turnabout of the IMF on the issue of capital controls? And didn't the Fund Research Department, under the guidance of its Director Olivier Blanchard, produce work questioning, among other sacred cows in neoliberal U.S. economics circles, the link between financial liberalization and income inequality, the size of fiscal multipliers, the merits of state-led investment in infrastructural projects, and the growth-retarding effect of austerity programs?[35]

---

32. Grabel 2011, 821–22.

33. Broome 2010, 49.

34. At several points in its history, the Fund set up new facilities with minimal conditions to provide quick infusions for members facing problems due to adverse changes in their external economic environment. But demand for the new facilities was generally weak: the two Oil Facilities survived for only two years in the mid-1970s, the Buffer Stock Financing Facility (created in 1969 to help governments deal with commodity-price fluctuations) was eliminated in 2000, and the Compensatory and Contingency Financing Facility was never used and expired in 2000.

35. See Ban 2015 for a discussion of the new thinking within the Fund Research Department.

Indeed, on both the capital controls and Research Department fronts the IMF has changed. IMF views on the merits of capital controls, although clearly different than the organizational view in the late 1990s, should not be overstated. The Fund leaned on member countries to remove restrictions but rarely used the tool of conditionality to pry open the financial systems of the borrowers.[36] It was not hesitant, however, to condemn the use of controls by the member states, most notably when Malaysia—a member state that has never borrowed from the Fund—imposed restrictions during the 1997–1998 regional crisis. When Iceland signed an agreement in October 2008, it had already imposed controls on capital outflows, and the IMF allowed the Icelandic authorities to retain the exchange restrictions. When Latvia came to the Fund in December 2008, it too was able to maintain controls that had been imposed as part of a deposit freeze at a failing bank.[37] The Fund is far from a proponent of capital controls, yet the institution has adapted to a changed post-crisis world by accepting that exchange restrictions ("capital flow management measures," in Fund parlance) are a legitimate part of the policy toolkit of member countries. New guidelines that sketch the evolving IMF view of capital controls (use them sparingly, and keep them temporary, transparent, and market-oriented) were approved by the Board in December 2012.[38]

And, although the IMF Research Department under Blanchard's leadership became much more willing to embrace unconventional positions, there is no reason to assume that a one-way transmission, bringing ideas from the research side into the operational departments of the Fund, always exists.[39] Intra-organizational silos (another pathological feature of IOs diagnosed by Barnett and Finnemore) often prevent the migration of new ideas from one part of the organization to another. Furthermore, the public faces of IOs frequently communicate views that deviate from the activities of the organizations.[40]

After the Crisis of 2008: Still Playing Favorites?

My argument that the changes have been small in the approach of the Fund to conditional lending for adjustment purposes raises the question: Does the pattern of favoritism in the IMF treatment of its borrowers persist? Spurred by this

36. Independent Evaluation Office of the IMF 2005.

37. Grabel 2011, 815.

38. Gallagher 2015, 133.

39. Alan Beattie, "Investment Is the Cure for Secular Stagnation," *Financial Times*, online ed., April 10, 2015, http://www.ft.com/intl/cms/s/0/8f7ce138-deb0–11e4–8a01–00144feab7de.html.

40. Weaver 2008.

question of whether the pattern holds in the post-2008 period, here I discuss some preliminary evidence on the covariates of the size of the programs signed in the first five years after the outbreak of the Global Financial Crisis. The preliminary nature of the evidence prevents me from moving much beyond speculation, but the initial results are broadly in line with the central argument of the book. The composition of the policy team of the borrowing government appeared to exert a sizable effect on the decisions taken by the Fund in the half-decade of economic turbulence that followed the shock of 2008.

To take a first cut at the question, I collected the same indicator of access—the size of the loan of a member relative to its quota (I took the logarithm to reduce the extreme dispersion in the measure)—for 104 new lending arrangements approved by the Executive Board between 2008 and 2013. The (raw) relative loan size indicator varied widely, as expected; the smallest loan in the post-2008 group was just 10 percent of the country quota and the largest was 2,399 percent of the quota. Using the coding rules from chapter 3, I then compiled the proportion neoliberal indicator for as many of the post-2008 program countries as possible, given the gaps in some policymakers' biographical records (or the absence thereof, in a few cases).

As an initial test of the relationship between the indicator of loan size and the ideational makeup of the policy team of the borrowing country, I looked at the bivariate correlation between the two indicators—which was modestly strong ($\rho = 0.32$) and highly statistically significant ($p = 0.001$). To see if the correlation between the updated proportion neoliberal variable and the size of the loans signed after 2008 held when I controlled for other factors, I added several other variables to the regression model. I used three indicators to control for the possibility that the correlation was due to fact that the richer and potentially more systemically important European countries needed larger tranches of lending—and that these richer countries also happened to have more neoliberals as members of their policy teams. The rationale for the inclusion of the first two additional indicators, per capita GDP and GDP (I took the logarithms of both in the analysis), is obvious. But I also controlled for membership in the OECD. Membership in the OECD is only for the privileged countries; it is, as Rawi Abdelal and Sophie Meunier point out, "symbolic of having achieved 'developed' status."[41] If the correlation was due to the confounding effect of country wealth and status on the terms of access to Fund resources, the inclusion of the three indicators should eliminate any substantively strong and statistically significant relationship between the loan size and proportion neoliberal variables. Two

---

41. Abdelal and Meunier 2010, 360.

other indicators of macroeconomic performance (and, hence, the demand for credit) are included as covariates: GDP growth and the current account balance (as a proportion of GDP).[42]

I added two other variables to the specification. First, I included a measure of foreign policy closeness of the borrower with the United States, based on UN General Assembly (UNGA) voting profiles, as a covariate. The indicator (U.S. affinity) recovers the foreign policy preferences of countries from their UNGA voting records.[43] The variable measures the unidimensional foreign policy "ideal point" of each country in each year, interpreted as the position of the country toward the U.S.-led liberal international order. Second, I included the measure that takes the value of 1 when a Paris Club debt restructuring agreement was reached in the six months preceding or following the initiation of a IMF program.

I estimated an ordinary least squares (OLS) model with robust, country-clustered standard errors—the results are reported in table 7.2. Model 1 includes ninety-four programs from sixty-six countries. The high R^2-statistic (0.651) indicates that the covariates in the model account for a large proportion (up to 65 percent) of the observed variation in the loan size/quota indicator.

Because the number of programs in the analysis is small and the findings have not been subjected to the kinds of robustness tests that I conduct in chapter 3, the statistical results should to be treated with the appropriate dose of caution. But the point estimate of the partial correlation between proportion neoliberal and the relative size of loans in the post-2008 era suggests that the pattern documented in the book persists. Based on the first model reported in table 7.2, increasing the value of the proportion neoliberal variable by one standard deviation (+0.23) and holding all other covariates in the specification constant yields a 16.5 percent increase in the size of the average program in the years between 2008 and 2013.

Furthermore, the statistical finding is not driven by the inclusion of a handful of very large programs in historically rich Northern countries (Greece, Iceland, Ireland, and Portugal). The structure of programs in the rich eurozone members was, in any case, historically unprecedented, with the Fund serving as a junior partner in the rescue programs alongside the European Commission and European Central Bank. But the inclusion of these observations, uniqueness of the arrangements notwithstanding, matters little for the statistical relationship: the

---

42. The economic indicators were taken from the World Bank's *World Development Indicators* database, http://data.worldbank.org/data-catalog/world-development-indicators.

43. I use this indicator, constructed by Bailey, Strezhnev, and Voeten (2015), instead of the UNGA-based foreign policy affinity measure that I use in chapter 3 (Gartzke 2006), which has not been updated to cover the 2008–2013 period covered in the statistical analysis reported in this chapter.

TABLE 7.2 Covariates of the size of IMF loans, 2008–2013

COVARIATES OF LOG(LOAN SIZE/QUOTA)	(1) FULL SAMPLE	(2) SPECIFICATION WITHOUT THE FOUR NORTHERN COUNTRIES[A]
Proportion neoliberal	$0.716^{0.037}$	$0.726^{0.031}$
	(0.337)	(0.329)
(log)GDP per capita	$0.320^{0.002}$	$0.308^{0.005}$
	(0.100)	(0.105)
(log)GDP	$0.656^{0.000}$	$0.666^{0.000}$
	(0.164)	(0.171)
GDP growth	$-0.029^{0.079}$	$-0.028^{0.103}$
	(0.016)	(0.017)
Current account balance	$-0.022^{0.179}$	$-0.021^{0.218}$
	(0.016)	(0.017)
UNGA affinity score	$0.286^{0.046}$	$0.298^{0.040}$
	(0.140)	(0.142)
Paris Club debt agreement	$0.372^{0.353}$	$0.380^{0.346}$
	(0.398)	(0.400)
OECD member	$-0.033^{0.881}$	$-0.176^{0.398}$
	(0.223)	(0.207)
R^2	0.65	0.58
Number of observations	94	89

Notes: Standard errors are reported in parentheses. The *p* values appear in the superscripts on the coefficients. OECD, Organization for Economic Cooperation and Development; UNGA, UN General Assembly.

[a] Greece, Iceland, Ireland, and Portugal.

proportion neoliberal variable is positively (and significantly) correlated with the relative size of the loans in both specifications (in fact, the relationship is slightly stronger in the second model, with the historically rich European countries excised from the sample).

This more recent evidence is far from definitive. Nevertheless, it suggests that the proximity of the beliefs of the members of the domestic policy team (captured, indirectly, by the proportion neoliberal variable) and Fund officials continues to be highly correlated with variation in at least one of the three elements of conditional lending.

Two other factors, on top of the statistical evidence presented here, suggest that the argument linking shared beliefs to IMF treatment will continue to be relevant for understanding IMF-borrower relations in the coming years. First, for all the changes to international and national economies wrought by the forces of market globalization, managing the difficult adjustment problems faced by countries that are suddenly cut off from the international sources of financing on which they depend, will remain an enduring policy problem. In fact, financial market integration makes dealing with the adjustment problem a *more* relevant issue in global economic governance; the multiplication of nodes for transmitting market instability across borders, coupled with the sheer size of the global pool of capital (into which governments running large current deficits hope to tap), have helped make economic crises more frequent events. The IMF possesses the resources and the (waning, perhaps) authority to help member countries manage their adjustment problems, but as I make clear in this chapter, the top decision makers of the Fund have not dislodged the institutionally embedded, neoliberal-oriented mode of understanding the proper solutions to the adjustment problems of countries and replaced it with something else. IMF officials seem to follow the first rule of wing walking: don't let go of one thing until you have hold of something else. And for IMF economists, most coming to the institution armed with graduate degrees from highly ranked U.S. economics departments, there is simply no credible alternative to the financial programming model that has been in place for years.[44]

The second reason why I am willing to speculate that my argument will remain a relevant framework for understanding the character of IMF-borrower relations is that the distance between the beliefs of individuals at the helm of the economies of the borrowing countries and the beliefs of Fund officials remains sizable in many settings—and fervent disagreement rather than concordance is as likely to be a feature of Fund-borrower negotiations in the future as it has been in past decades. Any degree of general convergence toward the view, shared by many IMF officials, that policymaking should be oriented to facilitating the free play of market forces was arrested by the outbreak of the Global Financial Crisis in 2008. Instead of convergence, the post-2008 environment is characterized by, as Kirshner puts its, a "new heterogeneity of thinking" about the relative balance of state and market, especially in the financial sector.[45] Olivier Blanchard acknowledges that the crisis heralded a swing of the policymaking pendulum in most countries back from markets toward the state, noting further, "the economic crisis has put into question many of our beliefs."[46] Just as they have many times in the past, Fund officials will sit across the negotiating table from national economic policymakers whose views reflect very different beliefs about how economies work (and what policymakers can and should do to make them work better). And if the argument in this book holds, the ride given by the Fund to those disputatious policymakers may well be a rough one.

---

44. Mussa and Savastano 2000, 101.
45. Kirshner 2014, 123–24.
46. Blanchard 2012, 225.

References

Abdelal, Rawi. 2001. *National Purpose in the World Economy: Post-Soviet States in Comparative Perspective*. Ithaca: Cornell University Press.

——. 2007. *Capital Rules: The Construction of Global Finance*. Cambridge, MA: Harvard University Press.

Abdelal, Rawi, Mark Blyth, and Craig Parsons. 2010. "Introduction: The Case for Constructivist Political Economy." In *Constructing the International Economy*, ed. Rawi Abdelal, Mark Blyth, and Craig Parsons, 1–19. Ithaca: Cornell University Press.

Abdelal, Rawi, and Sophie Meunier. 2010. "Managed Globalization: Doctrine, Practice and Problem." *Journal of European Public Policy* 17(3): 350–67.

Abrevaya, Jason. 1997. "The Equivalence of Two Estimators of the Fixed Effects Logit Model." *Economics Letters* 55: 41–43.

Acemoglu, Daron, Simon Johnson, Pablo Querubin, and James Robinson. 2008. "When Does Policy Reform Work? The Case of Central Bank Independence." *Brookings Papers on Economic Activity* 39(1): 351–429.

Acemoglu, Daron, Simon Johnson, James Robinson, and Yunyong Thaicharoen. 2003. "Institutional Causes, Macroeconomic Symptoms: Volatility, Crises, and Growth." *Journal of Monetary Economics* 50(1): 49–123.

Adolph, Christopher. 2013. *Bankers, Bureaucrats, and Central Bank Politics: The Myth of Neutrality*. New York: Cambridge University Press.

Aggarwal, Vinod. 1996. *Debt Games: Strategic Interaction in International Debt Rescheduling*. New York: Cambridge University Press.

Ahamed, Liaquat. 2014. *Money and Tough Love: On Tour with the IMF*. London: Visual Editions.

Amir, Sulfikar. 2008. "The Engineers versus the Economists: The Disunity of Technocracy in Indonesian Development." *Bulletin of Science, Technology & Society* 28(4): 316–23.

Arena, Richard. 2010. "From the 'Old' to the 'New' Keynesian-Neoclassical Synthesis: An Interpretation." In *The Return to Keynes*, ed. Bradley W. Bateman, Toshiaki Hirai, and Maria Cristina Marcuzzo, 77–93. Cambridge, MA: Harvard University Press.

Babb, Sarah. 2001. *Managing Mexico: Economists from Nationalism to Neoliberalism*. Princeton: Princeton University Press.

——. 2007. "Embeddedness, Inflation, and International Regimes: The IMF in the Early Postwar Period." *American Journal of Sociology* 113(1): 128–64.

Bailey, Michael, Anton Strezhnev, and Erik Voeten. 2015. "Estimating Dynamic State Preferences from United Nations Voting Data." *Journal of Conflict Resolution*. DOI: 10.1177/0022002715595700.

Ban, Cornel. 2015. "From Designers to Doctrinaires: Staff Research and Fiscal Policy Change at the IMF." In *Elites on Trial*, ed. Glenn Morgan, Paul Hirsch, and Sigurd Quack, 337–69. Research in the Sociology of Organizations No. 43. Bingley, UK: Emerald Group.

Barnett, Michael, and Liv Coleman. 2005. "Designing Police: Interpol and the Study of Change in International Organizations." *International Studies Quarterly* 49: 593–619.

Barnett, Michael, and Martha Finnemore. 1999. "The Politics, Power, and Pathologies of International Organizations." *International Organization* 53(4): 699–732.

——. 2004. *Rules for the World: International Organizations in Global Politics*. Ithaca: Cornell University Press.

Barro, Robert, and Jong-Wha Lee. 2005. "IMF Programs: Who Is Chosen, and What Are the Effects?" *Journal of Monetary Economics* 52: 1245–69.

Basu, Kaushik. 2003. *Analytical Development Economics: The Less Developed Economy Revisited*. Cambridge, MA: MIT Press.

——. 2011. *An Economist's Miscellany*. New York: Oxford University Press.

Beck, Nathaniel. 2001. "Time-Series Cross-Section Data: What Have We Learned in the Past Few Years?" *Annual Review of Political Science* 4: 271–93.

Beck, Nathaniel, Jonathan Katz, and Richard Tucker. 1998. "Beyond Ordinary Logit: Taking Time Seriously in Binary Time-Series Cross-Section Models." *American Journal of Political Science* 42: 1260–88.

Beck, Thorsten, George Clarke, Alberto Groff, Philip Keefer, and Patrick Walsh. 2001. "New Tools in Comparative Political Economy: The Database of Political Institutions." *World Bank Economic Review* 15(1): 165–76.

Beckert, Jens. 1996. "What Is Sociological about Economic Sociology? Uncertainty and the Embeddedness of Economic Action." *Theory and Society* 25(6): 803–40.

——. 2002. *Beyond the Market: Social Foundations of Economic Efficiency*. Princeton: Princeton University Press.

Besley, Timothy, and Marta Reynal-Querol. 2011. "Do Democracies Select More Educated Leaders?" *American Political Science Review* 105(3): 556–66.

Best, Jacqueline. 2005. *The Limits of Transparency: Ambiguity and the History of International Finance*. Ithaca: Cornell University Press.

——. 2012. "Ambiguity and Uncertainty in International Organizations: A History of Debating IMF Conditionality." *International Studies Quarterly* 56(4): 674–88.

Bienen, Henry, and Nicolas van de Walle. 1991. *Of Time and Power: Leadership Duration in the Modern World*. Princeton: Princeton University Press.

Biglaiser, Glen. 2002. "The Internationalization of Chicago's Economics in Latin America." *Economic Development and Cultural Change* 50(2): 269–86.

Bird, Graham. 1983. "The International Monetary Fund and Developing Countries: Retrospect and Prospect." *De Economist* 131(2): 161–95.

Bird, Graham, and Thomas D. Willett. 2004. "IMF Conditionality, Implementation, and the New Political Economy of Ownership." *Comparative Economic Studies* 46: 423–50.

Blanchard, Olivier. 2005. "An Interview with Stanley Fischer." *Macroeconomic Dynamics* 9(2): 244–62.

——. 2009. "(Nearly) Nothing to Fear but Fear Itself." *Economist*. http://www.economist.com/node/13021961.

——. 2012. "Concluding Remarks." In *In the Wake of the Crisis: Leading Economists Reassess Economic Policy*, ed. Olivier Blanchard, David Romer, Michael Spence, and Joseph E. Stiglitz, 225–28. Cambridge, MA: MIT Press.

Blanchard, Olivier, and Daniel Leigh. 2013. "Fiscal Consolidation: At What Speed?" *Voxeu.com*, 3 May. http://www.voxeu.org/article/fiscal-consolidatio n-what-speed.

Blossfeld, Hans-Peter, Katrin Golsch, and Gotz Rohwer. 2007. *Event History Analysis with Stata*. Mahwah, NJ: Lawrence Earlbaum.

Blustein, Paul. 2001. *The Chastening: Inside the Crisis That Rocked the Global Financial System and Humbled the IMF*. New York: PublicAffairs.

———. 2005. *And the Money Kept Rolling In (and Out): Wall Street, the IMF, and the Bankrupting of Argentina*. New York: PublicAffairs.

Blyth, Mark. 2002. *Great Transformations: Economic Ideas and Institutional Change in the Twentieth Century*. New York: Cambridge University Press.

———. 2006. "Great Punctuations: Prediction, Randomness, and the Evolution of Comparative Political Science." *American Political Science Review* 100(4): 493–98.

———. 2013. *Austerity: The History of a Dangerous Idea*. New York: Oxford University Press.

Boas, Taylor, and Jordan Gans-Morse. 2009. "Neoliberalism: From New Liberal Philosophy to Anti-Liberal Slogan." *Studies in Comparative International Development* 44(2): 137–61.

Bodea, Cristina, and Raymond Hicks. 2015. "Price Stability and Central Bank Independence: Discipline, Credibility, and Democratic Institutions." *International Organization* 69(1): 35–61.

Bonelli, Marcelo. 2004. *Un pais en deuda: La Argentina y su imposible relacion con el FMI*. Buenos Aires: Editorial Planeta.

Bourdieu, Pierre. 2003. *Firing Back: Against the Tyranny of the Market 2*. Trans. Loic Wacquant. New York: New Press.

Boughton, James. 2001. *Silent Revolution: The International Monetary Fund, 1979–1989*. Washington, DC: International Monetary Fund.

———. 2012. *Tearing Down Walls: The International Monetary Fund, 1990–99*. Washington, DC: International Monetary Fund.

Box-Steffensmeier, Janet M., and Bradford S. Jones. 2004. *Event History Modeling: A Guide for Social Scientists*. New York: Cambridge University Press.

Box-Steffensmeier, Janet M., Dan Reiter, and Christopher Zorn. 2003. "Nonproportional Hazards and Event History Analysis in International Relations." *Journal of Conflict Resolution* 47(1): 33–53.

Breen, Michael. 2014. "IMF Conditionality and the Economic Exposure of Its Shareholders." *European Journal of International Relations* 20(2): 416–36.

Broome, Andre. 2010. "The International Monetary Fund, Crisis Management and the Credit Crunch." *Australian Journal of International Affairs* 64(1): 37–54.

Broz, J. Lawrence, and Michael Brewster Hawes. 2006. "Congressional Politics of Financing the International Monetary Fund." *International Organization* 60(1): 367–99.

Bueno de Mesquita, Bruce, Alastair Smith, Randolph M. Siverson, and James D. Morrow. 2003. *The Logic of Political Survival*. Cambridge, MA: MIT Press.

Buira, Ariel. 1983. "IMF Financial Programs and Conditionality." *Journal of Development Economics* 12: 111–36.

Bulow, Jeremy. 2002. "First World Governments and Third World Debt." *Brookings Papers on Economic Activity* 1: 229–55.

Campbell, John L., and Ove K. Pedersen, eds. 2001. *The Rise of Neoliberalism and Institutional Analysis*. Princeton: Princeton University Press.

Caraway, Teri, Stephanie J. Rickard, and Mark S. Anner. 2012. "International Negotiations and Domestic Politics: The Case of IMF Labor Market Conditionality." *International Organization* 66: 27–61.

Cavallo, Domingo F. 1984. *Volver a Crecer*. Buenos Aires: Editorial Planeta.

Cavallo, Domingo F., and Joaquin A. Cottani. 1997. "Argentina's Convertibility Plan and the IMF." *American Economic Review* 87(2): 17–22.

Centeno, Miguel A. 1993. "The New Leviathan: The Dynamics and Limits of Technocracy." *Theory and Society* 22: 307–35.

Centeno, Miguel A., and Joseph N. Cohen. 2012. "The Arc of Neoliberalism." *Annual Review of Sociology* 38: 317–40.

Chinn, Menzie D., and Jeffry A. Frieden. 2011. *Lost Decades: The Making of America's Debt Crisis and the Long Recovery.* New York: W. W. Norton.

Chiozza, Giacomo, and Hein E. Goemans. 2004. "International Conflict and the Tenure of Leaders: Is War Still *Ex Post* Inefficient?" *American Journal of Political Science* 48(3): 604–19.

Chwieroth, Jeffrey. 2007a. "Neoliberal Economists and Capital Account Liberalization in Emerging Markets." *International Organization* 61: 443–63.

——. 2007b. "Testing and Measuring the Role of Ideas: The Case of Neoliberalism in the International Monetary Fund." *International Studies Quarterly* 51: 5–30.

——. 2010. *Capital Ideas: The IMF and the Rise of Financial Liberalization.* Princeton: Princeton University Press.

——. 2013. "'The Silent Revolution': How the Staff Exercise Informal Governance over IMF Lending." *Review of International Organizations* 8(2): 265–90.

Cohen, Benjamin J. 1969. *Balance of Payments Policy.* New York: Penguin Books.

Cohen, Joshua, and Charles F. Sabel. 2005. "Global Democracy?" *NYU Journal of International Law and Politics* 37(4): 763–97.

Cohen, Lauren, and Christopher J. Malloy. 2014. "Friends in High Places." *American Economic Journal: Economic Policy* 6(3): 63–91.

Colander, David. 2005. "The Making of an Economist Redux." *Journal of Economic Perspectives* 19(1): 175–98.

Colander, David, and Reuven Brenner, eds. 1992. *Educating Economists.* Ann Arbor: University of Michigan Press.

Colander, David, and Arjo Klamer. 1987. "The Making of an Economist." *Journal of Economic Perspectives* 12(4): 95–111.

Collier, Paul. 1997. "The Failure of Conditionality." In *Perspectives on Aid and Development,* ed. Catherine Gwin and Joan Nelson, 51–77. Washington, DC: Overseas Development Council.

Conaghan, Catherine M., and James Malloy. 1994. *Unsettling Statecraft: Democracy and Neoliberalism in the Central Andes.* Pittsburgh: University of Pittsburgh Press.

Conway, Patrick. 2006. "The International Monetary Fund in a Time of Crisis: A Review of Stanley Fischer's *IMF Essays from a Time of Crisis.*" *Journal of Economic Literature* 44 (1): 115–44.

——. 2007. "The Revolving Door: Duration and Recidivism in IMF Programs." *Review of Economics and Statistics* 89(2): 205–20.

Cooper, Richard N. 1971. *Currency Devaluation in Developing Countries.* Princeton Essays in International Finance No. 86. Princeton: Department of Economics, Princeton University.

Copelovitch, Mark. 2010. *The International Monetary Fund in the Global Economy.* New York: Cambridge University Press.

Corrales, Javier. 1997. "Why Argentines Followed Cavallo: A Technopol between Democracy and Economic Reform." In *Technopols: Freeing Politics and Markets in Latin America in the 1990s,* ed. Jorge Dominguez, 49–93. University Park: Pennsylvania State University Press.

——. 2002. *Presidents without Parties: The Politics of Economic Reform in Argentina and Venezuela in the 1990s.* University Park: Pennsylvania State University Press.

Cukierman, Alex. 1992. *Central Bank Strategy, Credibility, and Independence: Theory and Evidence.* Cambridge, MA: MIT Press.

Dagnino Pastore, José M., and Manuel Fernández López. 1988. "Los economistas en el gobierno argentino." In *Cronicas Economicas: Argentina, 1969–88,* ed. José Dagnino Pastore, 1–20. Buenos Aires: Crespillo.

Danner, Mark D. 1987. "The Struggle for a Democratic Haiti." *New York Times Magazine,* June 21.

Dardot, Pierre, and Christian Laval. 2013. *The New Way of the World: On Neo-Liberal Society.* Trans. Gregory Elliott. London: Verso.

Davis, Paul, and Gustav F. Papanek. 1984. "Faculty Ratings of Major Economic Departments." *American Economic Review* 74(1): 225–30.

Denzau, Arthur, and Douglass North. 1994. "Shared Mental Models: Ideologies and Institutions." *Kyklos* 47(1): 3–31.

de Pablo, Juan Carlos. 1977. *Los Economistas y la Economía Argentina.* Buenos Aires: Ediciones Macchi.

Dequech, David. 2007–2008. "Neoclassical, Mainstream, Orthodox, and Heterodox Economics." *Journal of Post Keynesian Economics* 30(2): 279–302.

de Vries, Margaret Garritsen. 1985. *The International Monetary Fund, 1972–1978: Cooperation on Trial.* Vol. 1. Washington, DC: International Monetary Fund.

———. 1987. *Balance of Payments Adjustment, 1945 to 1986: The IMF Experience.* Washington, DC: International Monetary Fund.

Di Tella, Rafael, and Ingrid Vogel. 2004. "The 2001 Crisis in Argentina: An IMF-Sponsored Default?" Harvard Business School Case 704-004. Revised January. Harvard University.

Dixit, Avinash K., and Jörgen Weibull. 2007. "Political Polarization." *Proceedings of the National Academy of Science* 104(18): 7351–56

Dominguez, Jorge, ed. 1997. *Technopols: Freeing Politics and Markets in Latin America in the 1990s.* University Park: Pennsylvania State University Press.

Dominguez, Kathryn M. E., and Linda L. Tesar. 2007. "International Borrowing and Macroeconomic Performance in Argentina." In *Capital Controls and Capital Flows in Emerging Economies: Policies, Practices, and Consequences,* ed. Sebastian Edwards, 297–342. Chicago: University of Chicago Press.

Dornbusch, Rudiger, and Juan Carlos de Pablo. 1990. "The Austral Plan." In *Developing Country Debt and Economic Performance, vol. 2: The Country Studies—Argentina, Bolivia, Brazil, Mexico,* ed. Jeffrey D. Sachs, 91–114. Chicago: University of Chicago Press.

Dosman, Edgar J. 2008. *The Life and Times of Raul Prebisch, 1901–1986.* Montreal and Kingston: McGill-Queen's University Press.

Dreher, Axel. 2004. "The Influence of IMF Programs on the Reelection of Debtor Governments." *Economics and Politics* 16(1): 53–75.

Dreher, Axel, and Nathan Jensen. 2007. "Independent Actor of Agent? An Empirical Analysis of the Impact of U.S. Interests on IMF Conditions." *Journal of Law and Economics* 50(1): 105–24.

Dreher, Axel, Jan-Egbert Sturm, and Jakob de Haan. 2008. "Does High Inflation Cause Central Bankers to Lose Their Job? Evidence Based on a New Data Set." *European Journal of Political Economy* 24: 778–87.

Dreher, Axel, and Roland Vaubel. 2004. "The Causes and Consequences of IMF Conditionality." *Emerging Markets Finance and Trade* 40(3): 26–54.

Drezner, Daniel W. 2014. *The System Worked: How the World Stopped Another Great Depression.* Oxford: Oxford University Press.

Duménil, Gérard, and Dominique Lévy. 2011. *The Crisis of Neoliberalism*. Cambridge, MA: Harvard University Press.

Dusansky, Richard, and Clayton J. Vernon. 1998 "Rankings of U.S. Economics Departments." *Journal of Economic Perspectives* 12(1): 157–70.

Easterly, William. 2006. "An Identity Crisis? Examining IMF Financial Programming." *World Development* 34(6): 964–80.

Eaton, Kent. 2005. "Menem and the Governors: Intergovernmental Relations in the 1990s." In *Argentine Democracy: the Politics of Institutional Weakness*, ed. Steven Levitsky and María Murillo, 88–114. University Park: Pennsylvania State University Press.

Eckaus, Richard. S. 1986. "How the IMF Lives with Its Conditionality." *Policy Sciences* 19: 237–52.

Edwards, Martin. 2005. "Investor Response to IMF Program Suspensions: Is Noncompliance Costly?" *Social Science Quarterly* 86(4): 857–73.

Edwards, Sebastian. 2010. *Left Behind: Latin America and the False Promise of Populism*. Chicago: University of Chicago Press.

———. 2014. *Toxic Aid: Economic Collapse and Recovery in Tanzania*. New York: Oxford University Press.

Edwards, Sebastian, and Roberto Steiner. 2000. "On the Crisis Hypothesis of Economic Reform: Colombia 1989–91." *Cuadernos de Economía* 37(112): 445–93.

Eichengreen, Barry. 2002. *Financial Crises and What to Do about Them*. New York: Oxford University Press.

———. 2005. "The IMF Adrift on a Sea of Liquidity." In *Reforming the IMF for the 21st Century*, ed. Edwin M. Truman, 495–99. Washington, DC: Institute for International Economics.

Epstein, Edward C. 1987. "Recent Stabilization Programs in Argentina, 1973–86." *World Development* 15(8): 991–1005.

Erro, Davide G. 1994. *Resolving the Argentine Paradox: Politics and Development, 1966–1992*. Boulder: Lynne Rienner.

Faccio, Mara. 2006. "Politically Connected Firms." *American Economic Review* 96(1): 369–86.

Fairbrother, Malcolm. 2014. "Economists, Capitalists, and the Making of Globalization: North American Free Trade in Comparative-Historical Perspective." *American Journal of Sociology* 119(5): 1324–79.

Fearon, James D. 1988. "International Financial Institutions and Economic Policy Reform in Sub-Saharan Africa." *Journal of Modern African Studies* 26(1): 113–37.

Fearon, James D., and David Laitin. 2003. "Ethnicity, Insurgency, and Civil War." *American Political Science Review* 97(1): 75–90.

Fearon, James D., and Alexander Wendt. 2002. "Rationalism v. Constructivism: A Skeptical View." In *Handbook of International Relations*, ed. Walter Carlsnaes, Thomas Risse, and Beth A. Simmons, 52–72. Thousand Oaks: Sage.

Feldman, David Lewis. 1985. "The United States' Role in the Malvinas Crisis, 1982: Misguidance and Misperception in Argentina's Decision to Go to War." *Journal of InterAmerican Studies and World Affairs* 27(2): 1–24.

Fenochietto, Ricardo. 2003. "Comment." In *Latin American Macroeconomic Reforms: The Second Stage*, ed. José Antonio González, Vittorio Corbo, Anne O. Krueger, and Aaron Tornell, 392–96. Chicago: University of Chicago Press.

Fernandez, Roque B. 1985. "The Expectations Management Approach to Stabilization in Argentina during 1976–82." *World Development* 13(8): 871–92.

Fischer, Stanley. 2001. "The International Financial System: Crises and Reform." Lord Robbins Lectures Delivered at the London School of Economics, October 29–31.

Fisman, Raymond. 2001. "Estimating the Value of Political Connections." *American Economic Review* 91(4): 1095–102.

Fligstein, Neil, and Adam Goldstein. 2011. "The Roots of the Great Recession." In *The Great Recession*, ed. David B. Grusky, Bruce Western, and Christopher Wimer, 21–56. New York: Russell Sage Foundation.

Fourcade, Marion. 2006. "The Construction of a Global Profession: The Transnationalization of Economics." *American Journal of Sociology* 112(1): 145–94.

———. 2009. *Economists and Societies: Discipline and Profession in the United States, Britain, and France, 1890s to 1990s*. Princeton: Princeton University Press.

Frieden, Jeffry. 1991. *Debt, Development, and Democracy: Modern Political Economy and Latin America, 1965–1985*. Princeton: Princeton University Press.

Friedman, Thomas L. 2005. *The World Is Flat: A Brief History of the Twenty-First Century*. New York: Farrar, Straus, and Giroux.

Furtado, Celso. 1976. *Economic Development of Latin America*. 2nd ed. Trans. Suzette Macedo. New York: Cambridge University Press.

Gallagher, Kevin P. 2015. *Ruling Capital: Emerging Markets and the Reregulation of Cross-Border Finance*. Ithaca: Cornell University Press.

Gallardo, Julio Lopez, and Ricardo Mansilla. 2007. "The Latin American Theory of Inflation and Beyond." In *Ideas, Policies, and Economic Development in the Americas*, ed. Esteban Perez Caldentey and Matias Vernengo, 81–97. New York: Routledge.

Gartzke, Erik. 2006. *The Affinity of Nations Index, 1946–2002*. Version 4.0. Data set. March. University of California, San Diego. http://dss.ucsd.edu/datasets.htm.

Ghosh, Atish, Manuela Goretti, Bikas Joshi, Alun Thomas, and Juan Zalduendo. 2008. "Modeling Aggregate Use of IMF Resources—Analytical Approaches and Medium-Term Projections." *IMF Staff Papers* 55(1): 1–49.

Gibson, Edward. 1996. *Class and Conservative Parties: Argentina in Comparative Perspective*. Baltimore: Johns Hopkins University Press.

Gibson, Edward, and Ernesto Calvo. 2000. "Federalism and Low-Maintenance Constituencies: Territorial Dimensions of Economic Reform in Argentina." *Studies in Comparative International Development* 35(3): 32–55.

Giuliano, Paola, Prachi Mishra, and Antonio Spilimbergo. 2013. "Democracy and Reforms: Evidence from a New Dataset." *American Economic Journal: Macroeconomics* 5(4): 179–204.

Goemans, Hein E. 2008. "Which Way Out? The Manner and Consequences of Losing Office." *Journal of Conflict Resolution* 52(6): 771–94.

Goertz, Gary, and James Mahoney. 2012. *A Tale of Two Cultures: Qualitative and Quantitative Research in the Social Sciences*. Princeton: Princeton University Press.

Gold, Joseph. 1975. "Uniformity as a Legal Principle of the International Monetary Fund." *Law & Policy in International Business* 7: 765–811.

———. 1988. "Mexico and the Development of the Practice of the International Monetary Fund." *World Development* 16(10): 1127–42.

Goldstein, Judith, and Robert Keohane, eds. 1993. *Ideas and Foreign Policy*. Ithaca: Cornell University Press.

Goldstein, Morris. 2003. "IMF Structural Programs." In *Economic and Financial Crises in Emerging Market Economies*, ed. Martin Feldstein, 363–437. Chicago: University of Chicago Press.

Gootenberg, Paul. 2004. "Between a Rock and a Softer Place: Reflections on Some Recent Economic History of Latin America." *Latin American Research Review* 39(2): 239–57.

Gore, Charles. 2000. "The Rise and Fall of the Washington Consensus as a Paradigm for Developing Countries." *World Development* 28(5): 789–804.

Gould, Erica. 2003. "Money Talks: Supplementary Financiers and International Monetary Fund Conditionality." *International Organization* 57(3): 551–86.

——. 2006. *Money Talks: The International Monetary Fund, Conditionality, and Supplementary Financiers*. Stanford: Stanford University Press.

Grabel, Ilene. 2000. "The Political Economy of 'Policy Credibility': The New-Classical Macroeconomics and the Remaking of Emerging Economies." *Cambridge Journal of Economics* 24(1): 1–19.

——. 2011. "Not Your Grandfather's IMF: Global Crisis, 'Productive Incoherence' and Development Policy Space." *Cambridge Journal of Economics* 35: 805–30.

Graeber, David. 2011. *Debt: The First 5,000 Years*. London: Melville House.

Graves, Phillip E., James Marchand, and Randall Thompson. 1982. "Economics Departmental Rankings: Incentives, Constraints, and Efficiency." *American Economic Review* 72(5): 1131–41.

Haas, Ernst B. 1990. *When Knowledge Is Power: Three Models of Change in International Organizations*. Berkeley: University of California Press.

Hackman, J. Richard. 2003. "Learning More by Crossing Levels: Evidence from Airplanes, Hospitals, and Orchestras." *Journal of Organizational Behavior* 24: 905–22.

Harberger, Arnold C. 2003. "Foreword." In *Latin American Macroeconomic Reforms: The Second Stage*, ed. José Antonio González, Vittorio Corbo, Anne O. Krueger, and Aaron Tornell. vii–xii. Chicago: University of Chicago Press.

Harvey, David. 2005. *A Brief History of Neoliberalism*. Oxford: Oxford University Press.

Helleiner, Eric. 1994. *States and the Reemergence of Global Finance: From Bretton Woods to the 1990s*. Ithaca: Cornell University Press.

——. 2014a. *Forgotten Foundations of Bretton Woods: International Development and the Making of the Postwar Order*. Ithaca: Cornell University Press.

——. 2014b. *The Status Quo Crisis*. New York: Oxford University Press.

Helleiner, Gerald K. 1983. "Lender of Early Resort: The IMF and the Poorest." *American Economic Review* 73(2): 349–53.

Heras, Raul Garcia. 2008. *El Fondo Monetario y el Banco Mundial en la Argentina. Liberalismo, populismo y finanzas internacionales*. Bunos Aires: Lumiere.

Heredia, Mariana. 2004. "El Proceso como bisagra. Emergencía y consolidación del liberalismo tecnocratico: FIEL, FM y CEMA." In *Empresarios, tecnocratas y militares: La trama corporative de la ultima dictadura*, ed. Alfredo Raul Pucciarelli, 313–77. Buenos Aires: Siglo XXI Editores Argentina.

Heymann, Daniel. 1991. "From Sharp Disinflation to Hyperinflation, Twice: The Argentine Experience, 1985–89." In *Lessons of Economic Stabilization and its Aftermath*, ed. Michael Bruno, Stanley Fischer, Elhanan Helpman, and Nissan Liviatan, 104–30. Cambridge, MA: MIT Press.

Hira, Anil. 1998. *Ideas and Economic Policy in Latin America: Regional, National, Organizational Case Studies*. Westport, CT: Praeger.

Hirsch, Barry T., Randall Austin, John Brooks, and J. Bradley Moore. 1984. "Economics Departmental Rankings: Comment." *American Economic Review* 74(4): 822–26.

Hirschman, Albert O. 1981. "The Rise and Decline of Development Economics." *Essays in Trespassing: Economics to Politics and Beyond*, 1–24. New York: Cambridge University Press.

Hogan, Timothy. 1984. "Economics Departmental Rankings: Comment." *American Economic Review* 74(4): 827–33.

Humphreys, Macartan. 2005. "Natural Resources, Conflict, and Conflict Resolution: Uncovering the Mechanisms." *Journal of Conflict Resolution* 49(4): 508–37.

Hurd, Ian. 2008. "Constructivism." In *Oxford Handbook of International Relations*, ed. Christian Reus-Smit and Duncan Snidal, 298–316. New York: Oxford University Press.

Independent Evaluation Office (IEO) of the International Monetary Fund. 2004. *Report on the Evaluation of the Role of the IMF in Argentina, 1991–2001*. Washington, DC: International Monetary Fund. http://www.imf.org/External/NP/ieo/2004/arg/eng/.

——. 2005. *Evaluation Report: The IMF's Approach to Capital Account Liberalization*. Washington, DC: International Monetary Fund.

——. 2011. *IMF Performance in the Run-Up to the Financial and Economic Crisis*. Washington, DC: International Monetary Fund.

International Monetary Fund (IMF). 1978. *Conditionality in the Upper Credit Tranches—Suggested Guidelines*. Memorandum to the Executive Board No. SM/78/296, December 15. Washington, DC: International Monetary Fund.

——. 1997. *Review of Experiences under ESAF-Supported Arrangement—Staff Studies*. Vol. 2. Staff Memorandum for the Executive Board No. EBS/97/112, Suppl. 2, July 7. Washington, DC: International Monetary Fund.

——. 2000. *Report to the IMF Executive Board of the Quota Formula Review Group*. April 28. http://www.imf.org/external/np/tre/quota/2000/eng/qfrg/report/dload/EBAP52.pdf.

——. 2003. *Lessons from the Crisis in Argentina*. Internal Staff Report No. SM/03/345. October 9. Washington, DC: International Monetary Fund.

——. 2006. *Global Financial Stability Report: Market Development and Issues*. Washington DC: International Monetary Fund.

——. 2007. *Staff Handbook of the International Monetary Fund*. Washington, DC: International Monetary Fund.

——. 2012. *The 2011 Review of Conditionality Overview Paper*. Prepared by the Strategy, Policy and Review Department, June 19. Washington, DC: International Monetary Fund.

——. 2013. *Greece: Ex Post Evaluation of Exceptional Access under the 2010 Stand-By Arrangement*. Washington, DC: International Monetary Fund.

James, Harold. 1996. *International Monetary Cooperation since Bretton Woods*. Washington, DC: International Monetary Fund.

Jolly, Richard, Louis Emmerij, and Thomas Weiss. 2009. *UN Ideas That Changed the World*. Bloomington: Indiana University Press.

Joyce, Joseph P. 2013. *The IMF and Global Financial Crises: Phoenix Rising?* New York: Cambridge University Press.

Kahler. Miles. 1990. "The United States and the International Monetary Fund: Declining Influence or Declining Interest?" In *The United States and Multilateral Institutions*, ed. Margaret P. Karns and Karen A. Mingst, 91–114. Boston: Unwin Hyman.

——. 1992. "External Influence, Conditionality, and the Politics of Adjustment." In *The Politics of Economic Adjustment*, ed. Stephan Haggard and Robert Kaufman, 89–136. Princeton: Princeton University Press.

——. 1993. "Bargaining with the IMF: Two-Level Strategies and Developing Countries," in *Double-Edged Diplomacy*, ed. Peter Evans, Harold K. Jacobson, and Robert D. Putnam, 363–94. Berkeley: University of California Press.

Katzenstein, Peter J., Robert O. Keohane, and Stephen D. Krasner. 1998. "International Organization and the Study of World Politics." *International Organization* 52(4): 645–85.

Kaufman, Robert. 1990. "Stabilization and Adjustment in Argentina, Brazil, and Mexico." In *Economic Crisis and Policy Choice: The Politics of Adjustment in the Third World*, ed. Joan M. Nelson, 63–112. Princeton: Princeton University Press.

Kedar, Claudia. 2013. *The International Monetary Fund and Latin America: The Argentine Puzzle in Context*. Philadelphia: Temple University Press.

Keefer, Philip, and David Stasavage. 2003. "The Limits of Delegation: Veto Players, Central Bank Independence, and the Credibility of Monetary Policy." *American Political Science Review* 97(3): 407–23.

Kenen, Peter B. 1986. *Financing, Adjustment, and the International Monetary Fund*. Washington, DC: Brookings Institution.

Keynes, John M. 1921. *A Treatise on Probability*. London: Macmillan.

Kiguel, Miguel. 1991. "Inflation in Argentina: Stop and Go since the Austral Plan." *World Development* 19(8): 969–86.

Killick, Tony. 1995. *Aid and the Political Economy of Policy Change*. New York: Routledge.

Kirshner, Jonathan. 1999. "Keynes, Capital Mobility, and the Crisis of Embedded Liberalism." *Review of International Political Economy* 6(3): 313–37.

——. 2007. *Appeasing Bankers: Financial Caution on the Road to War*. Princeton: Princeton University Press.

——. 2014. *American Power after the Financial Crisis*. Ithaca: Cornell University Press.

——. 2015. "The Economic Sins of Modern IR Theory and the Classical Realist Alternative." *World Politics* 67(1): 155–83.

Klamer, Arjo, and David Colander. 1990. *The Making of an Economist*. Boulder: Westview Press.

Knight, Frank. 1921. *Risk, Uncertainty, and Profit*. New York: Houghton Mifflin.

Kogut, Bruce, and J. Muir Macpherson. 2008. "The Decision to Privatize: Economists and the Construction of Ideas and Policies." In *The Global Diffusion of Markets and Democracy*, ed. Beth Simmons, Frank Dobbin, and Geoffrey Garrett, 104–40. New York: Cambridge University Press.

Koremenos, Barbara, Charles Lipson, and Duncan Snidal. 2001. "The Rational Design of International Institutions." *International Organization* 55(4): 761–99.

Krasner, Stephen D. 1968. "The International Monetary Fund and the Third World." *International Organization* 22(3): 670–88.

Krueger, Anne O. 2003. "IMF Stabilization Programs." In *Economic and Financial Crises in Emerging Market Economies*, ed. Martin Feldstein, 297–362. Chicago: University of Chicago Press.

Laeven, Luc, and Fabian Valencia. 2008. "Systemic Banking Crises: A New Dataset." IMF Working Paper No. WP/08/224, November. International Monetary Fund, Washington, DC.

Lago, Ricardo. 1991. "The Illusion of Pursuing Redistribution through Macropolicy: Peru's Heterodox Experience, 1985–1990." In *The Macroeconomics of Populism in Latin America*, ed. Rudi Dornbusch and Sebastián Edwards, 263–323. Chicago: University of Chicago Press.

Leiva, Fernando Ignacio. 2008. *Latin American Neostructuralism: The Contradictions of Post-Neoliberal Development*. Minneapolis: University of Minnesota Press.

Lin, Justin Yifu. 2012. "New Structural Economics: A Framework for Rethinking Development." In *New Structural Economics: a Framework for Rethinking Development and Policy*, ed. Justin Yifu Lin, 13–47. Washington, DC: World Bank.

Lindbeck, Assar. 1991. "Public Finance for Developing Countries." In *Liberalization in the Process of Economic Development*, ed. Lawrence B. Krause and Kim Kihwan, 102–42. Berkeley: University of California Press.

Lindert, Peter H., and Peter J. Morton. 1989. "How Sovereign Debt Has Worked." In *Developing Country Debt and Economic Performance, vol. 1: The International Financial System*, ed. Jeffrey D. Sachs, 39–106. Chicago: University of Chicago Press.

Little, Ian M. D. 1982. *Economic Development: Theory, Policy, and International Relations*. New York: Basic Books.

Londregan, John, and Keith Poole. 1990. "Poverty, the Coup Trap, and the Seizure of Executive Power." *World Politics* 42(2): 151–83.

Manzetti, Luigi. 1991. *The International Monetary Fund and Economic Stabilization: The Argentine Case*. New York: Praeger.

March, James G., and Johan P. Olsen. 1998. "The Institutional Dynamics of International Political Orders." *International Organization* 52(4): 943–69.

Marinov, Nikolay. 2005. "Do Economic Sanctions Destabilize Country Leaders?" *American Journal of Political Science* 49(2): 564–76.

Markoff, John, and Veronica Montecinos. 1993. "The Ubiquitous Rise of Economists." *Journal of Public Policy* 13(1): 37–68.

Marshall, Monty G. 2010. *Major Episodes of Political Violence (MEPV) and Conflict Regions, 1946–2008*. Vienna, VA: Center for Systemic Peace.

Marshall, Monty G., and Keith Jaggers. 2007. *Polity IV Project: Political Regime Characteristics and Transitions, 1800–2006. Dataset Users' Manual*. Vienna, VA: Center for Systemic Peace.

Martin, Lisa. 2006. "Distribution, Information, and Delegation to International Organizations: The Case of IMF Conditionality." In *Delegation and Agency in International Organizations*, ed. Darren G. Hawkins, David A. Lake, Daniel L. Nielson, and Michael J. Tierney, 140–64. New York: Cambridge University Press.

Maxfield, Sylvia. 1990. *Governing Capital: International Finance and Mexican Politics*. Ithaca: Cornell University Press.

Mazower, Mark. 2012. *Governing the World: The History of an Idea*. New York: Penguin Press.

McGuire, James W. 1997. *Peronism without Peron: Unions, Parties, and Democracy in Argentina*. Stanford: Stanford University Press.

McNamara, Kathleen. 1998. *The Currency of Ideas: Monetary Politics in the European Union*. Ithaca: Cornell University Press.

Mearsheimer, John. 1994. "The False Promise of International Institutions." *International Security* 19 (3): 5–26.

Meltzer, Allan H. 1982. "Rational Expectations, Risk, Uncertainty, and Market Reactions." In *Crises in Economic and Financial Structure*, ed. Paul Wachtel, 3–22. Lexington, MA: Lexington Books.

Mikesell, Raymond F. 1994. *The Bretton Woods Debates: A Memoir*. Princeton Essays in International Finance No. 192. Princeton: Department of Economics, Princeton University.

Minsky, Hyman. 2008. *Stabilizing an Unstable Economy*. New York: McGraw Hill.

Mirowski, Philip. 2013. *Never Let a Serious Crisis Go to Waste: How Neoliberalism Survived the Financial Meltdown*. London: Verso.

Momani, Bessma. 2007. "IMF Staff: Missing Link in Fund Reform Proposals." *Review of International Organizations* 2(1): 39–57.

Momani, Bessma, and Aidan Garrib. 2010. "Iraq's Tangled Web of Debt Restructuring." In *From Desolation to Reconstruction: Iraq's Troubled Journey*, ed. Bessma Momani and Mokhtar Lamani, 157–76. Waterloo, Canada: Wilfrid Laurier University Press.

Morrisson, Christian, and Fabrice Murtin. 2009. "The Century of Education." CEE Discussion Papers 109. Centre for the Economics of Education, London School of Economics and Political Science.

Mosley, Layna. 2006. "Constraints, Opportunities, and Information: Financial Market-Government Relations around the World." In *Globalization and Egalitarian Redistribution*, ed. Pranab Bardhan, Samuel Bowles, and Michael Wallerstein, 87–119. Princeton: Princeton University Press.

Mudge, Stephanie Lee. 2008. "What Is Neo-Liberalism?" *Socio-Economic Review* 6: 703–31.

Mussa, Michael. 2002. *Argentina and the Fund: From Triumph to Tragedy*. Washington, DC: Institute for International Economics.

——. 2006. "Reflections on the Function and Facilities for IMF Lending." In *Reforming the IMF for the 21st Century*, ed. Edwin M. Truman, 413–54. Washington, DC: Institute for International Economics.

Mussa, Michael, and Miguel Savastano. 2000. "The IMF Approach to Economic Stabilization." In *NBER Macroeconomics Annual 1999*, ed. Ben S. Bernanke and Julio J. Rotemberg, 79–122. Cambridge, MA: MIT Press.

Nelson, Joan. 1992. "Good Governance: Democracy and Conditional Economic Aid." In *Development Finance and Policy Reform*, ed. Paul Mosley, 309-316. New York: St. Martin's Press.

Nelson, Stephen C. 2010. "Does Compliance Matter? Assessing the Relationship between Sovereign Risk and Compliance with International Monetary Law." *Review of International Organizations* 5(2): 107–39.

——. 2014a. "The International Monetary Fund's Evolving Role in Global Economic Governance." In *Handbook of Global Economic Governance*, ed. Manuela Moschella and Kate Weaver, 156–70. New York: Routledge.

——. 2014b. "Playing Favorites: How Shared Beliefs Shape the IMF's Lending Decisions." *International Organization* 68(2): 297–328.

——. 2016. "International Financial Institutions and Market Liberalization in the Developing World." In *Oxford Handbook of Politics of Development*, ed. Carol Lancaster and Nicolas van de Walle. New York: Oxford University Press.

Nelson, Stephen C., and Peter J. Katzenstein. 2014. "Uncertainty, Risk, and the Financial Crisis of 2008." *International Organization* 68(2): 361–92.

Oatley, Thomas, and Jason Yackee. 2004. "American Interests and IMF Lending." *International Politics* 41(3): 415–29.

Page, Scott E. 2008. "Uncertainty, Difficulty, and Complexity." *Journal of Theoretical Politics* 20(2): 115–49.

Pastor, Manuel, and Carol Wise. 1999. "Stabilization and its Discontents: Argentina's Economic Restructuring in the 1990s." *World Development* 27(3): 477–503.

Pepinsky, Thomas. 2009. *Economic Crises and the Breakdown of Authoritarian Regimes: Indonesia and Malaysia in Comparative Perspective*. New York: Cambridge University Press.

Pessino, Carola. 2003. Comment. In *Latin American Macroeconomic Reforms: The Second Stage*, ed. José Antonio González, Vittorio Corbo, Anne O. Krueger, and Aaron Tornell, 422–26. Chicago: University of Chicago Press.

Polak, Jacques J. 1991. *The Changing Nature of IMF Conditionality*. Essays in International Finance No. 184. Princeton: Princeton University, International Finance Section.

Pop-Eleches, Grigore. 2009a. *From Economic Crisis to Reform: IMF Programs in Latin America and Eastern Europe*. Princeton: Princeton University Press.

———. 2009b. "Public Goods or Political Pandering: Evidence from IMF Programs in Latin America and Eastern Europe." *International Studies Quarterly* 53: 787–816.

Powell, Andrew. 2003. "Argentina's Avoidable Crisis: Bad Luck, Bad Economics, Bad Politics, Bad Advice." *Brookings Trade Forum* 2002: 1–58.

Powell, Walter W., and Jeanette A. Colyvas. 2008. "Microfoundations of Institutional Theory." In *The Sage Handbook of Organizational Institutionalism*, ed. Robin Greenwood, Christine Oliver, Roy Suddaby, and Kerstin Sahlin-Andersson, 276–98. Los Angeles: Sage.

Ramirez, Hernán. 2000. *La Fundación Mediterranea y de como construir poder: La genesis de un proyecto hegemonico*. Cordoba: Ferreyra Editor.

Ray, James Lee. 2003. "Explaining Interstate Conflict and War: What Should We Control For?" *Conflict Management and Peace Science* 20: 1–31.

Reinhart, Carmen R., and Christoph Trebesch. 2015. "The International Monetary Fund: 70 Years of Reinvention." NBER Working Paper No. 21805. National Bureau of Economic Research, Cambridge, MA.

Remmer, Karen. 1986. "The Politics of Economic Stabilization: IMF Standby Programs in Latin America, 1954–1984." *Comparative Politics* 19(1): 1–24.

Remmer, Karen, and Eric Wibbels. 2000. "The Subnational Politics of Economic Adjustment: Provincial Politics and Fiscal Performance in Argentina." *Comparative Political Studies* 33(4): 419–51.

Reus-Smit, Christian. 2007. "International Crises of Legitimacy." *International Politics* 44: 157–74.

Reynaud, Julien, and Julien Vauday. 2009. "Geopolitics and International Organizations: An Empirical Study on IMF Facilities." *Journal of Development Economics* 89: 139–62.

Rickard, Stephanie J., and Teri L. Caraway. 2014. "International Negotiations in the Shadow of National Elections." *International Organization* 68(3): 701–20.

Rodrik, Dani. 2014. "When Ideas Trump Interests: Preferences, Worldviews, and Policy Innovations." *Journal of Economic Perspectives* 28(1): 189–208.

Ross, Michael. 2001. "Does Oil Hinder Democracy?" *World Politics* 53(3): 325–61.

Sachs, Jeffrey D. 1989. "Conditionality, Debt Relief, and the Developing Country Debt Crisis." In *Developing Country Debt and Economic Performance, vol. 1: The International Financial System*, ed. Jeffrey D. Sachs, 255–98. Chicago: University of Chicago Press.

Sachs, Jeffrey, and Andrew Warner. 1995. "Economic Reform and the Process of Global Integration." *Brookings Papers on Economic Activity* 1: 1–118.

———. 2001. "The Curse of Natural Resources." *European Economic Review* 45: 827–38.

Santiso, Javier, and Laurence Whitehead. 2012. "Ulysses and the Sirens: Political and Technical Rationality in Latin America." In *Oxford Handbook of Latin American Political Economy*, ed. Javier Santiso and Jeff Dayton-Johnson, 403–56. New York: Oxford University Press.

Sarfaty, Galit. 2012. *Values in Transition: Human Rights and the Culture of the World Bank*. Stanford: Stanford University Press.

Schamis, Hector. 2003. "The Political Economy of Currency Boards: Argentina in Historical and Comparative Perspective." In *Monetary Orders*, ed. Jonathan Kirshner, 125–49. Ithaca: Cornell University Press.

Schamis, Hector, and Christopher Way. 2003. "Political Cycles and Exchange Rate-Based Stabilizations." *World Politics* 56(1): 43–78.

Schlefer, Jonathan. 2012. *The Assumptions Economists Make.* Cambridge, MA: Harvard University Press.

Schmidli, William Michael. 2013. *The Fate of Freedom Elsewhere: Human Rights and U.S. Cold War Policy toward Argentina.* Ithaca: Cornell University Press.

Schultz, Kenneth, and Barry Weingast. 2003. "The Democratic Advantage." *International Organization* 57(1): 3–42.

Scott, Loren C., and Peter Mitias. 1996. "Trends in Rankings of Economic Departments in the U.S.: An Update." *Economic Inquiry* 34(2): 378–400.

Seabrooke, Leonard. 2007. "Legitimacy Gaps in the World Economy: Explaining the Sources of the IMF's Legitimacy Crisis." *International Politics* 44(2–3): 250–68.

Seers, Dudley. 1962. "Why Visiting Economists Fail." *Journal of Political Economy* 70(4): 325–38.

Shapiro, Helen, and Lance Taylor. 1990. "The State and Industrial Strategy." *World Development* 18(6): 861–78.

Sikkink, Kathryn. 1991. *Ideas and Institutions: Developmentalism in Brazil and Argentina.* Ithaca: Cornell University Press.

Silva, Patricio. 2008. *In the Name of Reason: Technocrats and Politics in Chile.* University Park: Pennsylvania State University Press.

Simmons, Beth, Frank Dobbin, and Geoffrey Garrett. 2006. "Introduction: The International Diffusion of Liberalism." *International Organization* 60 (4): 781–810.

Sjaastad, Larry. 1989. "Argentine Economic Policy, 1976–81," in *The Political Economy of Argentina, 1946–83,* ed. Guido di Tella and Rudiger Dornbusch, 254–75. Pittsburgh: University of Pittsburgh Press.

Smith, William C. 1989. *Authoritarianism and the Crisis of the Argentine Political Economy.* Stanford: Stanford University Press.

——. 1990. "Democracy, Distributional Conflicts and Macroeconomic Policymaking in Argentina, 1983–89." *Journal of InterAmerican Studies and World Affairs* 32(2): 1–42.

——. 1991. "State, Market and Neoliberalism in Post-Transition Argentina: The Menem Experiment." *Journal of InterAmerican Studies and World Affairs* 33(2): 45–82.

Southard, Frank A. 1979. *The Evolution of the International Monetary Fund.* Princeton Essays in International Finance No. 135. Princeton: Department of Economics, Princeton University.

Spiller, Pablo T., and Mariano Tommasi. 2007. *The Institutional Foundations of Public Policy in Argentina.* New York: Cambridge University Press.

Spraos, John. 1986. *IMF Conditionality: Ineffectual, Inefficient, Mistargeted.* Princeton Essays in International Finance No. 166. Princeton: Department of Economics, Princeton University.

Starr, Pamela K. 1997. "Government Coalitions and the Viability of Currency Boards: Argentina under the Cavallo Plan." *Journal of InterAmerican Studies and World Affairs* 39: 83–133.

Stiglitz, Joseph. 2003. *Globalization and Its Discontents.* New York: W. W. Norton.

——. 2008. "Is There a Post-Washington Consensus Consensus?" In *The Washington Consensus Reconsidered: Towards a New Global Governance,* ed. Narcis Serra and Joseph Stiglitz, eds. 41–56. Oxford: Oxford University Press.

Stiles, Kendall W. 1987. "Argentina's Bargaining with the IMF." *Journal of InterAmerican Studies and World Affairs* 29(3): 55–85.

Stone, Randall. 2002. *Lending Credibility: The International Monetary Fund and the Post-Communist Transition.* Princeton: Princeton University Press.

———. 2004. "The Political Economy of IMF Lending in Africa." *American Political Science Review* 98(4): 577–91.

———. 2008. "The Scope of IMF Conditionality." *International Organization* 62 (4): 586–620.

———. 2011. *Controlling Institutions: International Organizations and the Global Economy.* New York: Cambridge University Press.

Strange, Susan. 1973. "IMF: Monetary Managers." In *The Anatomy of Influence; Decision Making in International Organizations,* ed. Robert W. Cox and Harold K. Jacobsen, 263–97. New Haven: Yale University Press.

Swedberg, Richard. 1986. "The Doctrine of Economic Neutrality of the IMF and World Bank." *Journal of Peace Research* 23: 377–90.

Tanzi, Vito. 2003. "Taxation Reform in Latin America in the Last Decade." In *Latin American Macroeconomic Reforms: The Second Stage,* ed. José Antonio González, Vittorio Corbo, Anne O. Krueger, and Aaron Tornell, 327–56. Chicago: University of Chicago Press.

———. 2007. *Argentina: An Economic Chronicle, How One of the Richest Countries in the World Lost Its Wealth.* New York: Jorge Pinto Books.

Taylor, John B. 2007. *Global Financial Warriors: The Untold Story of International Finance in the Post-9/11 World.* New York: W. W. Norton.

Taylor, Lance. 1988. *Varieties of Stabilization Experiences: Towards Sensible Macroeconomics in the Third World.* Oxford: Clarendon Press.

———. 2004. *Reconstructing Macroeconomics: Structuralist Proposals and Critiques of the Mainstream.* Cambridge, MA: Harvard University Press.

Tenembaum, Ernesto. 2004. *Enemigos: Argentina y el FMI: La Apasionante Discusion entre un Periodista y uno de los Hombres Clave del Fondo en los Noventa.* Buenos Aires: Grupo Editorial Norma.

Thacker, Strom. 1999. "The High Politics of IMF Lending." *World Politics* 52(1): 38–75.

Tirole, Jean. 2002. *Financial Crises, Liquidity, and the International Monetary System.* Princeton: Princeton University Press.

Toye, John, and Richard Toye. 2003. "The Origins and Interpretation of the Prebisch-Singer Thesis." *History of Political Economy* 35(3): 437–67.

———. 2004. *The UN and Global Political Economy: Trade, Finance, and Development.* Bloomington: Indiana University Press.

U.S. States Agency for International Development (USAID). 2012. "U.S. Overseas Loans and Grants: Obligations and Loan Authorizations, July 1, 1945–September 30, 2010." http://gbk.eads.usaidallnet.gov/data/detailed.html.

Valdes, Juan Gabriel. 1995. *Pinochet's Economists: The Chicago School of Economics in Chile.* New York: Cambridge University Press.

Van den Steen, Eric. 2010a. "Culture Clash: The Costs and Benefits of Homogeneity." *Management Science* 56(10): 1718–38.

———. 2010b. "On the Origin of Shared Beliefs (and Corporate Culture)." *RAND Journal of Economics* 41(4): 617–48.

van der Veer, Koen, and Eelke de Jung. 2006. "Paris Club Involvement: Helping or Harming IMF's Attempts to Catalyse Private Capital Flows?" Unpublished manuscript, Radboud University, Nijmegen.

van de Walle, Nicolas. 2001. *African Economies and the Politics of Permanent Crisis, 1979–1999.* New York: Cambridge University Press.

Vaubel, Roland. 1991. "The Political Economy of the International Monetary Fund: A Public Choice Approach." In *The Political Economy of International*

Organizations: A Public Choice Approach, ed. Roland Vaubel and Thomas D. Willett, 204–44. Boulder: Westview Press.

Veigel, Klaus. 2005. "Governed by Emergency: Economic Policymaking in Argentina, 1973–1991." PhD diss., Princeton University.

———. 2009. *Dictatorship, Democracy, and Globalization: Argentina and the Cost of Paralysis, 1973–2001.* University Park: Pennsylvania State University Press.

Venugopal, Rajesh. 2015. "Neoliberalism as a Concept." *Economy and Society* 44(2): 165–87.

Vetterlein, Antje. 2010. "Lacking Ownership: The IMF and Its Engagement with Social Development as a Policy Norm." In *Owning Development: Creating Policy Norms in the IMF and the World Bank*, ed. Susan Park and Antje Vetterlein, 93–112. New York: Cambridge University Press.

Vreeland, James R. 2003. *The IMF and Economic Development.* Princeton: Princeton University Press.

———. 2006. "IMF Program Compliance: Aggregate Index versus Policy Specific Research Strategies." *Review of International Organizations* 1(4): 359-378.

Wacziarg, Romain, and Karen Welch. 2008. "Trade Liberalization and Growth: New Evidence." *World Bank Economic Review* 22(2): 187–231.

Wade, Robert. 2013. "The Art of Power Maintenance: How Western States Keep the Lead in Global Organizations." *Challenge* 56(1): 5–39.

Weaver, Catherine. 2008. *Hypocrisy Trap: The World Bank and the Poverty of Reform.* Princeton: Princeton University Press.

Weiss, Thomas G. 2005. "Transcript of Interview with Richard Jolly." United Nations Intellectual History Project, July 20. http://www.unhistory.org/CD/PDFs/Jolly.pdf.

Wibbels, Eric. 2006. "Dependency Revisited: International Markets, Business Cycles, and Social Spending in the Developing World." *International Organization* 60(2): 433–68.

Willett, Thomas D. 2002. "Towards a Broader Public Choice Analysis of the International Monetary Fund." Claremont Institute for Economic Policy Studies Working Paper No. 2002–25. Claremont Colleges, Claremont, CA.

Williamson, John. 1980. "Economic Theory and International Monetary Fund Policies." *Carnegie-Rochester Conference Series on Public Policy* 13: 255–78.

Woll, Cornelia. 2008. *Firm Interests: How Governments Shape Business Lobbying on Global Trade.* Ithaca: Cornell University Press.

Woods, Ngaire. 2006. *The Globalizers: The IMF, the World Bank, and Their Borrowers.* Ithaca: Cornell University Press.

Wynia, Gary. 1992. *Argentina: Illusions & Realities.* 2nd ed. New York: Holmes & Meier.

Zajonc, Robert B. 1980. "Feeling and Thinking: Preferences Need No Inferences." *American Psychologist* 35(2): 151–75.

Zamora, Stephen. 1989. "Sir Joseph Gold and the Development of International Monetary Law." *International Lawyer* 23(4): 1009–26.

Zeckhauser, Richard. 2014. "New Frontiers beyond Risk and Uncertainty: Ignorance, Group Decision, and Unanticipated Themes." In *Handbook of the Economics of Risk and Uncertainty*, ed. Mark Machina and W. Kip Viscusi, xvii–xxix. Amsterdam: Elseveier.

Index

Abdelal, Rawi, 193, 199
access to funds
  in Argentine case study
    neoliberal phases, 97, 99, 138–40, 144,
      149, 153, 155–56, 157, 158–60
    non-neoliberal phases, 112, 115
    semi-neoliberal phase, 122, 128
    during collapse, 160, 161–62
  decision-making process, 11, 12, 32–33
  economic beliefs as determinant of, 4–7,
    40–49
  in quantitative analysis, 70–76, 205–8
    measurement methodology, 51–52
accountability, 188
Adolph, Christopher, 58n18, 68, 171
Africa, neoliberalism in, 168
Alemann, Roberto, 103–5
Alfonsín, Raúl, administration of, 47,
    109–35
  non-neoliberal phase (1983–1985), 109–16
  semi-neoliberal phase (1985–1989), 47,
    118–35
Alfonsístas, 152, 156–57
Alsogaray, Álvaro, 136
Alvarez, Chacho, 155
Argentina (case study)
  overview of, 87–88, 162–65
  economic views in, 92–95
  neoliberal policymaking phases
    military regimes (1976–1981), 89–91,
      95–102, 103–5, 116, 117
    Menem administration (1991–1999),
      135–51
    de la Rúa administration (1999–2001),
      152–61
  non-neoliberal policymaking phases
    military regimes (1981–1983), 94–95,
      102–3, 105–9
    Alfonsín administration (1983–1985),
      109–16
    after collapse, 161–62
  semi-neoliberal policymaking phase
    Alfonsín administration (1985–1989),
      118–35
Arriazu, Ricardo, 91
Article VIII, 9–10

attitudes towards the IMF, 1, 3–4, 13, 109,
    112–13
austerity, in Argentina
  Alfonsín administration, 121–23, 126,
    128, 129
  Menem administration, 139, 144
  de la Rúa administration, 154, 157
  military regimes, 95–96, 104
autonomy
  of IMF staff, 4, 20–21, 36–37, 191
  of international organizations, 17–20

Baker, James Jr. 130
banks (in Argentine case study)
  bailouts of, 15, 98–100, 131
  debt reduction by, 141
  failure of, 101, 160
  lending from, 13, 97, 104–5, 106, 107–8,
    127–28, 156
  pressure on IMF from, 98–99, 107–8, 109,
    127–28
Barnett, Michael, 15, 24, 65, 190n3, 193, 205
Bergsten, Fred, 90
Beveridge, William A., 99
Beza, Sterie, 113, 138
Bird, Graham, 54
Blanchard, Olivier, 23, 204, 205, 209
blindaje (shield), 155–57
Blyth, Mark, 9n24
bonds. *See* debt: Argentine
Bonelli, Marcelo, 92, 156
borrowers, use of term, 2n4
borrowing governments
  conditionality preferences, theories about,
    19–20, 43–44
  importance of, in quantitative analysis
    (log(GDP) variable), 66, 70, 77, 81, 83
  potential IMF influence on, 6, 13, 30–31,
    46–47, 116, 117, 118, 166–88
    quantitative analysis of, 173–87
  See also regime type; treatment of borrowers
Boughton, James, 131
Bourdieu, Pierre, 14
Brachet, Christian, 103, 106, 109
Brazil, 106
Brodersohn, Mario, 130

CPSIA information can be obtained
at www.ICGtesting.com
Printed in the USA
BVOW03*1515150117

473068BV00003B/2/P

9 781501 705120